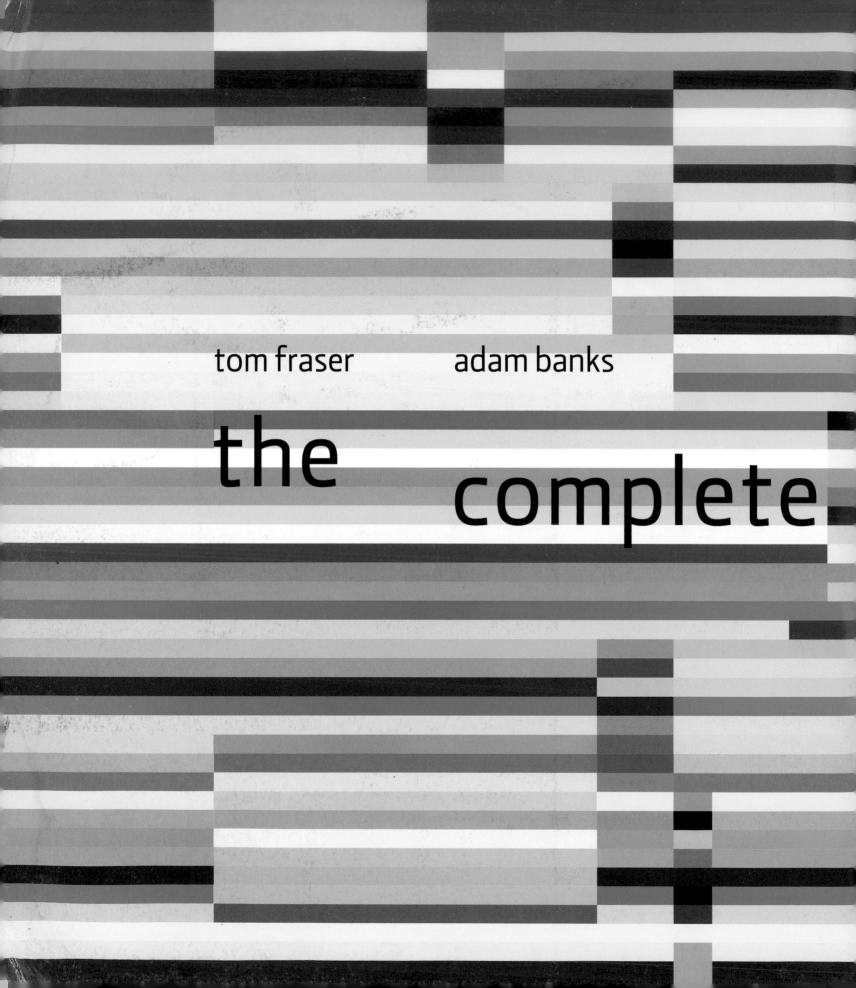

tom fraser   adam banks

the   complete

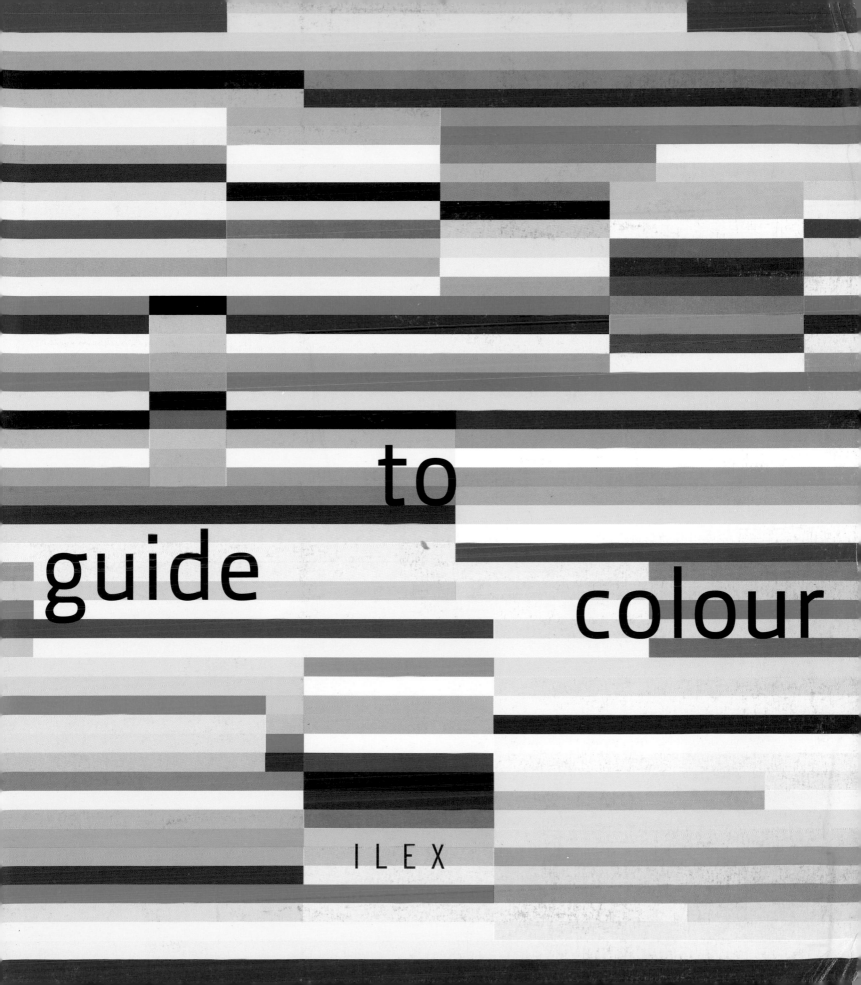

guide to colour

ILEX

First published in the United Kingdom in 2004 by
I L E X
The Old Candlemakers
West Street
Lewes
East Sussex BN7 2NZ

I L E X is an imprint of The Ilex Press Ltd
Visit us on the web at:
www.ilex-press.com

I L E X Editorial, Lewes:
Publisher: Alastair Campbell
Executive Publisher: Sophie Collins
Creative Director: Peter Bridgewater
Editorial Director: Steve Luck
Editor: Caroline Earle
Design Manager: Tony Seddon
Designer: Jonathan Raimes
Artwork Assistant: Joanna Clinch

I L E X Research, Cambridge:
Development Art Director: Graham Davis
Technical Art Editor: Nicholas Rowland

British Library Cataloguing-in-Publication Data
A catalogue record for this book is available
from the British Library

ISBN 1-904705-22-7

Printed and bound in China

For more information on this title please visit:
www.cobeuk.web-linked.com

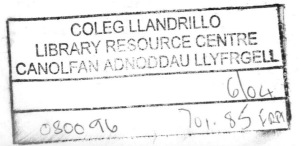
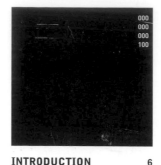
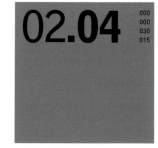
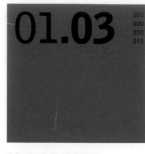
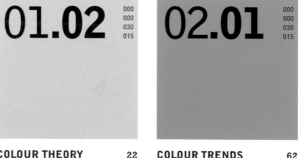

CONTENTS

02.05

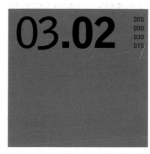

03.02

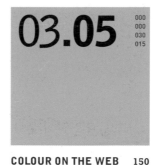

03.05

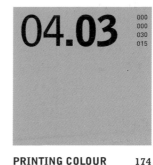

04.03

04.05 CONTINUED

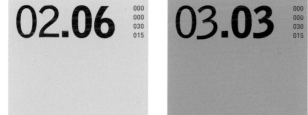

02.06

03.03

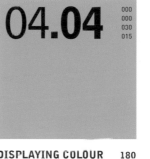

04.01

04.04

04.06

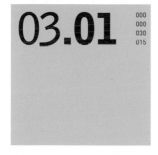

03.01

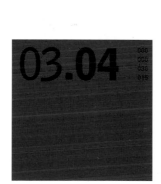

03.04

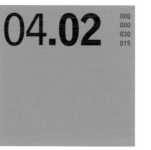

04.02

04.05

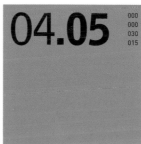

THE COMPLETE GUIDE TO COLOUR

Frank Zappa said writing about music was 'like dancing about architecture'. Writing about colour might seem similarly futile. This book aims to combine key elements of colour theory and practice to provide not just a how-to guide, but an exploration of the issues that anyone working with colour should consider before reaching for their paintbrush, mouse or other tool of choice.

The science of colour is disconcertingly tricky. For centuries it was assumed that the spectrum must make simple sense, that colours could be neatly categorized and diagrammed. As we will see, this could hardly be further from the truth. The more we pry into the mechanisms of colour perception, the more the certainties of red, green and blue give way to the vagaries of biology. Having found our way into this maze, we will need to find our way out.

Colour influences everything we encounter, shaping our perception by accident or design. It may communicate complex interactions of association and symbolism, or a simple message conveyed more plainly than in words. If you go to a game knowing nothing about football, make sure yours isn't the only red shirt in a sea of blue. Colour is as sensitive a subject as religion or politics, and it is often bound up with both. Are there universal truths about our interpretation of colours, or is everything relative? Semiotics, psychology, and mysticism tell conflicting stories.

Out of our many different ways of seeing colour come ways of using colour to shape our environment, and we go on to explore the application of colour in the home, in buildings, in art and in design. Throughout history, our attitudes to colour – whether personal or professional – have been shaped by prevailing tastes and norms. But when are these part of a coherent and distinctive worldview, and when are they mere prejudices that would be better cast aside?

Rather than risk an unpredictable effect on others, we are often tempted to avoid colour altogether. We dress in black for work to avoid sending unwanted messages. We paint our houses in neutrals before moving out to avoid putting off prospective buyers. In architecture, too, a tendency towards 'chromaphobia' is apparent in our offices, schools and shopping centres. Rather like the standard beige computer, contemporary buildings are often breathtakingly drab.

Working with colour can be extremely difficult – more so than experimentation with form. It is not, however, as dangerous as is sometimes imagined. True, to describe something as colourful is at best a backhanded compliment. But many people warmly embrace new and exciting uses of colour. When Apple launched a bright blue computer, it sold faster than any other.

The willingness to use colour must be matched by the ability to create and control it. The history of art and design is inextricably linked with the technology of pigment production, and our expectations of colour are still influenced by the technical limitations that beset our forebears. In the early twenty-first century, the rise of digital reprographics has brought about a revolution in colour. Our children grow up with colour in their lives where things were once black and white, and their experiences in turn will influence the future of colour in design.

The contemporary graphic designer, equipped with powerful computers and cheap colour printing, has more need than ever for principles to govern the use of colour. After showcasing more than 250 examples of colour in everything from buildings to Web sites, we demonstrate how colour can be manipulated in software such as Photoshop to achieve professional results in the smallest number of steps. With this complete package of inspiration and information, you should emerge equipped to apply colour with confidence.

DEFINITIONS

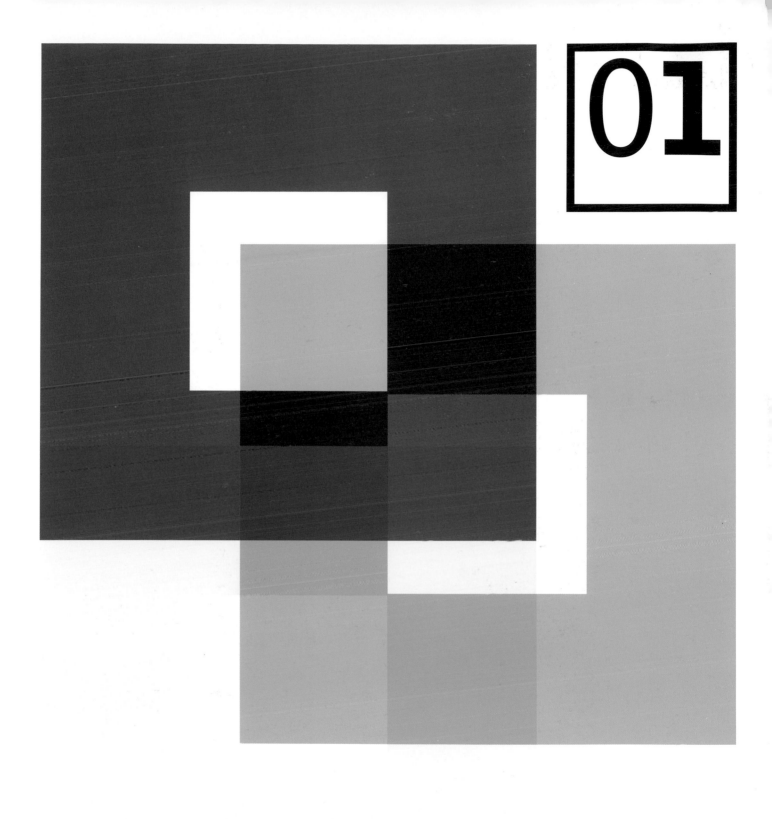

01

PART 01. DEFINITIONS

CHAPTER ONE

COLOUR IN CONTEXT

The world around us is full of colour, yet all of it is in our heads. We experience colour through only one sense: vision. Something that is wet can be seen, heard (think of the trickle of water from a tap) and felt to be wet; but something that is yellow can only be seen to be yellow. You can't hear or smell yellow; you can't touch it or taste it. This suggests that colour is not something that is fixed to an object or surface, but an event that is triggered only in the observer.

The act of seeing something comes before the process of reacting to it. Some people are unable to see colours, and other people see colours differently from the majority (see pages 28–29 for more on colour deficiency and perception), but generally our eyes all work in the same way, and the same stimulus produces the same response in everyone's visual system. What happens after that is another matter. Once our eyes have allowed us to experience a colour, it is everything else about ourselves that determines the meaning we attach to it.

Colour associations differ between cultures and individuals. Take the colour blue, for example. You could have three people sitting together in the same room, and to each of them, blue might signify something profoundly different. A Western pilot might associate blue with his air-force colours. To him, its connotations could be evocative of extreme speed and power. A Sikh might wear a blue turban to indicate that he's a Nihang, following a doctrine very different from the pilot's military code. A blues guitarist's heroes will have led lives that are very different from the role models of the Sikh.

A colour, or a composition in colours, can mean something quite different to every person who looks at it. We might say that colour is not simply formed on the eye, but also on the 'I'. For further reading in this area, there is no better source than the work of the French philosopher Maurice Merleau-Ponty (1908–61). He advocated a seeing-seen dynamic in which seeing is a double phenomenon: an encounter with the world and an encounter with oneself.

color

Inspired by the endless palette of the natural world, we have learned over tens of thousands of years to create and manipulate colour ourselves. Yet its effects on our psyches remain mysterious.

COLOUR IN MODERN LIFE Urban existence is often depicted as grey or monochromic. In most cities, nothing could be further from the truth. Most buildings feature painted timber, red or yellow brick, mosaic inserts or coloured panels of glass or plastic. Street furniture, shop signs and hoardings are coloured to catch the eye, and the vehicles passing between them gleam in a spectrum of shades. If you stumble across a surviving wilderness of unadorned concrete, you can be sure someone will have decorated it with rainbow-hued graffiti.

It is no coincidence that the strongest use of colour is often found where someone is trying to sell you something. If you think of a well-known brand, you will probably automatically think of the colour or colours that identify it. Some would argue that colour is the most important brand-recognition device, and it certainly is hard to think of a brand that does not have a colour or colour combination associated with it. Coke is red, Pepsi is blue, and – whatever your preference – that is the first reason why you will never pick up the wrong bottle.

Such use of colour is partly 'empty': one hue is chosen over another merely to differentiate a brand, not to make any literal or symbolic associations. In law, colours are not, in themselves, subject to trademark or copyright protection. A company can only act to prevent others from using its 'own' colour – as Pepsi has done with blue – if deliberate imitation has occurred. Picking a colour that has no intrinsic connection with the product makes it harder for competitors to dismiss imitation as coincidence.

But advertisers frequently use colour in ways designed to resonate with the consumer's unconscious desires. The mobile phone company Orange appropriated a colour in both name and hue to create one of the most successful new brands of the 1990s. Its slogan – 'The future's bright. The future's Orange' – spelled out the message of optimism and progress that the company hoped would be conveyed.

Deliberately constructed colour associations are not confined to commerce, in fact we use them in everyday life. Attaching a concept to a colour helps it carry around all the meanings we want it to contain. We talk about the 'black' economy, 'blue' movies, 'grey' power, the 'pink' dollar. Journalists, who have to convey meanings as concisely as possible, are especially prone to coining such terms.

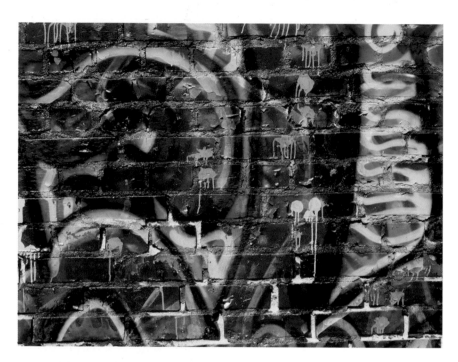

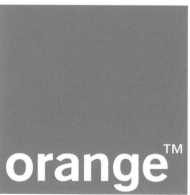

orange™

Above: Graffiti may be destructive, but it can also be interpreted as a positive response to the concrete jungle. Its colours and patterns at least try to communicate and engage, unlike the often faceless urban architecture on to which it's painted.

Left: Corporate colours represent a more insidious kind of communication. Carefully chosen, they can help get a message across that would otherwise be difficult to express – and perhaps appear less credible – in words alone.

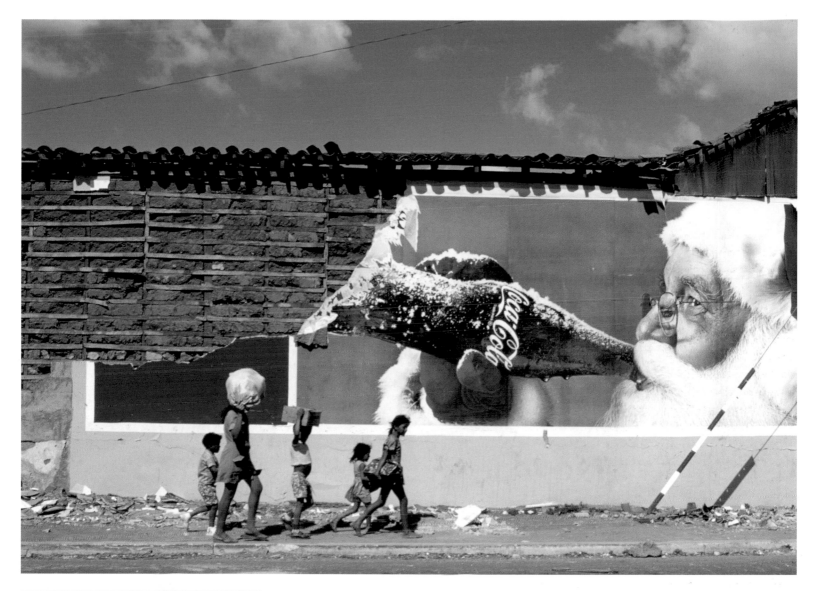

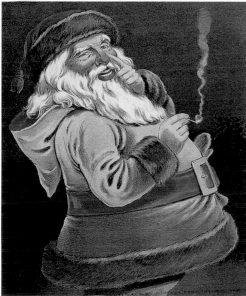

Above and left: **Traditionally, the colours you wear or display indicate your allegiance. Flags are still known in the military as 'colours'. Today, Santa Claus wears the colours of Coca-Cola, and the meaning is not lost even on those of us who may have little knowledge of the significance of Christmas. But Santa wasn't always so closely aligned with Coke, as the image on the left shows. By imposing a distinctive colour scheme, Coca-Cola appropriated a secular icon, transferring its associations to a branded product.**

Writers, such as Naomi Klein in her best-selling book *No Logo*, have argued that ubiquitous corporate branding and the colonization of colours are ultimately harmful to society. While the psychological effects continue to be debated, the physical ones are inescapable. Both Coca-Cola and PepsiCo, along with other companies, have been fined thousands of dollars for defacing the scenic Rohtang Pass in the Himalayas by painting their logos onto the rock. The effect of endless advertising plastered over every vertical surface may be seen as a little less destructive of the urban environment.

It can certainly be frustrating for designers to have to work around existing colour associations generated by saturation marketing. Until the 1930s, Santa Claus could be depicted any way an illustrator felt like, but after the Coca-Cola Company dressed him in its corporate colours as part of a campaign to sell chilled drinks in the middle of winter, red and white became the only widely accepted palette for his wardrobe.

COLOUR, CULTURE AND CREATIVITY

In the course of history, people have developed many different traditions of representation. Styles of image-making vary according to culture, technology and location, and the kinds of images designers and illustrators create are governed by their own ideas, beliefs and perceptions.

In Western art history, Christian symbolism has been a primary influence on colour use. The church has its own traditions of using colour to represent aspects of the faith. Colours were related to liturgical seasons as early as the fourth century and were systematized into a palette of black, white, red, green and violet around 1200 by Pope Innocent III. The same colours are used to this day, officially referred to by their Latin names. White (*albus*) is worn for festivals such as Christmas and Easter and on saints' days. Red (*ruber*), symbolizing blood, is worn and displayed on feast days associated with martyrdom. Green (*viridis*) represents life and is worn for everyday occasions, while violet (*violaceus*) is worn during Advent and Lent, signifying a time of reflection and penitence. Black (*niger*) is reserved for certain funeral masses, masses in remembrance of the dead and Good Friday, the day on which Christ was crucified.

In the Islamic tradition, colours are conceived of on a metaphysical level, deriving from the idea that light and darkness are two eternal possibilities pervading the universe. Islam attaches a particular significance to the number seven, which determines the construction of the conventional Islamic colour palette. This is composed of three levels, containing two arrangements of the seven basic colours and a further set of twenty-eight.

On the first level, for example, colours are gathered in a group of three and a group of four. The group of three comprises white, black, and sandalwood. White is described as the light of the sun, which allows colours to

Below: Different cultures endow colours with different meanings. Each religion has its own palette, which is often integral to expressions of faith and acts of worship. The coloured vestments of the Roman Catholic Church, for example, each have a specific liturgical significance. Although this use of colour developed over many centuries, it has been formalized by decrees which allocate more or less arbitrary connotations to each hue.

flow forth into the world. Black carries the concept of concealment, deriving from a notion of God hiding within his own radiance. Sandalwood can be viewed as a neutral base for all the colours of nature. The group of four comprises green, yellow, blue and red. Each is associated with an element: green is water, yellow is air, blue is earth and red is fire.

Notice how most of these pairings differ from the traditions that inform today's commercial colour symbolism: water is usually blue (check the logo of your water company) – a colour also associated with air – while earth is linked with orange and green.

In film and television, colour may be deeply symbolic, referring to and emphasizing particular themes or characters and – as in advertising – attempting to provoke or reinforce emotional responses. The audience may overlook many

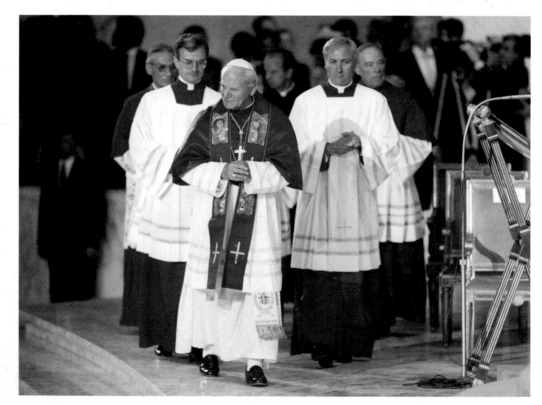

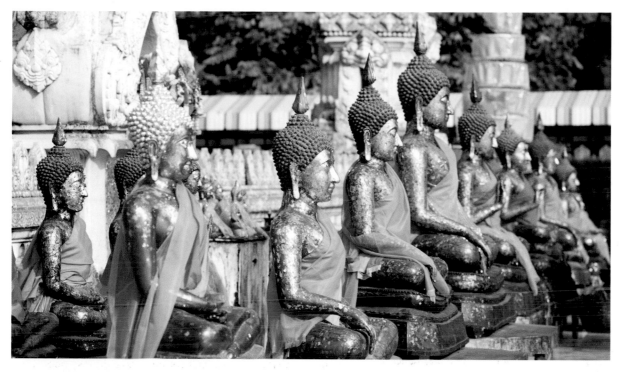

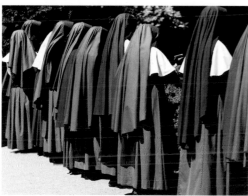

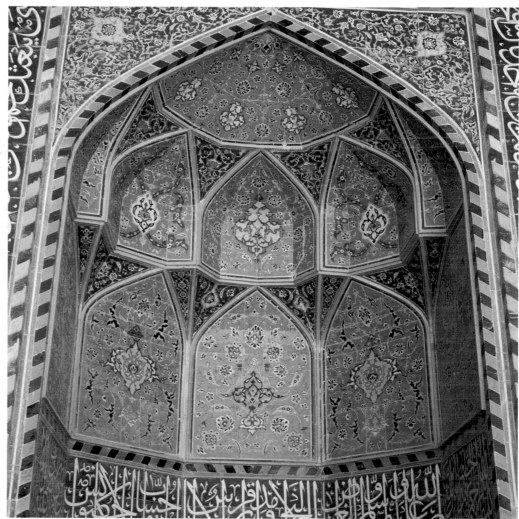

Left and below left: **Five primary colours – white, yellow, blue, red and green – are highly symbolic in Buddhism. Monastic robes are traditionally orange, avoiding any of these colours and indicating humility. Brown is similarly worn by some Christian orders as a sign of righteous poverty. Blue is often worn by nuns.**

Below: **Painting and sculpture have been the pre-eminent art forms in European civilization, but Islam favours media such as mosaics, textiles and glass. Figurative art does exist, but never in a religious context. Calligraphy (see the bottom and sides of this picture) is considered the most noble art form because of its association with the Koran, which is written in Arabic. Colour conventions link hues to abstract metaphysical concepts.**

symbolic colour references – hence the number of guides, available on the Internet and in books, explaining how to 'read' certain scenes in films.

Some directors would assert that audiences unconsciously register the meaning of colours in their work (*see page 94*). Even without accepting that colour associations are fixed, we can argue that repeatedly linking a colour with a character or type of event in a narrative will create connections in the viewer's mind. Red is used much more frequently than any of the other hues and often relates to themes of passion, obsession and desire. Green, a colour rarely used in branding, is often used in film to represent envy, awkwardness or discomfort.

COLOUR IN NATURE

From black-and-white zebras to brilliantly kaleidoscopic butterflies, from the most mundane piece of moss to the most exotic bird's display, nature is awash with incredible colour. The more nature is disrupted by human technology, the more we are made aware of how intricately its connections work and how easily they can be disturbed. Colour is a part of this intricacy.

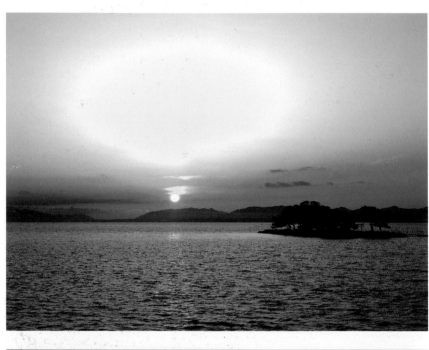

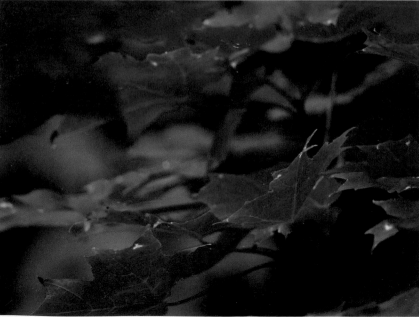

In nature, red, often combined with yellow or black, suggests poison or danger. Some cunning nonpoisonous animals use false markings to convince predators that they are toxic. Meanwhile, flowers and fruits that require pollination compete to attract insects and animals with their colourful displays.

When we decorate ourselves and our homes with colour, we send similar messages: 'I'm cool', 'I'm sexy', or 'I'm a good homemaker'. In nature, females generally prefer more colourful males. Charles Darwin (1809–82), in his work on natural selection, maintained that plumage colours indicate the strength of the genetic line – although scientists are still figuring out how this might work. One theory suggests that because animals' colours are made from rare pigments called carotenoids that are also used to fight disease, a male that uses his stock for display must be healthy, and therefore a good potential mate.

Some animals can change their colours. They may need to do this to defend against predators, communicate with others, attract potential mates, repel rivals, signal alarm, gain protection from the environment or deceive approaching prey. Camouflage is the best-known form of colour adaptation and of course is a technique borrowed by humans.

We discovered long ago how to control at least some of nature's colours. Garden designers use techniques as subtle as those of any painter. Packing plants together closely can increase the saturation of their colour. Different kinds of leaf

Above left: Our experience of the natural world lends significance to certain colours and colour combinations. The reds and yellows of a sunset can be used in art and design to evoke warmth and restfulness.

Left: The red and yellow colours of leaves during the autumn are believed to occur because of a reduction of chlorophyll production, but they may also serve to ward off predatory insects. Either way, these colours contribute to our feelings about this time of year.

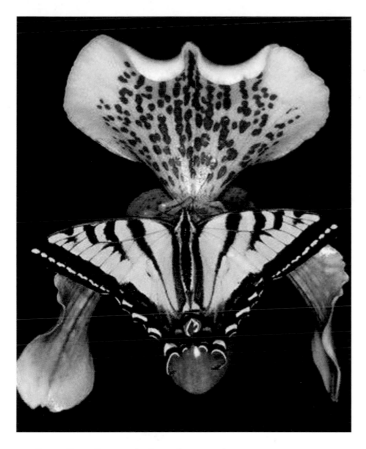

Left: While most animals lack our full-colour vision, some insects can see ultraviolet, a part of the electromagnetic spectrum which human eyes cannot see. This allows them to perceive colours that we can never experience.

Below: Colour serves many different purposes in the animal kingdom. 'Advertising coloration' attracts the attention of potential mates or of helpers, as with flowers and bees. 'Protective coloration' allows its wearer to blend in to the background, sometimes further assisted by 'protective resemblance': the stick insect, for example, mimics its environment in both colour and shape. 'Protective warning coloration' acts as a Keep off! sign to predators.

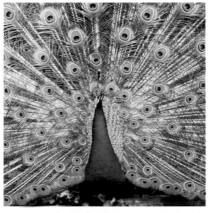

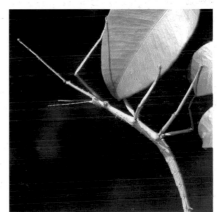

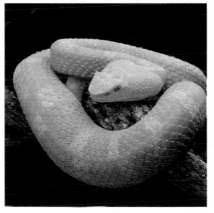

surface affect the way light is dispersed: coarse leaves chop up the light with shadow, while smooth leaves reflect it more directly. Unlike a painting, a garden goes through a steady process of change. Even the time of day has a great impact. Flowers open and close at different hours. Sunlight gets warmer during the day and goes through dramatic colour changes at dawn and dusk, completely altering a garden's appearance and atmosphere.

Gertrude Jekyll (1843–1932), one of Britain's greatest garden designers, was influenced by prevailing ideas about colour theory. She had studied to be a painter but turned to garden design when her eyesight started to fail. (Although colour is paramount, a garden also engages other senses.) Some of her schemes were planned to exploit features of the way we perceive colour. Of her own gardens at Munstead Wood, in Surrey, she wrote:

"The Grey garden is so called because most of its plants have grey foliage … the flowers are white, lilac, purple, and pink … Perhaps the Grey garden is seen at its best by reaching it through the orange borders. Here the eye becomes filled and saturated with the strong red and yellow colouring. This [makes] the eye eagerly desirous for the complementary colour, so that … suddenly turning to look into the Grey garden, the effect is surprisingly—quite astonishingly— luminous and refreshing."

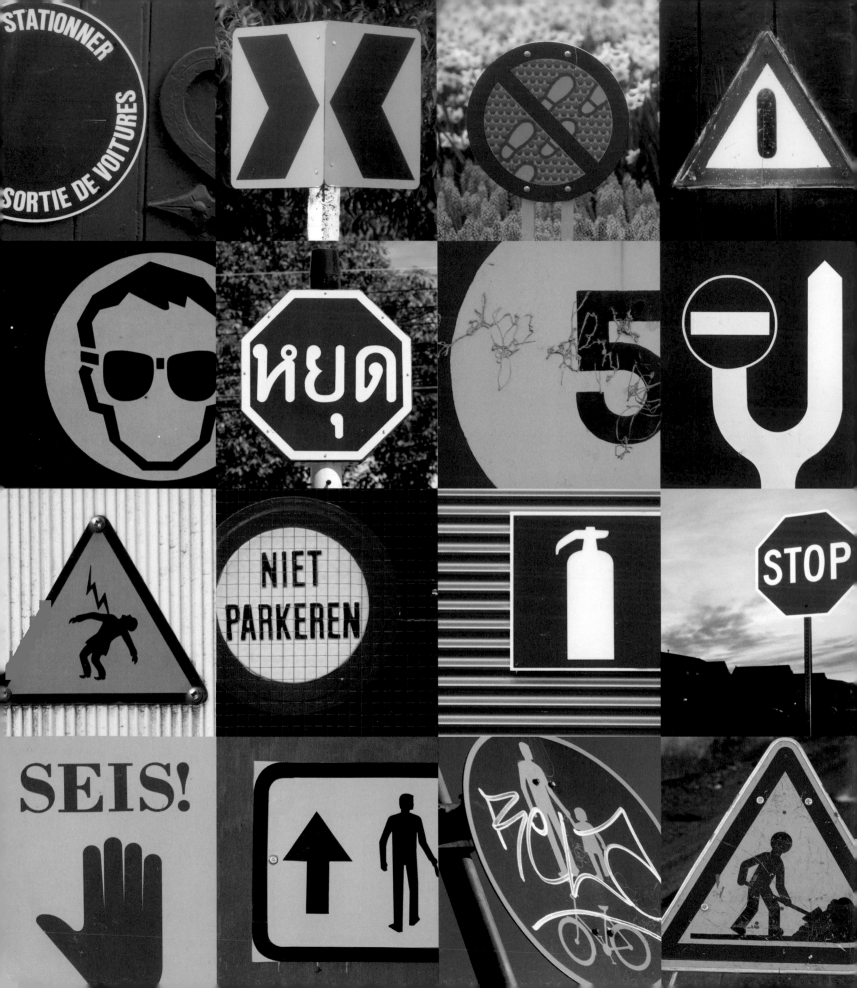

IN SEARCH OF COLOUR

An important way to understand how we conceptualize the language of colour is to compare it with the way we understand other languages. All theories of colour are in some sense theories of language, and how we 'speak', 'hear' or 'read' colours tells us a great deal about how we understand the world.

Left: Whether or not it uses words, a street sign needs to convey messages clearly in less time than it would take to read and digest a description of its meaning. In this context, colours have precise connotations: blue tells you what to do, red what not to do, yellow to beware.

Right. This hand signal means 'OK' or 'perfect' in North America and Britain, but in many countries it is a vulgar gesture. The interpretation of colours can vary just as much between cultures. For example, in many parts of the Far East, white is the colour of mourning and has negative implications, but for Buddhists in that region it represents purity and higher consciousness. Dark blue is popular (and sometimes patriotic) in the West, but it represents low caste in India, and in China it is politically charged because of its association with the nationalist Kuomintang.

Semiotics aims to be an objective and scientific way of viewing language and, through it, culture. It was central to the initial wave of structuralism in early twentieth-century European philosophy, before its big ideas collapsed into poststructuralism and its crazy sister, postmodernism.

The most important figure in the development of semiotics – or semiology, as the French call it – was the Swiss linguist Ferdinand de Saussure (1857–1913), whose work, summarized in the *Course in General Linguistics*, originated the key concepts of the *sign*, the *signifier* and the *signified*. Meaning was previously considered in terms of language and objects (the things referred to by language). But what if the thing was not an object but a feeling, a theory or a colour? Saussure redefined the relationship between language and objects by creating his concept of the semiotic sign.

A signifier can be a word, a sentence, an image, a sound or even a colour. The signified is whatever is referred to by the signifier. A sign is the combination of the two. If I ask a friend to 'meet me back at my house', 'my house' is a signifier and my actual house is the signified. I could make a different sign communicating the concept of 'my house' to my friend by standing and pointing at it or by drawing a picture of it.

Saussure tells us that signs are arbitrary. It does not matter if you call a potato an 'onion' or a 'zorb'. There is nothing intrinsically potatoey about the word potato. As long as all communicating parties agree on their sign system, they will understand each other.

Applying this idea to colour, if we decide the particular significance of a colour (*see page 20*) is arbitrary as the letters that make up its name, we start to realize that all the values colours hold are merely ones we have ascribed to them. A red traffic light means stop because that is what we have agreed it will mean. This is a very different understanding from the theories proposed by colour therapists and colour psychologists (*see page 48*), who believe colours carry intrinsic, universal meanings.

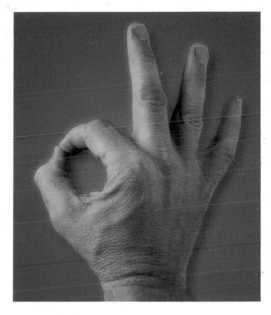

Once established, the arbitrary meanings of colours persist. Red simultaneously 'means' everything that has ever been assigned to it – by town planners, mystics, interior designers, religious groups and so on. Sometimes we know which value is being invoked because of context. Nobody interprets a red car as a stop signal. In fact, red bodywork tends to imply speed and power. If I write about a blue sky, you will probably see an image of a sky in your mind, and you may expect me to be describing a happy scene. If I say a 'blue mood', something else is triggered.

People often choose colours because of personal associations, whereas illustrators, designers, and architects usually do not. Regardless, that building is grey, or silver, or pink for a reason; that woman's clothes are black for a reason, or even many reasons. Figure out what those reasons are – and what combinations of signs are involved – and you will become more sophisticated in your own uses of colour.

COLOUR PSYCHOLOGY How do colours make us feel? We know that they can affect our emotions, but the question is whether this happens purely as a result of meanings conveyed through signs, or if there is a deeper link between colours and mental states. Can colours stimulate us not by prompting an association, but by acting directly on some aspect of our bodies or brains?

Most scientists would suggest that even emotional or subconscious responses to colour have some basis in linguistic association. But others claim that certain 'natural' meanings of colour exist that affect us regardless of social and cultural conditioning. The psychoanalyst Carl Jung (1875–1961) famously said that 'colours are the mother tongue of the subconscious'. While colour symbols may differ between cultures and religions, as we have seen, a great deal of colour meanings are recognized around the world. Even the pat advice on colour psychology that is frequently found in paint manufacturers' brochures and in

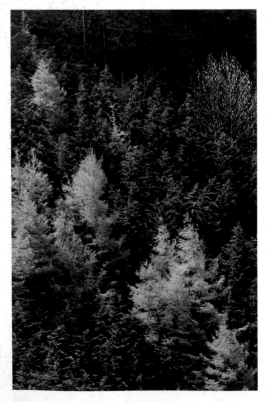

home decoration books tends to derive from Jewish, Islamic, Hindu, Tao, Buddhist, Christian or folk traditions, among many others.

That many colours are treated similarly by different ancient cultures may suggest that they have some level of intrinsic or collective meaning. If so, these meanings could come from natural phenomena. Red is an accepted colour of the sun, which gives life but can also take it away, and it is, of course, the colour of blood. In nature, red also often signifies danger. So perhaps there is no need for semiotics in order to explain why this colour can make people feel anxious, passionate, or angry. Blue – the colour of the sky and the sea, vast expanses that give a sense of freedom and perspective – is said to make people feel calm. However, it is also said to be a 'cold' colour and a lonely one, too. The 'bluest' experience must be to sit in a little boat far out at sea contemplating the sky. Freedom and calm, or cold loneliness? It all depends.

One objection to the idea of fixed colour effects is that there are no fixed colours. Even among people without any form of colour blindness, perception of colour is highly subjective. What I say is yellow, you may well say is orange. Where does yellow end and orange begin? John Gage, in *Color and Meaning: Art, Science, and Symbolism* (University of California, 1999), notes that as recently as the Middle Ages, languages such as Old French had words that could mean either blue or yellow, or red or green – hues that, both scientifically and psychologically, we can now only think of as irreconcilable opposites.

Naming colours is one way of manipulating their psychological impact. Paint manufacturers know that the titles of their colour swatches can affect sales at least as much as their pigments. Considerable investment is made in dreaming up evocative names for different paint colours, which may even be registered as trademarks. While their blurbs may pay lip service to universal colour meanings, apparently it can never do any harm to help along our responses with a few linguistic pointers.

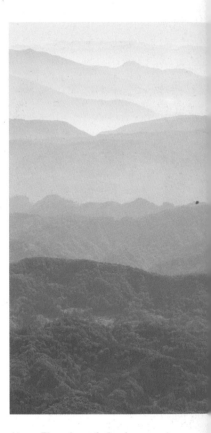

Above: The colour of a landscape gives us practical information, but also triggers emotional responses. Here, hazy blues speak of vast distances and imminent nightfall; though the picture may have been shot in a hot climate, it sends a shiver down the spine.

Left: Vivid green naturally evokes health and vitality. Yet when associated with, say, human flesh, the colour has quite different implications and much less wholesome associations.

SILVER

Moonlight, alchemy, spiritual powers, anything fluid (quicksilver) and mysterious. Intellect, harmony and self-awareness (mirrors). Like gold, this 'colour' depends on texture to differentiate it from, say, grey.

GOLD

One of the perceived colours of the sun and the traditional colour of money. A precious, ostentatious colour evoking feelings of security and abundance. A warm, syrupy colour that makes people feel relaxed.

RED

Passion, danger, anger, love, sex, power – red evokes strong feelings of whatever kind. According to Indian mysticism and holistic therapists, red is the colour of the lowest of the seven chakras, or energy centres, which lies at the base of the spine.

GREEN

Nature, luck, renewal, new beginnings (seedlings, plants), oxygen, money, prosperity, healing, employment, fertility, success, health, harmony.

BLUE

Calmness, coldness, serenity (the Virgin Mary), introspection, wisdom, solitude, space, truth, beauty, calculation, icyness.

TURQUOISE

According to British New Age guru David Icke, turquoise is the 'mystic colour of the universe'. In 2002, scientists at Johns Hopkins University announced that the real colour of the universe, calculated by averaging the light of the observed galaxies, was approximately turquoise. Sadly, they later revised this to a pale beige. Emotionally, turquoise is linked with feelings of elation, generosity, riches and expansiveness. Turquoise is to silver what purple is to gold.

BROWN

Earth, wood, solidity, stability, warmth. Overwhelmed by red (fire), but complements green or blue.

PART 0I. DEFINITIONS

CHAPTER TWO

COLOUR THEORY

To use colour effectively, we need to understand what it is and how it works. After developing his law of universal gravitation, Isaac Newton (1642–1727) became interested in theories of light and colour. At that time, many people believed colour to be a mixture of light and darkness. One scientist posited that the colour scale ranged from a brilliant red, which was proposed to be pure light, to blue and then black (darkness). Newton surmised that this must be wrong, since a white page with black writing did not appear coloured when it was viewed from a distance. Instead, the black and white blended together and appeared grey.

During the latter half of the seventeenth century, many scientists were experimenting with prisms. The general view was that a prism 'coloured' the light, accounting for the rainbow dot seen when light was projected through a prism onto a surface. In 1665, Newton performed his own experiments, refracting light through the prism onto a surface much farther away. The results confirmed that, rather than colouring the light, the prism was splitting it into the colours of the rainbow: red, orange, yellow, green, blue, indigo and violet. In 1666, Newton created a circular chart with the seven colours laid out around its circumference. As a tool for understanding and selecting colour, the colour wheel remains essentially unchanged to this day.

Newton assumed that light was made from particles, or 'corpuscles'. Meanwhile, however, the Dutch physicist Christiaan Huygens (1629–95) was developing the idea that light exists in waves. Newton's theory explained the reflection and refraction of light and the casting of shadows, but the wave theory explained why the edges of shadows were not sharp.

In 1864, Scottish physicist James Clerk Maxwell (1831–79) suggested that light was of an electromagnetic nature, propagating as a wave from source to receiver. By the end of the century, after Heinrich Hertz (1857–94) had discovered radio waves and Wilhelm Röntgen (1845–1923) had discovered X-rays, scientific thinking about light had been revolutionized. Visible light lies on a spectrum that also includes radio waves (longer wavelengths) and X-rays (shorter wavelengths), with the colours of the spectrum appearing in order of decreasing wavelength.

Albert Einstein (1879–1955) would later suggest that light might actually consist of particles after all, setting physicists a puzzle they have yet to solve.

Artists laboured for centuries to mix colours and create colour effects without really knowing what colour was or how it worked. Their successes were remarkable, but only a scientific understanding of the spectrum enabled advances such as colour photography.

THE TRICHROMATIC THEORY The prism proved that colour was a real phenomenon, yet at the same time it confirmed colour's subjectivity. As Newton said, 'Rays, properly expressed, are not coloured.' The question of how light created the impression of colour in the mind remained to be answered.

At the beginning of the nineteenth century, Thomas Young (1773–1829), an English physician, postulated that the eye must contain receptors made up of particles that 'oscillated' with particular wavelengths of light. An infinite number of particles would be required to cover the entire spectrum, but this was clearly impossible, so the receptors must instead be sensitive to only a limited number of colours. All the other colours we 'see' would then be made up of combinations of these. Young's trichromatic theory initially identified the three colours as red, yellow and blue, but he later

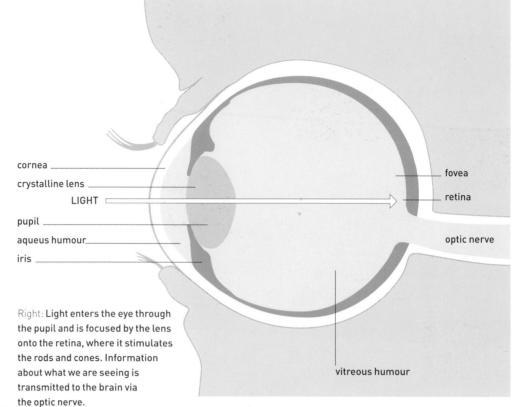

Below: **Within the retina, a complex arrangement of specialized cells processes information from the photoreceptors (rods and cones). Note the relatively small number of blue cones: the signal from these is somehow boosted to play a roughly equal role in colour vision, but the exact mechanism is not known.**

Right: **Light enters the eye through the pupil and is focused by the lens onto the retina, where it stimulates the rods and cones. Information about what we are seeing is transmitted to the brain via the optic nerve.**

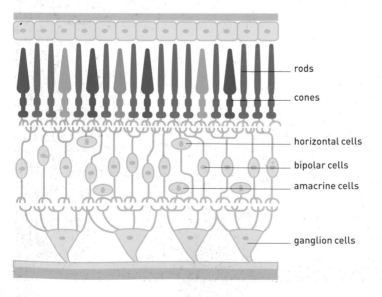

changed the yellow to green. The theory was further developed by German scientist Hermann von Helmholtz (1821–94), a pioneer of sensory physiology.

In the 1960s, scientists were able to confirm the existence of the receptors Young and von Helmholtz had described. These 'cones' (*at left*) are divided into three types sensitive to specific wavelengths corresponding to red (570 nanometers), green (535 nm) and blue (425 nm).

The combination of the three primary colours of light to re-create the entire spectrum is now referred to as additive mixing. Starting from an absence of light (darkness), light of each primary is added to produce progressively lighter tones, varying the proportion to create different colours. Mixing an equal amount of each primary results in 'white' light. You can see additive mixing in action on the TV, computer or movie screen, and in theatrical lighting.

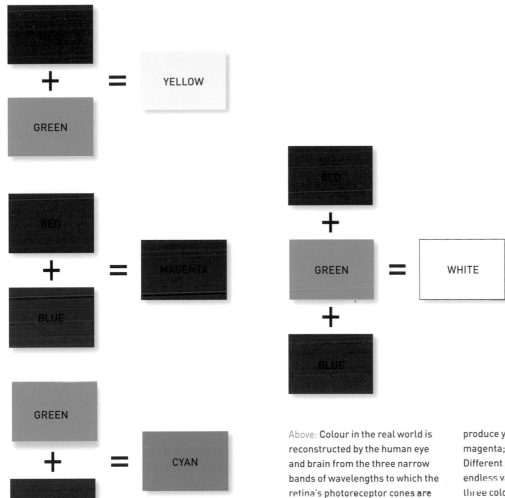

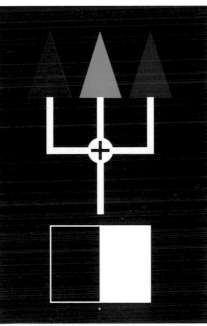

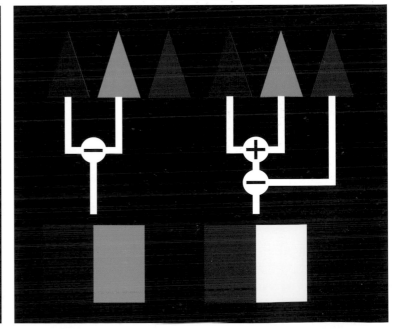

Although the Young–von Helmholtz trichromatic theory explained many observations about colour, it left other questions unaddressed. In the 1870s, Ewald Hering (1834–1918), a contemporary of von Helmholtz, studied the subjective impression of colour. He pointed out that yellow, which is supposed to be produced by a combination of red and green, is in fact perceived as an elementary colour, not a reddish green or a greenish red: we are not physically able to visualize such combinations. This led him to reject the trichromatic model in favour of a system of four colour sensations: yellow, red, blue and green, plus black and white, which generate colours by an 'opponent process.'

Subsequent research has shown that both the trichromatic theory and the opponent-process theory are correct. They deal with what happens at different stages of visual processing in the eye and brain. So colour systems based on both models are still used by scientists, artists, illustrators and designers, each system proving appropriate for different purposes.

Above: Colour in the real world is reconstructed by the human eye and brain from the three narrow bands of wavelengths to which the retina's photoreceptor cones are sensitive. For example, red and green light, in equal proportions, produce yellow; red and blue, magenta; and green and blue, cyan. Different proportions produce endless variation. Combining all three colours equally gives a neutral grey which, at its brightest, is white.

Right: Although we don't yet have a complete model of the way colour information is processed by the eye and brain, tests show that an 'opponent process' is at work. There are three opposing pairs: dark/light, red/green and blue/yellow. Within each pair, it's impossible to register both sensations at once, which explains why no combination of green and red will ever give the impression of 'greenish red'; instead, when green and red cones are stimulated but not blue, the result is yellow.

ACHROMATIC SYSTEM

CHROMATIC SYSTEM

ADDITIVE AND SUBTRACTIVE MIXING
Any child can tell you that the three primary colours are red, yellow and blue, and he or she has the paint box to prove it. Yet, as we have seen, the true primary colours of light – those that stimulate the receptors in our eyes – have been identified as red, green and blue. The reason for the difference is that when we see the colours of a painting, we are not looking at light emitted at those wavelengths, but at light reflected from the surface.

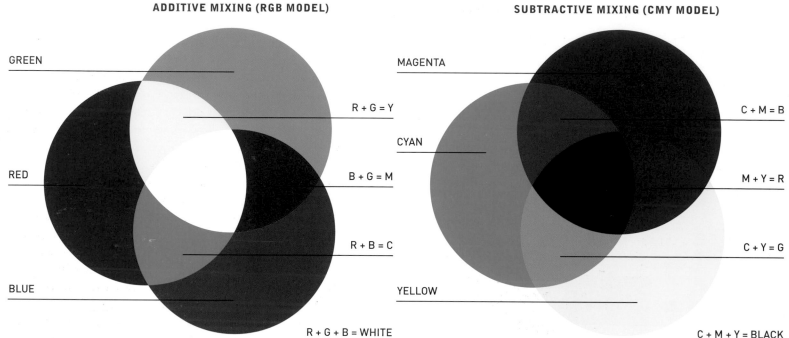

ADDITIVE MIXING (RGB MODEL)

GREEN

R + G = Y

RED

B + G = M

R + B = C

BLUE

R + G + B = WHITE

SUBTRACTIVE MIXING (CMY MODEL)

MAGENTA

C + M = B

CYAN

M + Y = R

C + Y = G

YELLOW

C + M + Y = BLACK

The primaries are not the only colours that can be mixed, of course. We can use prisms or coloured filters to produce any wavelength of light and combine it with any other to give a particular colour. Equally, we can mix paint colours and see what results. The reason for using the primaries is that if the proportions are right, we can accurately produce any colour within the visible spectrum. Start with a different set of colours, and this is not guaranteed.

In mixing paints, or pigments, we are manipulating light indirectly. When light strikes the pigmented surface, some wavelengths are absorbed and others reflected. The reflected wavelengths determine the colour we see. So what we call red paint is paint that absorbs green and blue

Above left: When working with emitted light, colours can be mixed from the three primary colours to which our eyes respond: red, green and blue. The diagram shows the theoretical results, with yellow, magenta and cyan produced as secondary colours where two primaries are equally mixed, and white as the result of mixing all three primaries at full strength. Note that what we mean by 'white' is a neutral grey, which seems lighter when more illumination is present (or when the contrast between the illuminated area and its surroundings is greater).

Above right: Cyan pigments absorb only red light, magenta only green and yellow only blue, so we can use these colours to mix reflected light as purely as possible. Modern colour printing uses these primaries.

light, while green paint absorbs red and blue. Now, we know from trichromatic theory that mixing red and green should produce yellow. It is not going to work that way with our pigments. Each absorbs more light than it reflects, so mixing two together can only make a darker colour: the combination of red and green in fact produces a muddy brown. Mixing paint in all three primaries, rather than making white, as with light, will make something close to black.

The solution is subtractive mixing. Instead of pigments that absorb all but a certain primary, we use pigments that only absorb a certain primary. Starting from white (the assumed colour of our canvas), we can then reverse the additive process

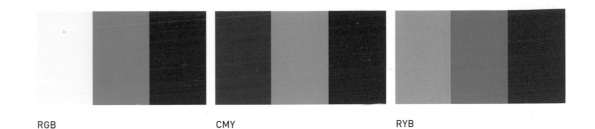

Right: Comparing the secondary colours produced by different mixing methods indicates the range and purity of colours that can be obtained. RGB mixing generates very pure CMY secondaries. CMY mixing results in RGB secondaries that are duller than pure red, green and blue light. RYB mixing results in even duller tones, and a smaller range of hues.

RGB   CMY   RYB

SUBTRACTIVE MIXING (RYB MODEL)

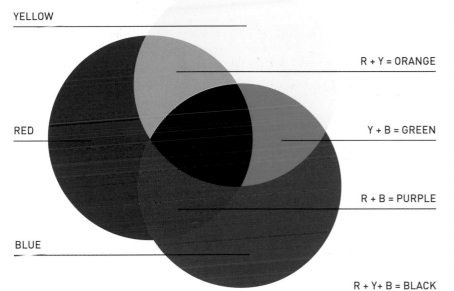

YELLOW

RED

BLUE

R + Y = ORANGE

Y + B = GREEN

R + B = PURPLE

R + Y + B = BLACK

Above: Mixing red, yellow and blue, the traditional artist's primaries, creates a limited colour spectrum. Because magenta and cyan are true primaries, absorbing only one wavelength, they can't be recreated by combining these colours.

by applying more pigment, subtracting more of each primary, until we finally reach black. The colours that absorb the primaries are their complements. Cyan (a blue-green colour) absorbs red; magenta (a pinkish colour) absorbs green; and yellow absorbs blue.

In mechanical colour printing, cyan, magenta, yellow and black – CMYK – are now used as primaries to generate a reasonably broad spectrum of colours (*see chapter 04.03*). Why have painters not followed suit? One reason is the availability of suitable pigments: the traditional artist's primaries of pure reds, yellows and blues have long been available (*see chapter 01.04*), while magenta and cyan are harder to come by. Another is that red and blue seem stronger and more useful colours in themselves than magenta and cyan.

As the pigment wheel of red/yellow/blue combinations demonstrates (*see page 40*), this system, although still used by painters, is limited in the range of colours that can be produced by mixing the primaries. Magenta and cyan are missing. Fortunately, painters have an ace up their sleeve: white pigment. By adding a 'colour' that reflects the maximum amount of all wavelengths, the possible range of colour impressions is greatly increased. As any child can also tell you, mixing white with blue gives light blue. With a touch of yellow, this becomes cyan.

Right: To fully understand subtractive mixing, compare these illustrations with the subtractive mixing diagram above left. A magenta surface is one which absorbs green wavelengths, reflecting red and blue. A yellow surface absorbs blue, reflecting red and yellow. A cyan surface absorbs red, reflecting blue and green. In each case more light is reflected than absorbed, so the reflected colour appears as bright as possible.

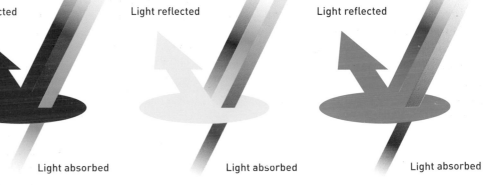

Light reflected   Light reflected   Light reflected

Light absorbed   Light absorbed   Light absorbed

SEEING COLOUR DIFFERENTLY Looking at the field of red and purple flowers photographed here, most of us see a bright, deep, passionate red contrasting with a cooler, calming, subdued and gentle purple, both pleasingly balanced by a wash of green created by the millions of different shades in the surrounding stalks and leaves. To someone with a colour deficiency (commonly called colourblindness), the scene would not look the same.

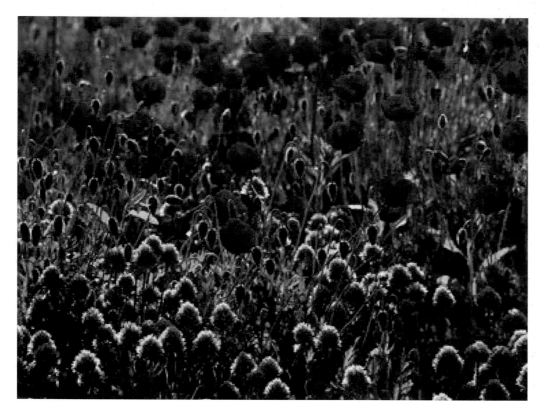

The three cones in the normal eye are known as the L-cone, M-cone and S-cone, and they recognize mostly long (red) wavelengths, medium (green) wavelengths and short (blue) wavelengths, respectively. Most colour deficiencies affect the L-cones or the M-cones, and the most severe deficiencies, when one cone type is completely absent, are collectively termed dichromatism, since only two colour receptors remain.

If the L-cone is affected, the condition is called protanopia, and if the M-cone is impaired, it is called deutanopia (or deuteranopia). Tritanopia, or absence of the S-cone, is extremely rare, as is monochromasty: the complete inability to perceive colour. More common is a reduced functioning of the L- or M-cone, termed anomalous trichromatism. In the L-cone it is called protanomaly, and in the M-cone deutanomaly. There is no variant in the S-cone.

Above: **This photograph represents the world as most of us see it. Red, green and blue cones are stimulated to various degrees by each point in the image, creating an impression of colour that spans the visible spectrum. To a hawkmoth, which would normally see ultraviolet, this image would look wrong.**

About 8 percent of all men have some sort of colour deficiency; in women, the figure is only about 0.5 percent. The common L- and M-cone deficiencies are known as red-green colour blindness, because the deficiencies reduce the ability to distinguish those two colours. The rare absence of the S-cone, sometimes called blue blindness, makes it difficult to differentiate between blue and yellow.

Looking at our scene, someone with protanopia would pick up bluer tones in the purple flowers and would see no red at all. Instead, the red flowers would become green, like the leaves, but a few shades darker. Someone with deutanopia would still not see the red. To him or her, the red flowers would look yellowish-green – brighter than in the previous case, but still only a few shades lighter than the leaves – and the purple flowers would appear blue, their redness removed.

Since their physiology is different, animals do not see colour the same way we do. It is often claimed that dogs see in black and white, but that is not strictly true. While human vision is trichromatic, dogs and most mammals have dichromatic vision. This means they cannot distinguish between some colours, rather like someone with severe colour blindness. Rodents, on the other hand, are monochromats, completely colour blind. Dogs are compensated by having superior night vision: to nocturnal predators, this is more important than good colour vision.

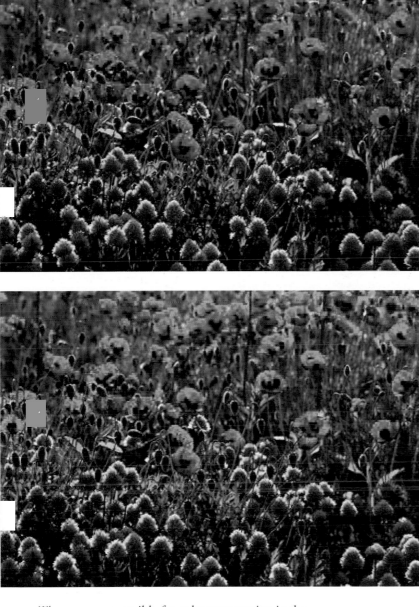

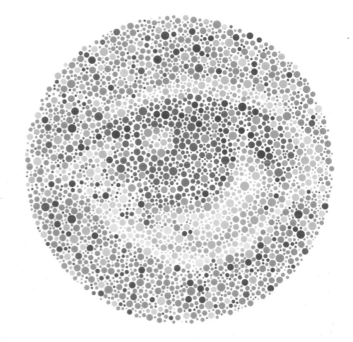

Left, above: **People with the colour deficiency known as protanopia don't see red, so the flowers would be harder to distinguish. Red surfaces may seem dark, and red lights – as in traffic lights – are all but invisible.**

Left, below: **Deutanopia also affects the distinction between red and green. Red, orange and green will all seem similar in hue, as will violet, purple and blue.**

Above: **The Ishihara tests for colour blindness are commonly used to identify red-green problems. Subjects are shown several images and asked to identify shapes formed by differently coloured dots within them. Those with anomalous colour vision may see no pattern, or a different pattern from those with normal vision.**

Below: **In low light, the cones in the retina are less responsive, and our vision relies mostly on the rods, which don't differentiate between wavelengths. As a result, we see an almost monochromic world. The lack of contrast, which is also noticeable, is a real phenomenon, as opposed to a neurological one.**

The cones responsible for colour perception in the human eye function poorly in low light, so in such conditions a different group of receptors, called rods, takes over. Rods do not distinguish between wavelengths, so vision becomes monochromic, creating the blue-grey visual world we associate with nighttime. Many nocturnal insects, however, can identify colours at night. A recent experiment with elephant hawkmoths shows that they are able to pick out artificial yellow and blue flowers from a selection that includes shades of grey.

Hawkmoths have three separate colour receptors: blue, green and ultraviolet. Like ours, these do not function well at night, but the moth's anatomy compensates by providing, among other things, a mirror-type structure at the base of the eye that replays images a second time, providing more information to be processed.

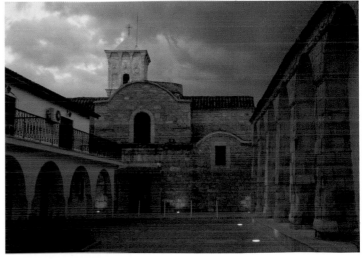

OPTICAL ILLUSIONS

Optical illusions provide some fascinating insights into how we perceive and interpret colour. The term illusion, of course, is in itself problematic, as it has pejorative implications. Are our eyes really being fooled, or is what we see in these illusions actually a kind of reality? Who's to say that an optical illusion is less real than anything else we see?

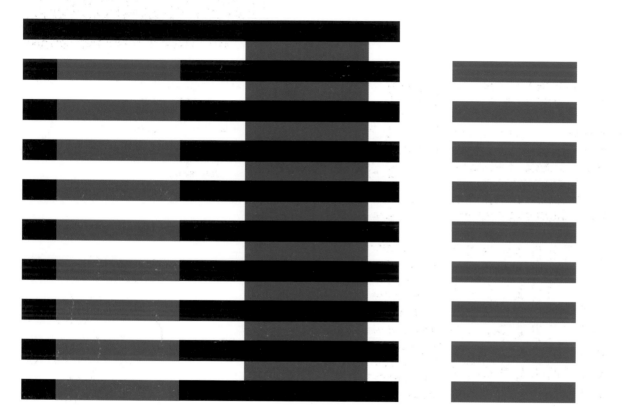

For reasons that are still not completely understood, we can be made to see colour even in black-and-white images. Benham's Top, a popular toy since the late nineteenth century, consists of a disc marked with a black-and-white pattern that, when spun rapidly, creates an illusory colour spectrum. Another example of this is the McCollough Effect, in which exposure to two different primaries alternated respectively with horizontal and vertical black stripes causes the viewer to see false colours in black-and-white stripes of the same orientation. We can also be induced to see white spaces filled with colours that are not present at all. This is demonstrated by the neon spreading illusion: when sections of a gridline pattern are coloured differently from the rest, we seem to see a continuous glowing band of a third colour.

Above: Although the wavelengths of light reflected from two points within a scene may be the same, our eye and brain may interpret their colour differently, depending on their surroundings; this is known as the Munker-White effect. Here (above left), the blue bars on the left are clearly lighter than those on the right. When the same bars are reproduced independently of the black lines, however, it becomes obvious that they are identical.

Certain kinds of optical illusion have proved particularly significant in our understanding of how colour works in artistic compositions. Among the earliest to be explored were the effects of placing different colours next to one another. Leonardo da Vinci (1452–1519) – who had already identified white, black, red, green, blue and yellow as primary colours – noticed that certain colours intensified each other. Leonardo referred to these as 'contrary' colours; we now refer to them as complementary colours, or complements. Complementary colours produce a neutral colour when mixed.

part 01. definitions

French chemist Michel Chevreul (1786–1889), who was employed by the famous Gobelins tapestry studio, investigated more thoroughly the possibilities of this effect. He examined another optical illusion: afterimaging. If you stare at a strongly coloured surface for a few seconds, then look away, you will see a block of a different colour. This is a negative afterimage, and its colour will be the complement of the one you were looking at. The effect is called successive contrast. But afterimaging occurs, albeit less dramatically, whenever we look at colours, and it affects the way colour fields appear when juxtaposed.

Right and below: **What is now known as the McCollough effect was first described by Celeste McCollough in a paper in** Science **in 1965. Gaze at the coloured grids for at least a couple of minutes, then look at the black-and-white grids. You should see a green haze around the horizontal lines and a magenta haze around the verticals. This isn't just an afterimage caused by fatigued neurons. The precise cause is unclear, but neuro-transmitters are involved, which may explain why the effect can last for several hours. For more on this phenomenon, visit http://research.lumeta.com/ches/me/.**

Above and left: **Stare at the blue square for a couple of minutes. Now stare at the small grey square and note the colour illusion. The colour you should be able to 'see' around the grey square is blue's complementary colour.**

Our visual system seems to 'expect' the complement of whatever colour we see. If the complement is present, the combination looks especially vibrant; if absent, we produce it ourselves. (We now know that this effect is caused by inhibitory interactions in cells in the visual cortex of the brain that work on principles similar to Hering's opponent process.) This discovery is the basis of simultaneous contrast, an important principle in the use of colour in art and design.

PARTITIVE COLOUR Simultaneous contrast affects our perception of black-and-white images: a midgrey object will look darker on a white background than on a black background. Its effect on combinations of black and white with colours is slightly more complicated: not only will a given red, for example, look brighter on a black background, it will also appear warmer.

When colours are combined with each other, all sorts of interactions are set off (simultaneous colour contrast), and the impression generated by the colours within an image can be highly unpredictable. The same colour used in different positions, for example, may look completely different as a result of being juxtaposed with other colours.

Once these effects are understood, they can be harnessed to create an intensified colour experience, giving the impression of vibrant or luminous colour; or they can be deliberately cancelled. Because simultaneous contrast operates only in a small area around the division between two colours, the effect can be reduced or removed altogether by separating the colour fields with a black or white outline. A more subtle way to prevent unwanted interactions is to identify which is the weaker colour of a pair and add a small amount of the other colour's complement to it. By second-guessing the brain's response in this way, the artist is able to regain control of colour perception and produce a more predictable impression.

Another way to exploit colour interactions is partitive mixing. Instead of mixing pigments together before applying them to the canvas, the artist places fine dots or stripes of carefully chosen colours to create the impression of a new colour, which is mixed in the eye/brain rather than on the canvas. The process is a pseudoadditive one, since it

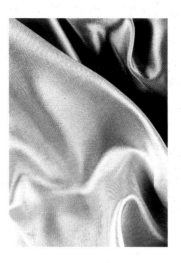

Above: **In shot silks, coloured threads are combined in such a way that the perceived colour of the fabric is constantly shifting.**

Below: **The simultaneous contrast effect is particularly strong at the junctions of complementary colour fields of similar brightness. These 'vibrating' colour combinations make text almost unreadable (left).**

attempts to combine the colours reflected by the pigments rather than combining the colours absorbed. Following French chemist Michel Chevreul (*see page 31*), several postimpressionist painters adopted variations on the method, most explicitly Georges Seurat (1859–91). Applying his pointillist technique, Seurat used colour dots of varying sizes to build up the hazy areas of colour that fill his often gigantic canvases.

It was his own research into optics and colour theory that led Seurat to this method, but it seems that he laboured under some fundamental misconceptions. Seurat believed that his dots of paired complementaries would create an impression of luminosity. Instead, they tend towards greyness. Red and green, for example, appear vibrant when fields of each are juxtaposed. But the effect does not occur when small dots are used to optically mix these colours.

Chevreul had already applied a better understanding of partitive colour to tapestry weaving. Many other fabric production techniques rely on partitive mixing to create rich colour effects, whether or not their originators understood the process at work. Although a tweed may look brown, its colour gains a special quality from being made up of threads of various colours, which are visible individually only when viewed close up. More dramatically, 'shot' fabrics interweave colours in such a way that the overall impression changes depending on how the light strikes the surface, giving a shimmering appearance to the material. This effect is called iridescence.

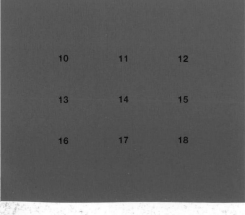

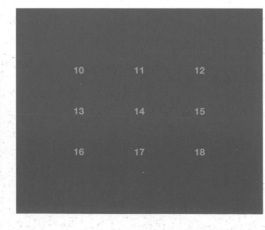

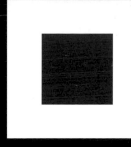 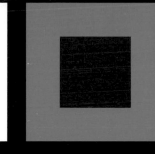 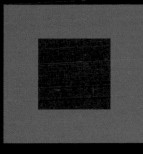

RED ON BLACK
On a black background, a field of red appears hot and vibrant, with clearly defined edges.

RED ON WHITE
The red colour appears duller against a white background. Observing the effects colours have on each other is the starting point for understanding the relativity of colour. The relationship between values, saturations and the warmth or coolness of respective hues causes noticeable differences in the perception of colour.

RED ON CYAN
Here the red colour looks brilliant against the cyan background, but the red square looks somewhat smaller than on the black background. This is another trick the eye plays on us. In fact, we have a very short memory for colours and are often unable to identify the same colour displayed in a different context. The effect is reduced by separating the colour fields with a black or white outline (right).

RED ON BROWN
As increasing amounts of magenta and yellow are added to the background colour, the red square begins to appear more and more lifeless.

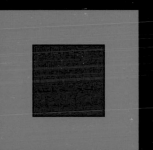

RED ON MAGENTA
When the red square is placed on a 100% magenta background, the two shapes become less and less distinguishable to the eye as distance increases.

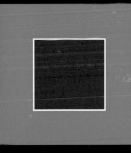

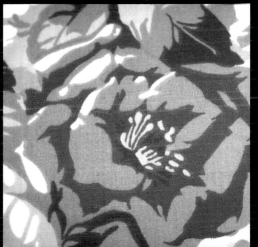

Left: **Tapestry was the medium in which Chevreul first explored partitive colour mixing. Properly understood and applied, the interactions between the colours of neighbouring threads can produce a tremendously rich palette.**

Below: **The repeated eye motif is made up of 100% cyan and 100% yellow ink in each case, but it gives very different impressions of colour depending on background. On yellow, for example, it seems quite dark, yet on purple it appears almost luminous.**

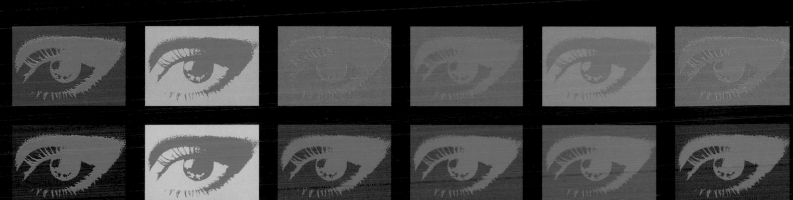

DIMENSIONS OF COLOUR

The wavelength of light involved is only one of the ways in which we differentiate colours. As we have seen (*see page 27*), blue paint can be light blue or dark blue. In either case, the colour may be either bright and strong or dull and greyish, and what dictates these nuances of colour are its hue, saturation and lightness. These qualities are all independent of each other, and to describe a colour fully, we need to measure all three.

The property of colour associated with wavelength is known as hue and is the trickiest to describe meaningfully. Although all people perceive colour in roughly the same way (unless they have a form of colour blindness) and will agree that a certain colour is red rather than green, they will not always agree on the exact colour that represents pure red or pure green. Most people's idea of red is slightly more orange than the red in the trichromatic model, for example, and the common perception of green is slightly yellower.

Similarly, to create an intermediate, or secondary, colour, such as orange (red/yellow), we should mix exactly equal proportions of two primaries. It turns out, however, that different proportions are needed to create secondaries that look balanced rather than appear biased towards one primary or the other.

The brightness (as opposed to darkness) of a color can also be referred to as value. A pigment of a given hue can be lightened or darkened by adding white or black, giving a tint. Untinted hues, as depicted in the colour wheel, are referred to as pure hues. Pure hues do not all share the same value, however, so it may be necessary to add white or black to one to make it similar in lightness to another. For example, pure green needs to be darkened to match pure red. Adjusting the value of a hue the opposite way – for example, adding white to blue or black to yellow – creates what artists and illustrators call a discord.

Variations in value bring light, shadow and depth to pictures. An area will tend to seem flat if the colours within it are of a similar value, even if their hues differ. Darker and lighter values can be used to add shadows and highlights, giving the illusion of three-dimensional objects within the two-dimensional canvas. In optical mixing (partitive) techniques, colours of similar value should be used, as these are blended most readily by the eye/brain.

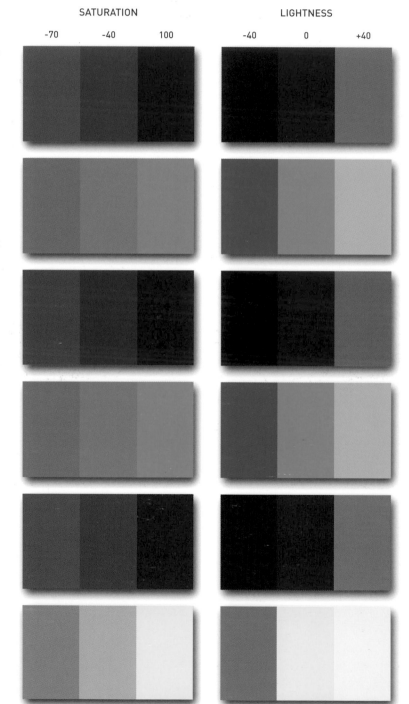

SATURATION			LIGHTNESS		
-70	-40	100	-40	0	+40

Left: The concepts of hue, saturation and lightness are best described visually. These swatches show computer-generated variations on the primary colours. A painter might reduce saturation by adding a colour's complement, or vary lightness by adding white or black.

Below: The Mac OS X Color Picker, as seen on Macintosh computers, usefully demonstrates the principles of hue, saturation and lightness. Hues are arranged around the colour wheel, with less saturated colours in the centre graduating to pure (fully saturated) hues at the outside edge. The slider on the right of the box controls lightness. In the centre image, lightness has been reduced to 50%; in the image on the right, it has been reduced to zero.

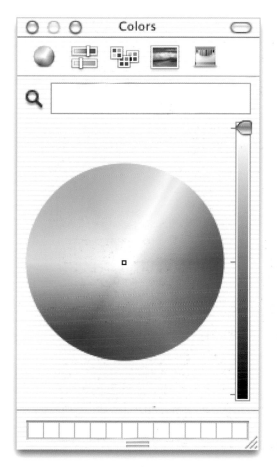
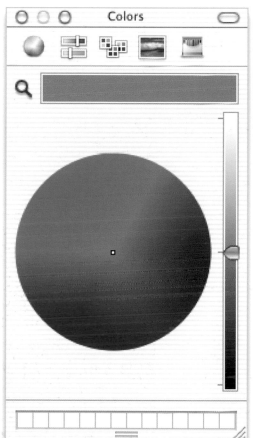
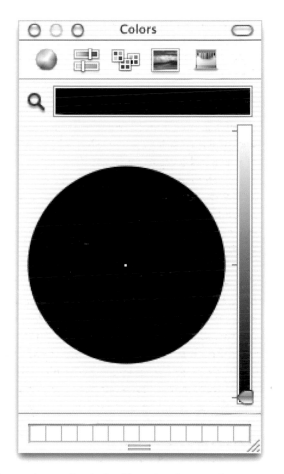

The final aspect or dimension of a colour is saturation. (The alternative term intensity is best avoided, since it can also refer to brightness.) More saturated colours might be described as brighter, stronger or more vivid. Pure hues, including primaries, are fully saturated. Desaturated colours are greyer and, as this suggests, can be mixed as pigments by adding both black and white to pure hues. The result is that a certain amount of light is reflected, most of which spans the full visible spectrum; the particular wavelengths that make up the desired hue dominate only marginally. Hues mixed with grey are called tones. In additive mixing, desaturated colours have nearly equal percentages of red, green and blue, with small variations producing the weakened impression of hue.

Other techniques for producing desaturated colours subtractively involve either two or three hues. Mixing a hue with a smaller proportion of its complement gives a shade. Mixing the three primary colours in unequal proportions gives a broken hue. Of course, larger numbers of different pigments can be combined ad infinitum, but the results will quickly become dark and muddy as more light is absorbed.

COLOUR AND ILLUMINATION In depicting a real-world scene, the artist or illustrator must consider the overall quality of the ambient light; the degree of illumination of each part of an object (light and shadow); the interaction of the colour of the light with the 'local colour' of the surface (that is, its reflective properties); and the working of the eye.

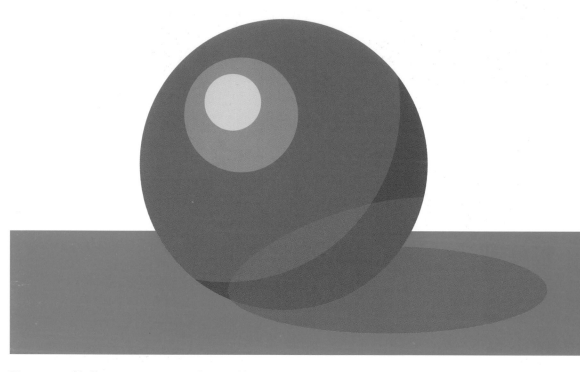

Left: The interaction of cast and reflected light in even a simple scene may be quite complex, but a basic understanding of colour-mixing principles will enable you to work it out. In practice, of course, artists will often pay more attention to observation than to theoretical calculations.

Picture a red ball sitting on a green plane and lit by a yellow lamp. To find out the colour result of the light striking the ball, we must combine our knowledge of additive and subtractive mixing (*see page 26*). A yellowish light is dominated by red and green wavelengths and is deficient in blue. A surface colour identified as red is one that predominantly absorbs green and blue light and reflects red. Accordingly, our red ball will strongly reflect the strong red component of the light striking it, weakly reflect the strong green component and weakly reflect the weak blue component. So the reflected light will contain a lot of red, a little green and hardly any blue. This additive mix gives an orange-red.

At its closest point to the light source, the ball will have a highlight: a small area of lighter colour. The more reflective (shinier) the object, the lighter and less saturated the highlight will be, since wavelengths are being reflected indiscriminately. On the opposite side, the ball will fall into shadow, which will be a darker shade.

We must also consider the interaction between the ball and the plane on which it rests. First, the ball will cast a shadow onto the green plane. This cast shadow will darken the green. Second, the plane will in turn be reflected in the ball, adding green. The strength and clarity of this reflection will depend on the shininess of the ball.

Shadows are not usually depicted as simple shades of the surface colours on which they fall. In reality, as Johann Wolfgang von Goethe (1749–1832) noted (*see page 48*), the colours of cast shadows are complicated by the presence of multiple light sources. For example, a shadow cast by a yellow lamp in a room dimly lit by daylight will look bluish, since the green and red tones contributed by the lamp are subtracted from the shadow area, while the level of blue is unchanged. Similar effects occur to a lesser degree in form shadows due to reflected light. Artists commonly approximate these effects using two rules of thumb: that a

Right: What colour is the centre square on the front face of this cube? You would probably say yellow, and, reading the image as a depiction of a real object, that would be correct. But try placing a sheet of paper over the page, then cutting a small hole over the centre square on each of the cube's three sides. They are all exactly the same shade of brown. Our ability to compensate for different levels of lighting affects our interpretation of colour. We must accordingly adjust colours in artwork to create the desired effect.

Below: When an object is simultaneously illuminated by lights of different colours, the colours of shadows can be surprising.
The principles are most clearly demonstrated with red, green and blue lights, but they can be conveyed more subtly when, for example, objects within a room are lit both by electric lamps and daylight.

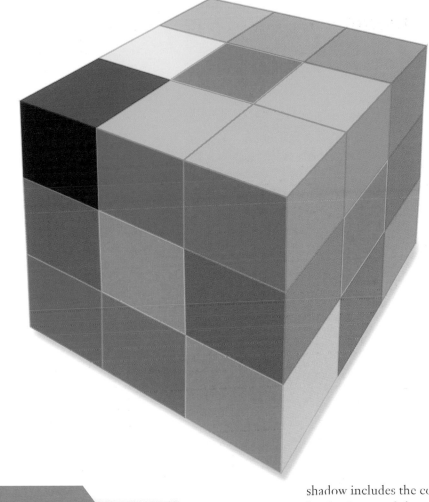

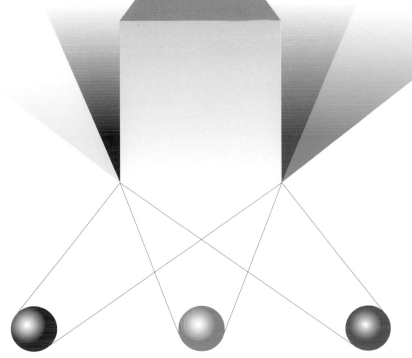

shadow includes the complement of the local colour; and that warm (yellow/red) light casts cold (blue/green) shadows, and vice versa.

When colour is applied in this way, some mixes may seem wrong. For example, darkening and desaturating yellow creates a brownish colour. This does not mean, however, that it will give the impression of brown within your composition, or that it cannot be used to represent a yellow object. To make sense of the world around us, our human visual system needs to recognize objects or colour fields as a whole, not as fragments of different tones. It does so by paying less attention to the absolute level of light received at each primary wavelength than to the ratio.

So we tend to see an object as red, for example, if it reflects more red light than nearby areas, and less blue and green, even though the actual proportion of red light that it reflects may be smaller than that of blue or green. This is called colour constancy.

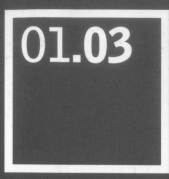

01.03

COLOUR SYSTEMS

Understanding the physics and physiology of colour is one thing; using colour in artwork is another. To help you select and combine colours, construct pleasing palettes and predict colour interactions, you will need a visual reference. Various colour systems have been devised to provide this, including wheels, triangles and more complex diagrams.

The attempt to formalize colour relationships dates back at least to Aristotle (384–322 BC), but it was begun in earnest by Leonardo da Vinci (1452–1519) and progressed steadily from the seventeenth century onwards. When Newton bent the visible spectrum around into a circle, he was able to note that mixing two colours from opposite positions on the wheel produced a neutral, or 'anonymous', colour. This demonstrated the principle of complements, which would later prove essential to many colour techniques. One of the most useful features of all colour wheels is that complements and other relationships (*see page 40*) are immediately obvious.

Like Newton's, most colour wheels show only pure hues, but some add variations with different lightness and/or saturation. To show all three aspects at once, a three-dimensional diagram is required, which makes such systems rather unwieldy to refer to. In computer graphics software, a colour picker commonly shows a spectrum of hues graduating from light to dark, with a slider to adjust saturation.

Other colour systems are concerned with defining exactly how to produce specific colours. In 1952, German scientist Alfred Hickethier (1901–67) proposed a cube of one thousand colours formed from different percentages of printing inks. Systems of this kind, including Trumatch and Focoltone, provide a palette of colours that can be reproduced on any printing press, although the result will match only if the inks and processes used conform to certain standards. The Pantone system provides a palette of formulas for premixed pigments, both for printing and for other media such as textiles and plastics.

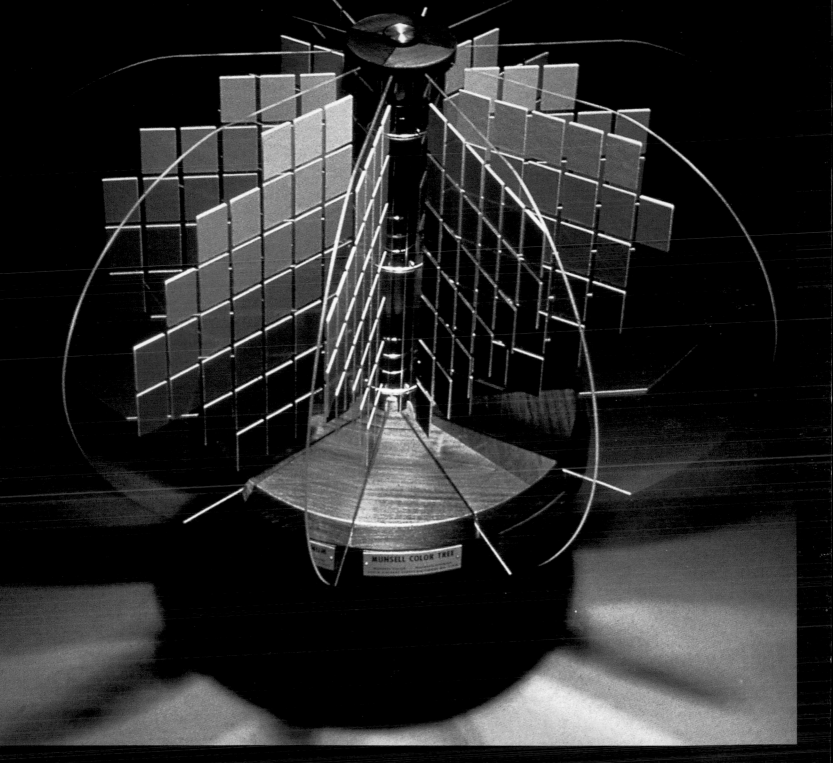

From the ancient Greeks onwards, theorists have looked for simple, logical order in the colour spectrum. In fact, however, colour perception is a rather complicated and messy business, as is demonstrated by the irregular shape of the Munsell Tree, the most successful modern colour model.

MUNSELL COLOR TREE

COLOUR WHEELS Newton's division of the spectrum into seven hues was, of course, arbitrary – there are no steps in the rainbow – and seems to have been dictated by his obsession with numerology, the mystic pseudoscience of number symbolism. The resulting colour wheel is slightly awkward: segments are of different sizes, and red, yellow and blue, the traditional primaries, are not evenly distributed around the circle.

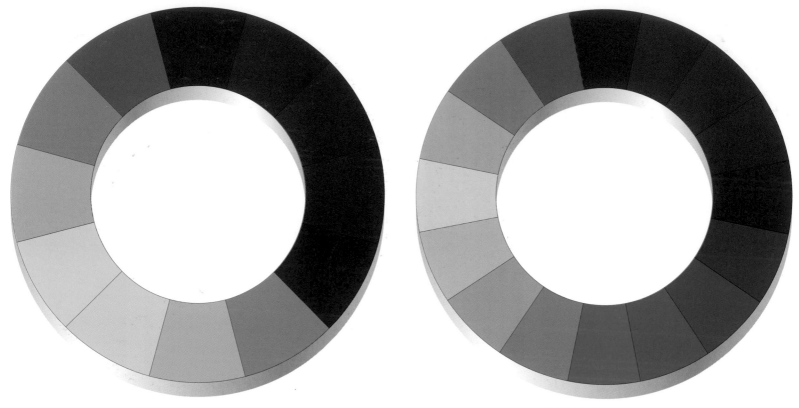

THE PIGMENT WHEEL   **THE ARTIST'S WHEEL**

Colour wheels produced by later theorists have almost always been based on an equidistant distribution of the primary colours – whichever those colours might be. The typical pigment wheel uses red, yellow and blue, the flawed subtractive mixing system generally adopted by those working with paint, fabrics or other reflective materials. Interspersed with the primaries on the wheel are three secondary colours, each representing a mix of the surrounding primaries. Six further tertiary colours are then interspersed to give a total of twelve hues.

　　The pigment wheel does not work well for partitive mixing. Here, the key relationship is between colours and their negative afterimages, but these pairs are not found opposite each other on the pigment wheel. A closer approximation of simultaneous contrast pairings is produced by adding green to the wheel as a fourth primary. The resulting visual wheel has been in use since the Renaissance, before the operation of partitive mixing was fully

Above left: **The traditional base colours used in mixing pigments are red, yellow and blue. A colour wheel based on these primaries shows the painter which hues should be combined to produce other colours. Note the limitation common to all basic colour wheels: Only pure hues are shown – that is, only one level of saturation and lightness – and only two primary combinations are offered.**

Above: **Adding green as a fourth primary colour creates an alternative colour wheel which is also widely used by artists. Although the overall range of hues produced is not significantly different, the complementary pairings – hues opposite each other on the wheel – vary slightly. Of course, painters will usually work from a palette of many pigments beyond the primary colours.**

Below: This simple colour wheel shows how red, green and blue light combine to give cyan, magenta and yellow secondary colours. Colour wheels in computer software are based on this, but show continuous graduation between hues rather than discrete steps.

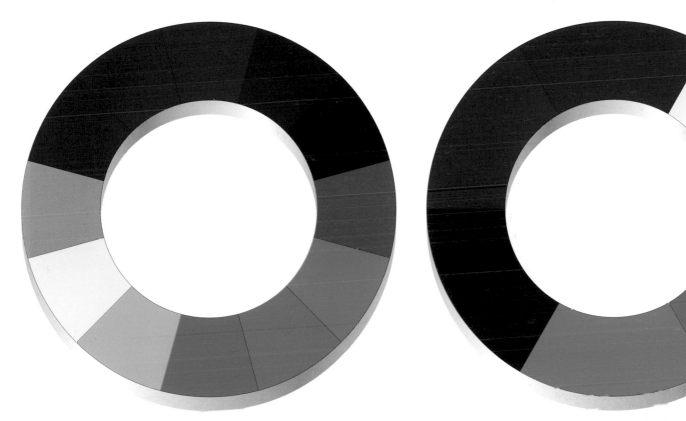

THE PROCESS WHEEL

THE LIGHT WHEEL

Above: When colours are mixed subtractively in colour printing, the user decides the percentage of each ink to apply. The lower the percentage, the lighter the colour. Pure hues are produced by using one or two inks. This wheel shows 100% magenta, cyan and yellow as primaries (clockwise from top); 100% of each pair as secondaries, making red, blue and green; and 100% + 50% combinations as tertiary colours.

understood. In the twentieth century, Albert Munsell (*see page 46*) tried to improve further on the pairing of complements by adding a fifth primary, violet.

Although colour wheels indicate which hues should be mixed in order to produce secondary and tertiary hues, they do not show how much of each will be required. Because the value and saturation of primaries varies, unequal proportions will be needed to produce a colour that is visually equidistant between its two components. Some painters, frustrated by the technical inaccuracy and practical unhelpfulness of standard colour wheels, have put together their own diagrams showing the exact location of specific paint colours within a colour wheel. Various examples of these

paint colour wheels can be found on the Web by typing 'colour wheel' into an Internet search engine.

The process colour wheel shows how cyan, magenta and yellow inks combine. Unlike other subtractive colour wheels, this one shows a full spectrum of colours, including red, green and blue (RGB) as relatively pure secondaries. Similar to this in reverse, the RGB additive colour wheel, or light wheel, shows the results of mixing light, with cyan, magenta and yellow appearing as secondaries. It is used by lighting designers and anyone working with translucent media.

RGB is also the usual model for colour specification on the computer, with values given as percentages, or on a scale from 0 to 255. Since it matches the primary colours detected by the human eye and makes mixing relatively simple, RGB is not a bad choice, but you must bear in mind that opposing colours on the wheel are not particularly good complements for simultaneous contrast effects.

COLOUR HARMONIES Whichever colour wheel you use, its main purpose is to point you towards hues that will work well together. The simplest relationships on the wheel are between analogous colours, which lie side by side, and between complements, found on opposite sides. But a number of other relationships can indicate pleasing colour schemes.

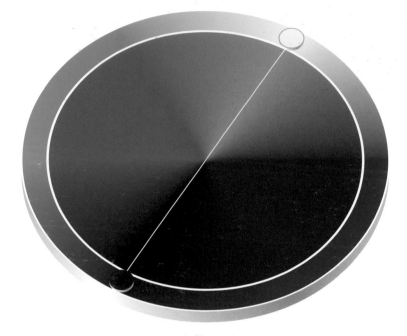

COMPLEMENTARY SCHEME
Two colours lying opposite each other on the colour wheel.

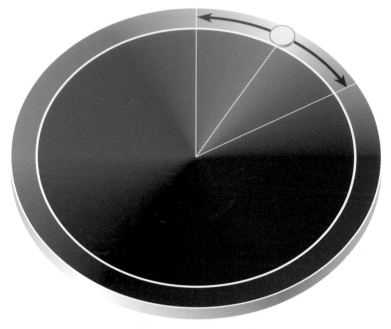

ANALOGOUS SCHEME
Two or more colours lying next to each other on the colour wheel.

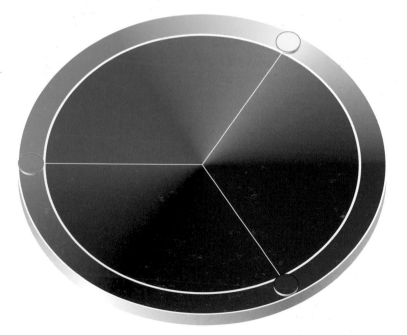

TRIADIC SCHEME
Three colours spaced evenly around the colour wheel.

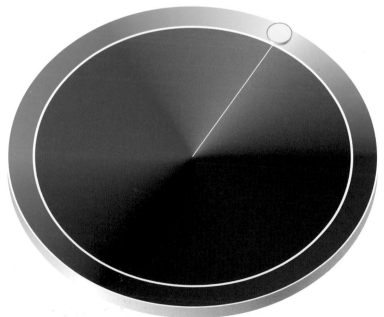

MONOCHROMATIC SCHEME
Shades and tints of a single colour, varying saturation and lightness instead of hue.

Colour schemes are sometimes described as harmonies. In this context, harmony relates to the eye/brain's expectation of overall balance or neutrality. When the colours in a composition add up to grey, harmony is achieved, and the image feels right – literally 'easy on the eye'. Of course, this is not to say that the colours used must themselves be neutral. The colour wheel will help you select colour combinations that balance each other.

A triadic scheme is based on three colours spaced equidistantly around the colour wheel. These could be primaries, but this scheme tends to be garish; a triad of secondary or tertiary colours is easier to handle. A more sophisticated three-colour scheme is the split complementary. This comprises any hue plus the two hues surrounding its complement.

A double complementary scheme uses two sets of complements. These may be at any angle to each other on the colour wheel, although the flexibility of the scheme means not all combinations formed this way will necessarily be pleasing.

To make these schemes work harmoniously, the lightness, saturation and/or extension (area of coverage) of the colours selected from the wheel will need to be adjusted to equalize their visual strengths. Goethe formulated a scale of relative strengths (see below) for this purpose. When you want to create a dramatic effect, you can either depart from the formula or exaggerate it – by using a very small area of a strong colour in a large field of a weak complement, for example.

Finally, a monochromatic scheme is based on a single hue, with variation created entirely by adjusting lightness or saturation. Here, Goethe's proportions for different hues cannot be applied, but note that black scores lowest in the system (meaning it can be used most freely) and white highest (meaning it should be used most sparingly). This suggests that darker tints should dominate monochrome compositions, and may indicate why designers often use monochrome imagery on a black background to give an impression of cool sophistication.

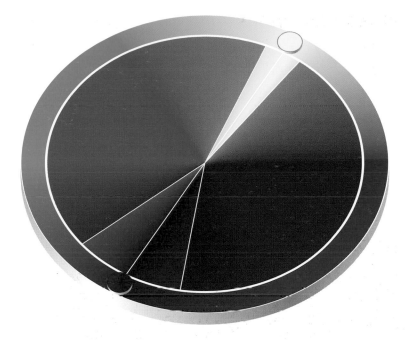

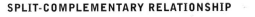

SPLIT-COMPLEMENTARY RELATIONSHIP
One hue accompanied by two equally spaced from its complement.

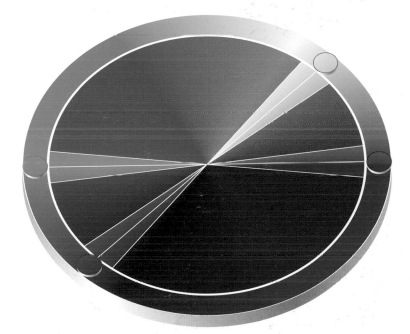

DOUBLE-COMPLEMENTARY RELATIONSHIP
Two complementary pairs lying opposite each other on the colour wheel.

Left: Goethe's colour ratio digram shows the relative visual strengths of six colours – yellow being the strongest and violet the weakest. To balance an area of yellow, for example, you would need just over twice the area of blue, which scores only 4 compared to 9.

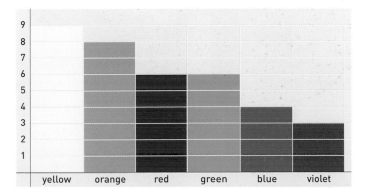

9					
8					
7					
6					
5					
4					
3					
2					
1					
yellow	orange	red	green	blue	violet

COLOUR AT THE BAUHAUS During the early twentieth century, the Bauhaus school of architecture and applied arts in Weimar, Germany, was an exceptional melting pot for artists and theorists. The two members of the school profiled here, Johannes Itten (1888–1967) and Josef Albers (1888–1976), both published key works on colour. Albers moved to the United States after the Bauhaus closed under pressure from the rising Nazi Party, bringing with him ideas that would influence leading modern artists.

From 1906, the Bauhaus provided a focus for a new kind of art, design and architecture that was simple and functional. Among several prominent painters working there in the early 1920s were Wassily Kandinsky (1866–1944), Paul Klee (1879–1940) and Johannes Itten. A pupil of Adolf Hoelzel (1853–1954), a Stuttgart teacher and painter whose theories profoundly influenced his work, Itten was initially responsible for the *Vorkurs* (foundation course), which stressed the importance of mysticism and experimentation as a means to self-discovery. His primary interest was in colour, and the legacy of his work still forms the backbone to colour-theory courses in art colleges.

Right: In Johannes Itten's colour wheel, based on red, yellow and blue primaries, the triangles bring colours together which are normally separated by their positions on the wheel.

Below: Itten's ideas about colour became, and remain, hugely influential as a result of his involvement with the Bauhaus. Although he acknowledged that a fully comprehensive analysis of colour perception eluded him and may indeed be impossible, his work is rigorous and, above all, useful to the practising artist or designer.

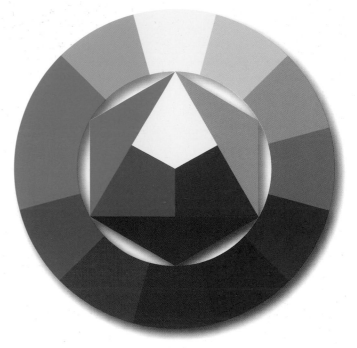

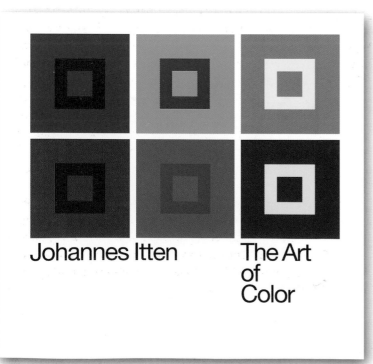

Johannes Itten   The Art of Color

Itten did not limit himself to examining colour scientifically, experimenting with light waves and reflections, or to a designer's perspective, exploring colour relationships and visual effects. Following the tradition initiated by Goethe (*see page 48*) and in line with the work of Kandinsky, he was convinced that colours could have psychological and spiritual effects on people and actively influence the way they felt.

Itten taught his students to appreciate colour harmony – not in the sense of one colour influencing another, but in terms of 'balance, a symmetry of forces'. This was achieved only when colours were mixed not to produce a new colour but to create grey. "Medium gray matches the required equilibrium condition of our sense of sight," he wrote in *The Art of Color* (John Wiley and Sons, 1960).

Itten believed that colour harmony is entirely subjective and that, given time to experiment, each person ultimately develops his or her own palette. He tested his ideas on his students and found confirmation in the fact that they all worked from different colour palettes, which they used time and time again.

Two colour wheels devised by Itten – both based on red, yellow and blue primaries – remain popular today. The first, a twelve-pointed star, shows light tints at the centre progressing

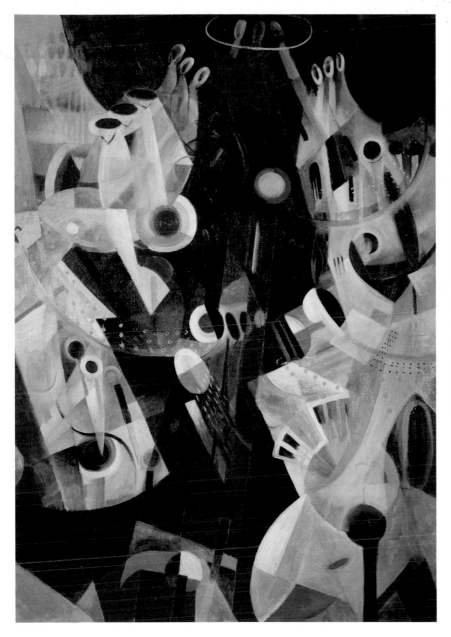

Interaction of Color — **Josef Albers**
Unabridged text and selected plates
Revised edition

Above: Johannes Itten's *Red Tower* (1917–18) combines the artist's interests in both colour and geometry.

Right: Itten's colour star expands the colour wheel to include variations in lightness. Forms such as spheres, cubes and pyramids have been used by theorists to vary hue, saturation and lightness into one diagram.

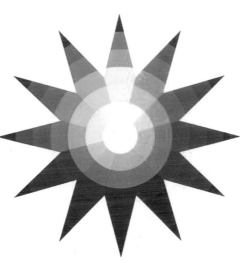

to dark at the edges. The second, an outer rim with a centre triangle of the three primaries and intermediate triangles of the complementary secondaries, shows combinations of hues.

Having studied under Itten, Josef Albers (1888–1976) taught on the Bauhaus's *Vorkurs* from 1923 to 1926. After developing in his art a very personal brand of abstraction in which mathematical proportions were used to create balance and unity, he left for the United States in 1933 along with other Bauhaus professors. He taught first at Black Mountain College in North Carolina, an experimental institution, and then at Yale. Albers's *Interaction of Color* (Yale University Press, 1963, pictured above) is regarded as a crucial text on colour theory. Focusing on investigating what happens when colours interact, his work provides a wonderful resource for anyone who wants to create subtle colour compositions.

Albers's principles gave rise to op art (short for optical art), a movement that was given its name in a *Time* article of 1964. Using tricks with colour and geometry, op art drew heavily on the emerging field of perceptual psychology. Besides Albers himself, two of the movement's best-known proponents were Victor Vasarely (1908–97) and Bridget Riley (b. 1931) (*see page 112*).

MUNSELL'S TREE

The most versatile colour model to date was created by Albert Munsell (1858–1918). His inspiration came from fellow American Ogden Rood (1831–1902), who took red, green and blue as his primaries and arranged them so that the complement of each hue matched its negative afterimage, helping the artist make full use of simultaneous contrast effects. He also developed the idea of a three-dimensional colour model – first proposed in 1810 by the German painter Philip Otto Runge (1777–1810) – with pure hues around the equator, lighter tints at the top and dark shades at the bottom.

Munsell's breakthrough was to realize that, because some hues are more saturated than others when pure, colour relationships get distorted when the spectrum is forced into a regular geometric shape. Instead of a sphere, he ended up with a 'tree', with hues arranged along its branches in order of saturation, or purity. Because the branches can be of different lengths, the saturation of each hue can progress along an equal scale, yet extend to its own natural limit. So yellow has a very long branch, while pink is much shorter.

The plan of Munsell's tree, which can be depicted as a wheel, is divided into five primaries, or principal hues, with a further five intermediates producing a total of ten divisions. (Commercial versions of the model are commonly subdivided into twenty sections.) Each primary is labelled with an initial: R (red), Y (yellow), G (green), B (blue), P (purple). Intermediates are labelled with the initials of the surrounding principals: YR, GY and so on. For more accurate specification, the hue circle is also divided into steps numbered clockwise from 5 at the top (red) to 100.

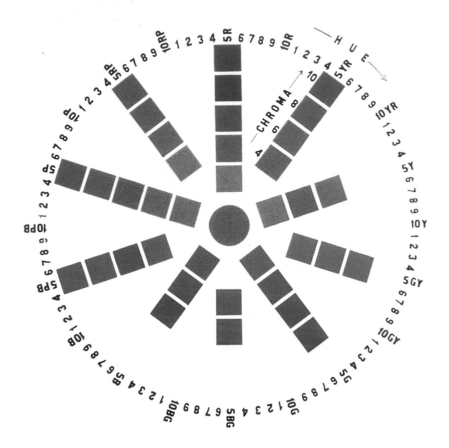

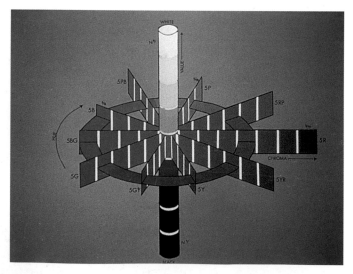

Above: **Munsell's three-dimensional colour model is based on a wheel with five primaries, adding purple to the red, green, yellow and blue of other systems. Like Itten's star, the wheel has an extra dimension, but in this case it is saturation (chroma) that varies from low at the centre to high at the outside edge. Any number of colours can be represented within the system.**

Left: **The wheel is extended vertically to produce a 'tree' of colours, with lightness varying from top to bottom. Colours can be depicted as 'branches' radiating from the centre at each lightness level.**

The tree is divided vertically into ten value steps, numbered from 0 (pure black) at the bottom to 10 (pure white) at the top. Branches are divided into equal steps, starting at zero at the centre for neutrals (greys) and radiating to numbers as high as 20 or more. Thanks to the open-ended scale, even fluorescent materials can find their true place.

A Munsell colour is specified by the notation HV/C, in which H is the hue, V is the value and C is the chroma, or saturation. To make the specs more readable, the hue number is accompanied by the initial(s) of the preceding principal hue.

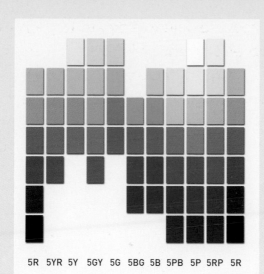

5R 5YR 5Y 5GY 5G 5BG 5B 5PB 5P 5RP 5R

So a bright red would be 5R 6/14. The notation changes for neutrals: the hue is given as N, and the chroma is omitted, so a black ink might be N1/.

The Munsell tree has proved extremely useful to manufacturers, artists, illustrators and designers, and it forms the basis of many industry-standard colour-specification systems. Its main drawback is that the selection of the actual colours in the tree owes as much to Munsell's subjective judgment as to his scientific method.

Munsell's work, however, influenced a highly scientific approach to colour-space modelling undertaken in the 1930s by the International Commission on Illumination (abbreviated to CIE, for Commission Internationale de l'Éclairage). A series of experiments established the response of a 'standard observer' – a Mr Average of colour perception, if you like – to colour stimuli, and this was used to plot the visible spectrum on a three-dimensional (XYZ) diagram. Like Munsell's tree, the result is an odd, lumpy shape.

The CIE model now underpins most technical descriptions of colour, including the handling of colour images by computers and digital devices such as cameras, scanners and printers. Although still imperfect, it firmly attaches a given numeric value to a precisely measured colour. Unfortunately, the model is quite useless to the artist.

Below: **The CIE XYZ colour space, based in part on Munsell's work, is the most widely adopted scientific model of colour perception to date, and the basis of colour management in modern digital systems.**

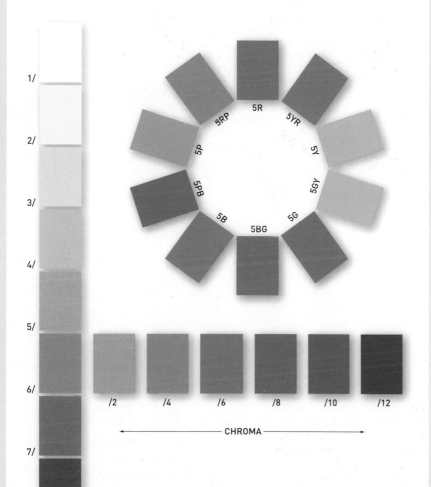

CHROMA

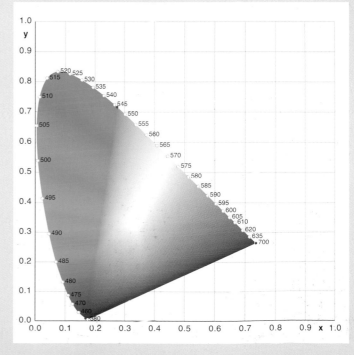

PSYCHOLOGICAL COLOUR SYSTEMS We have mentioned Itten's exploration of the psychological aspects of colour, which he put to practical use in his compositions. He was neither the first nor the last colour theorist to take this approach. Goethe, best known as Germany's most famous poet, playwright, and novelist, attached equal importance to his work in colour theory.

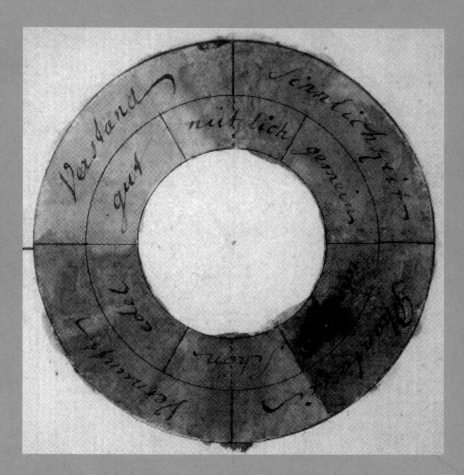

enable them to be combined in an equal visual proportion. His principles are still widely referred to by artists and designers.

While Goethe was interested in the way human nature makes us respond to colour, another question in colour psychology – presaged by Itten – is how personal colour preferences might relate to individual character. Max Lüscher (b.1923), head of the Institute of Psycho-Medical Diagnostics in Lucerne, Switzerland, is one of the most authoritative contemporary voices in the field of colour psychology, and his psychological test, or 'colour diagnostic', involving coloured cards has been in clinical use by psychiatrists, psychologists and physicians since 1947.

Eight differently coloured cards are placed in front of an individual, who chooses his or her 'favourite' colour, then another,

Goethe's *Zur Farbenlehre* (*Theory of Colours*), published in 1810, disagreed violently with Newton's conclusions about light and colour. His opposition was philosophical as well as practical. Goethe believed the division of the spectrum was symptomatic of science's tendency to break up the world into meaningless pieces, destroying any sense of unity.

Although his stated aim was to reduce the 'confusion' surrounding the use of colour in art, Goethe resorted to idiosyncratic language and concepts in expounding his ideas, alluding to 'sensual-moral effects', 'deprivation' and 'power'. Nonetheless, by approaching colour through observations of human perception rather than the physics of light, he covered a lot of ground that Newton could not, exploring simultaneous contrast, afterimaging, the colour of shadows and the effect of illumination on objects, as well as considering how colours can relate to emotional states. He also worked out ratios of the strengths of different hues to

Right: Johann Wolfgang Goethe, the German playwright and poet, significantly advanced colour theory. While Newton's theories explained colour in terms of the physical properties of light, they had nothing to say about the way colour is perceived and processed by the eye and brain. Goethe recognized the shortcomings of the Newtonian approach to colour, and – through experimentation and intuition, in the absence of detailed neurological theory – tried to clarify the effects of colour on the observer.

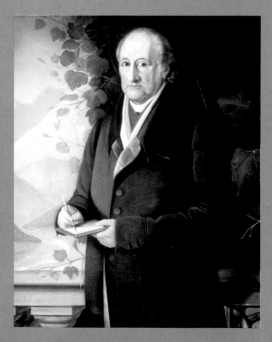

part 01. definitions

until all the cards have been used. The cards selected are analysed according to Lüscher's system in order to determine aspects of the subject's personality.

Whether or not the results are meaningful is a matter of conjecture, but you can judge for yourself by taking the test. Various interactive versions are available online, although none are authorized by Lüscher. For designers, particularly those working in fields such as corporate branding, marketing, packaging and interiors, what matters is how colour affects the mood and choices of the viewer. This is explored by colour consultancy services. One of the most influential is Colour Affects, founded in the 1980s by Angela Wright, author of *The Beginner's Guide to Colour Psychology* (Colour Affects Limited, 1998). Wright's system of four colour groups linked to personality types recalls Aristotle's four elements, the four humours of Hippocrates and Galen, and Jung's 'predominant

Below: Professor Max Lüscher's colour card test is widely used by psychologists, though it is also widely criticized. If you type 'Lüscher' into a search engine, you'll find a number of sites that run the test. The official Lüscher test is described and marketed at www.luscher-color.com.

functions' of thought, feeling, intuition and sensation. She has worked with the Colour and Imaging Institute of the University of Derby, to incorporate the system into a software package.

Colour Affects' basic principles and advice are of obvious practical value to designers. Wright warns, for example, that shape, layout and typeface are often considered first in packaging design, yet the consumer is likely to be more influenced by colour. The company's textual descriptions of the colour groups and their associations, which you can read at www.colour-affects.co.uk, may be helpful in considering the likely responses to a colour scheme.

GREY
Positive: Psychological neutrality.
Negative: Lack of confidence, dampness, depression, hibernation, lack of energy.

BROWN
Positive: Seriousness, warmth, nature, earthiness, reliability, support.
Negative: Lack of humour, heaviness, lack of sophistication.

VIOLET
Positive: Spiritual awareness, containment, vision, luxury, authenticity, truth, quality.
Negative: Introversion, decadence, suppression, inferiority.

BLACK
Positive: Sophistication, glamour, security, emotional safety, efficiency, substance.
Negative: Oppression, coldness, menace, heaviness.

BLUE
Positive: Intelligence, communication, trust, efficiency, serenity, duty, logic, coolness, reflection, calm.
Negative: Coldness, aloofness, lack of emotion, unfriendliness.

RED
Positive: Physical courage, strength, warmth, energy, basic survival, 'fight or flight', stimulation, masculinity, excitement.
Negative: Defiance, aggression, visual impact, strain.

GREEN
Positive: Harmony, balance, refreshment, universal love, rest, restoration, reassurance, environmental awareness, equilibrium, peace.
Negative: Boredom, stagnation, blandness, enervation.

YELLOW
Positive: Optimism, confidence, self-esteem, extraversion, emotional strength, friendliness, creativity.
Negative: Irrationality, fear, emotional fragility, depression, anxiety, suicide.

PART 01. DEFINITIONS

CHAPTER FOUR

MAKING COLOUR

We are surrounded by colour in the natural world, both in terms of animals and plants, but producing it to order is no small challenge. Throughout history, not only has the course of art been guided by the availability of pigments, but the demand for rare, fashionable or symbolic colours has provoked significant political, technical and commercial developments.

Pigments exist as a dry powder that is combined with a binder, such as water, wax or oil, to make it stick to a surface, or ground. The binder may either harden or evaporate. The impression of colour depends both on the pigment and on the ground.

Even the earliest known paintings demonstrate techniques of pigment production. Cave art of the late Paleolithic period (c. 20,000 BC) was created mainly using earth colours such as red and yellow ochres (iron oxides and hydroxides). But the preparation of some pigments may have been very complex. According to a *New Scientist* report, a white pigment found at the famous Lascaux caves in France, seems to have been made by heating animal bone to 400°C (752°F) to produce apatite, which was then mixed with calcite and heated to 1,000°C (1,832°F) to form tetracalcite phosphate.

Colour symbolism was integral to ancient Egyptian art. The green skin of Osiris represented his rebirth after death. Red was also an important colour, used in invocations. Egyptian blue, dating from 2500 BC, was blended from a precise mixture of lime, copper oxide and quartz, fired to around 900°C (1,652°F), then ground into a fine powder.

Chinese painting on silk, dating back as far as 770–256 B.C., is dominated by red and black inks. The red came from cinnabar (mercury sulphide), which at this time was a much sought-after pigment. When archaeologists excavated Herod the Great's palace in Jericho, dating from the first century BC, several powdered pigments were found, including cinnabar, which would have been imported at great expense – perhaps suggesting Roman support for his unpopular rule over Judaea.

Right: In the limited palette of pigments available to the ancient Egyptians, colours had symbolic meanings which varied between eras. In the Old Kingdom, for example, women are depicted as light-skinned and men as dark-skinned (reddish brown). Later, the darker colour was used to portray women of the elite class.

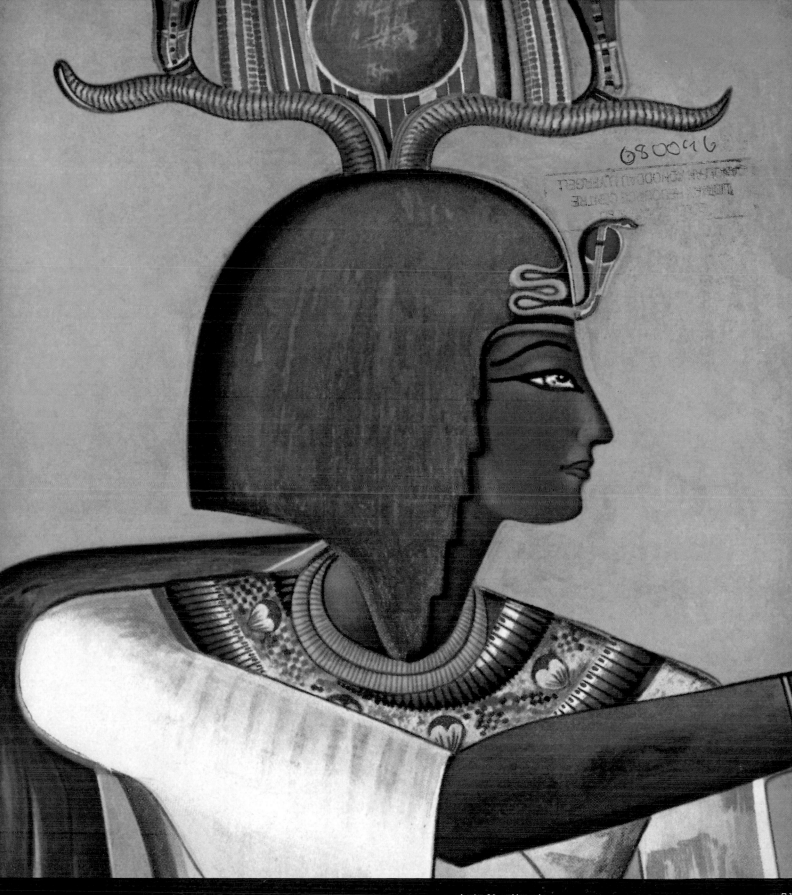

ART AND ALCHEMY By medieval times, European artists had a great many pigments at their disposal, not only extracted from plants and minerals but also man-made. Vermilion, for example, was synthesized from sulphur and mercury. Applying the pigments, however, still presented the artist with many difficulties. Watery binders such as egg tempera were laborious to mix, encouraged unpredictable reactions between ingredients and dried too quickly for comfort.

The Italian painter Cennino Cennini (c. 1370–c. 1440), in a treatise on the arts and crafts entitled *Il libro dell'arte* (c.1390), described the pigments and techniques of the Old Masters. His incredibly detailed work not only includes chemical and alchemical recipes for specific colours, but also advises on the 'correct' methods of depicting objects such as flesh and drapery. Like the perspective and proportion of the period, the use of colour was formulaic rather than realistic, and the choice of pigments was dictated largely by the patron's budget.

During the Renaissance, oils took over as the binder of choice, improving the usability of paints but also changing the character of pigments. Ultramarine (deep blue) became muddy and had to be lightened with white. Vermilion no longer appeared as brilliant, and 'lake' reds, from animal and vegetable extracts, regained favour. Glazing became integral to the painting process, with many layers of thinned oils applied to modify and enrich base colours.

Below left and below: These very different images of the Madonna show the varying approaches to colour in fifteenth-century painting. Titian's *Gypsy Madonna* (c.1512) (below left) is a good example of the artist's use of an expansive palette, while Leonardo da Vinci's *Madonna Benois* (c.1475–78) shows how Leonardo created equally rich effects using a narrow range of desaturated colours.

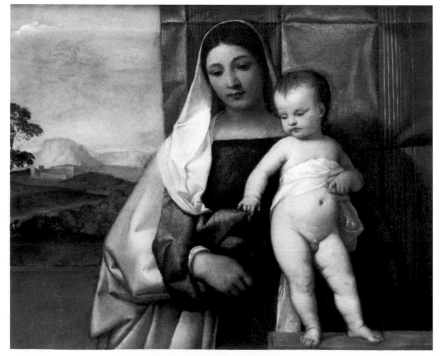

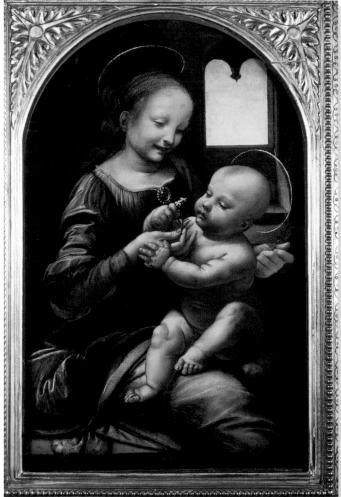

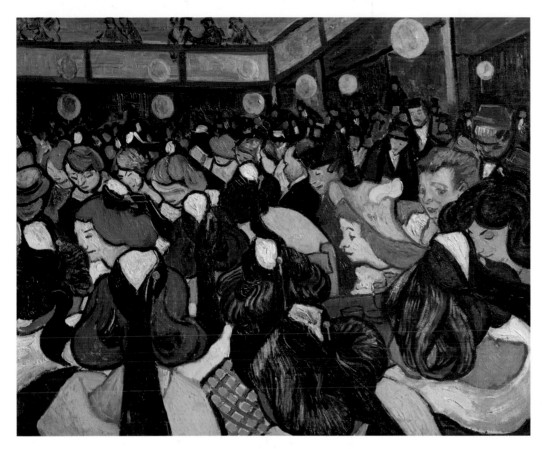

The variety of materials available encouraged considerable experimentation in the fifteenth century, with two kinds of colourist emerging: the Venetian, such as Titian, who fought to control and balance strong colours, and the Florentine, such as Leonardo, who used a more muted palette to create a subdued yet luminous impression of light and shade.

The seventeenth century saw a withdrawal from strong colour into a brownish palette, made possible by the introduction of new autumnal pigments and by the ability of oil-based paints to remain stable when many different pigments were mixed. The broken tints used by artists such as Rembrandt are in dramatic contrast to the medieval emphasis on purity, which valued the finest pigments for their inherent qualities rather than their contribution to an overall effect.

When painting burst into vibrant colour in the nineteenth century, it was largely thanks to the availability of new pigments developed mainly by French chemists. Vivid greens based on arsenic were taken up by both the Pre-Raphaelites and the impressionists, and unfortunately also by wallpaper manufacturers: Napoléon Bonaparte may have been among the victims of the toxic gases released when their products became damp. Less hazardous were emerald greens based on chromium – also a source of new yellows and oranges – while cobalt provided blues. The English paint-maker George Field devised a new and even brighter mercury-sulphide vermilion.

Above: In *The Dance Hall in Arles* (1888), as with all his oil masterpieces, Vincent van Gogh utilized vibrant new pigments developed by French chemists. He mixed these with barium sulphate, which he used as an inexpensive filler. The juxtaposition of complementary colours creates the vibrancy for which van Gogh's paintings are famous.

The twentieth century brought brilliant whites made from titanium dioxide. In the 1950s, quinacridone pigments were introduced, organic compounds that are more transparent than their mineral-based precursors and can be mixed to produce highly saturated rather than muddy colours. With a polymer binder, these and other organic pigments – including pthalocyanines, or pthalos – form the modern paint category of acrylics.

During the second half of the twentieth century, an increasing number of leading artists began to work with paints that were originally intended for domestic and industrial use. For so long a treasured and troublesome rarity, pigment had become a banal commodity.

PIGMENTS IN OTHER MEDIA

Clothes coloured using the rarest and most expensive dyes have been signifiers of status in most societies. Probably the most famously prized pigment in history is Tyrian purple, produced in Asia Minor from around 1600 BC. Ancient Greek literature mentions both garments of this colour and the dye's painstaking manufacture from a substance found in tiny quantities in the gland of a shellfish. In the Roman Empire, the colour was reserved by law for the highest-ranking officials and later exclusively for the emperor.

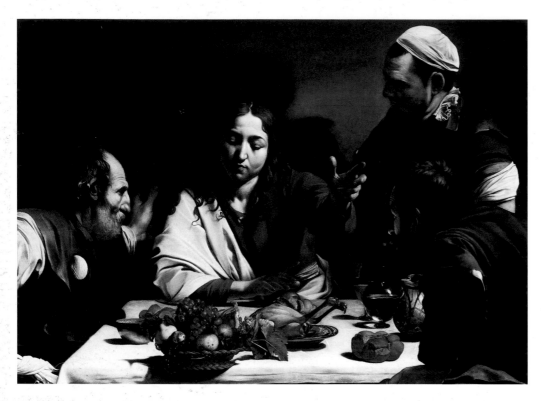

By the sixth century, purple had become a shorthand for power and prestige and was used in depictions of Christ. But the method of production was lost in the Middle Ages and rediscovered only in the 1850s, when interest in purple was piqued by the invention of murexide. This Roman purple mimicked the ancient version but was extracted rather more cheaply from guano.

By the late nineteenth and early twentieth centuries, pigment manufacturing had become big business, with chemists hired as colour consultants. Demand for purple – commentators spoke of a 'mauve decade' – encouraged an English chemistry student named William Henry Perkin to experiment with a new coal-tar extract called aniline. The aniline dye industry would give rise to corporations such as ICI (Imperial Chemical Industries), Ciba-Geigy and IG Farben. Today, the market is dominated by the aniline-related anthraquinone dyes, or 'azos'.

Above: **Nobody can be quite sure of the exact colour of the original Tyrian purple, but its association with high status survived as an artistic convention for centuries, preserved even in otherwise ground-breaking paintings such as Carravaggio's** *The Supper at Emmaus* **(1601).**

The development of paints and dyes has been characterized by a search for predictability. Yet some of the most extraordinary examples of colour are found in an ancient discipline that thrives on inconsistency: pottery. Techniques such as reduction-fired stoneware are closer to alchemy than a reliable industrial process, but in the right hands, they can produce extraordinary works of art.

In an oxygen-starved environment, the fuel – gas, oil or wood – draws out the chemically combined oxygen in the clay and causes the glaze to ignite. The very atmosphere in the kiln affects the way the finished pot will look. Years ago, when there were many small but thriving earthenware potteries in Devon, the pots produced there could vary in colour from one season to another. Early in the year, sap in the bracken used to fire the kilns caused it to burn less effectively than later in the year, when it was drier.

The wonderful glaze effects produced by studios like Devon's present-day Dartington Pottery rely on experimenting with the different minerals in the glaze. Pots are fired twice – first at a lower temperature, so that the water suspending the glaze is absorbed by the porous clay, then at a higher

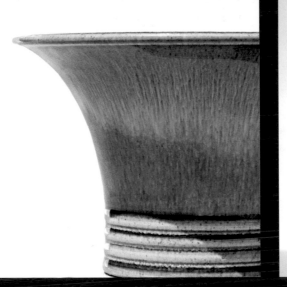

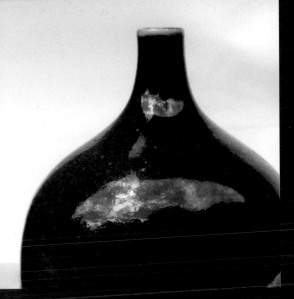

Right: **Pottery glazing is an ancient art which resists the tight control that technology can bring to media such as painting and printing. The variety and unpredictability of the colour effects that can be achieved encourage and reward experimentation. Even when a design is produced in large numbers, each piece is unique and often impossible to re-create.**

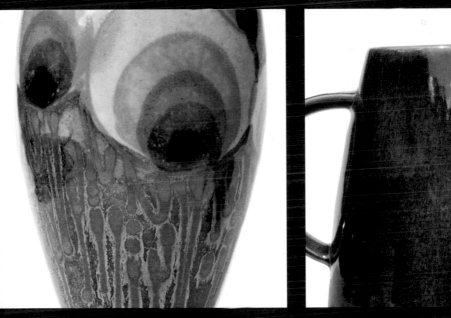

temperature to melt the glaze and vitrify the body. The minerals in the glaze react with each other during firing, and these reactions can be directed (though never entirely controlled) by the temperature, the length of the firing time and the way the glaze is applied.

Looking at the thrilling results of such methods, we see that it is worth considering the effects of the present-day ability to achieve near-perfect colour reproduction. Colour effects soon cease to be interesting when they are rolled out time and time again in precisely the same way. Holding up a glazed pot to the light to see the unique crystal formations and watching as the sunlight penetrates a glaze and completely alters its appearance – these are rare pleasures in a world filled with objects whose designers increasingly submit to the forces of standardization.

COLOUR PHOTOGRAPHY The invention of the camera came many centuries before that of film. In the fifth century BC, the Chinese philosopher Mo-tzu noted that when a tiny hole allowed light into a dark room, an inverted image of the outside scene was formed on the opposite wall. In the following century, Aristotle used the same principle to project the image of a partial solar eclipse.

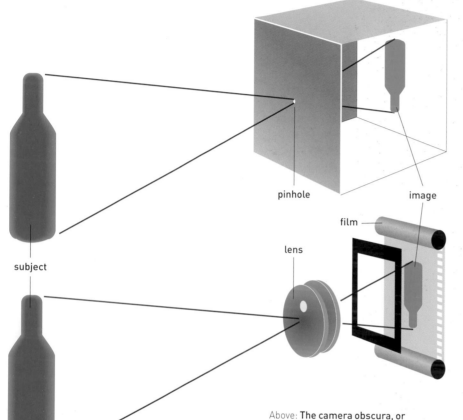

subject

pinhole

image

film

lens

The camera obscura was further developed during the Renaissance, when lenses and mirrors were added to produce drawing aids for the artist. It was not until the early nineteenth century, however, that it became possible to record a permanent, or fixed, image. By the 1860s, monochrome photography was becoming commonplace, and the work of James Clerk Maxwell (*see page 84*) suggested ways the process might be adapted to produce colour images.

Maxwell made three monochrome photographs of a tartan ribbon, using a different filter (red, blue and green) in front of

Above: **The camera obscura, or 'pinhole camera' (top), provided the first evidence that a two-dimensional image could be produced directly from the real world. The addition of a lens enabled the size and focus of the image to be controlled, and some paintings of the Renaissance and Baroque periods may have been produced by tracing over a projected image of a real scene. It was only with the invention of light-sensitive plates in the nineteenth century, and the subsequent development of film, that images could be made permanent.**

Right: **Modern colour film contains three emulsion layers, each sensitive to different wavelengths of light, enabling the full visible spectrum to be recorded.**

the camera for each, and projected the three images using lanterns with similar filters. The result was a colour image, although not a very good one. Given that Maxwell's photographic plates in fact reacted almost exclusively to blue light, it was only due to a combination of luck and inaccuracy that the experiment worked at all. Nonetheless, the principle was successfully established.

Autochrome, the first commercially viable colour photographic system, was invented by the Lumière brothers at the turn of the twentieth century. Glass plates were coated with a powder formed from grains of potato starch that had been dyed red, green and blue. When light was allowed onto the plate, a black light-sensitive layer behind the starch was selectively lightened: only red light passed through the red grains, and so on. The plate was then chemically fixed and could be held up to the light for viewing. Light would pass through the areas corresponding to each colour, reconstructing the image by additive partitive mixing (*see chapter 01.02*), sometimes referred to as a mosaic process.

Modern colour photographic processes, however, are not partitive and rely on subtractive rather than additive colour mixing. Most colour film contains three layers of light-sensitive emulsion, known as an integral tripack. (For technical reasons there are many more layers,

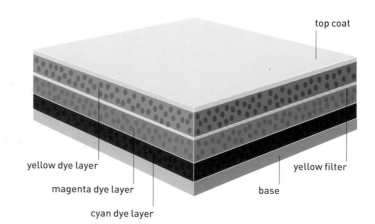

top coat

yellow dye layer

magenta dye layer

cyan dye layer

yellow filter

base

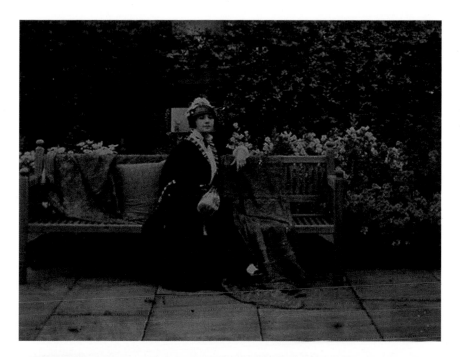

Left: Autochrome was the first commercial system for colour photography. The image was formed in a light-sensitive material masked by differently coloured grains and viewed as a transparency. Although the colours were quite dull, the quality of the images was surprisingly high.

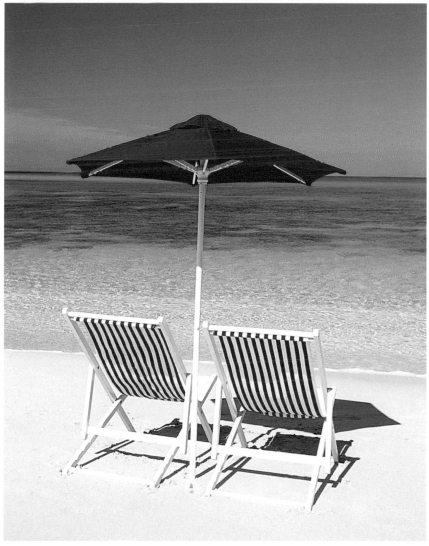

Left: Modern photographic materials offer a large tonal range and a high degree of colour fidelity. In both consumer and commercial photography, the requirement is often for colours as bold and vibrant as possible; those trying to use colour differently often have to choose different film stock and processing methods from the norm.

but the principle is based on these three.) When a picture is taken by exposing the film to light, the relevant wavelengths are recorded continuously across each layer, forming a latent image that is not yet visible to the eye.

Each emulsion contains dye couplers, chemicals that produce dyes of a certain colour when combined with a developer solution. The blue layer is manufactured to produce yellow dyes, the green layer magenta and the red layer cyan. When the exposed film is immersed in developer, a visible negative image is formed by the dyes produced. This image is then fixed by immersion in another solution that stabilizes the dyes. A print can be made by shining light through the negative onto photographic paper, which itself contains similar light-sensitive dyes. Transparency film differs in that the CMY image produced is positive rather than negative.

The balance of colour in a photo can be dramatically affected by the way it is developed and processed. This can be exploited for special effects (*see chapter 04.05*), but it more often needs to be carefully controlled to preserve the colours originally captured.

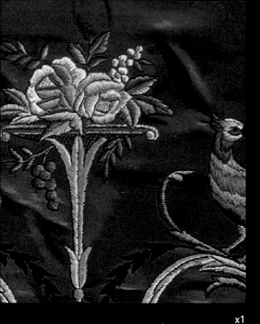
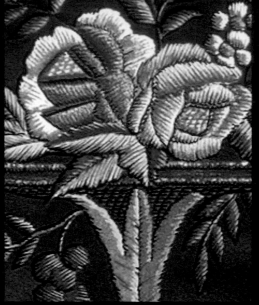
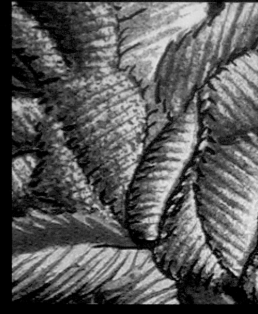

x1

x5

x10

Above: **Chromolithography** was a planographic colour-printing method used from the early nineteenth century to produce full-colour artwork. As many as twenty plates would be used, each created by hand, and the resulting prints often showed astonishing quality and richness, with very fine detail visible on close inspection. The method fell out of favour with the rise of photographic reproduction.

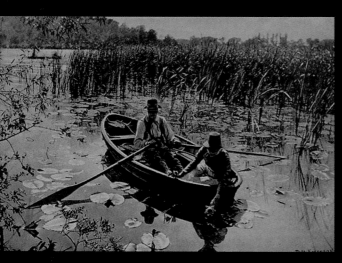

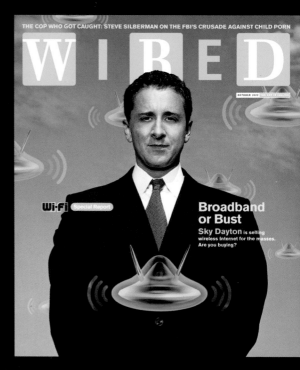

Above: **Photogravure allowed black-and-white photos to be reproduced in ink on paper. The process was later adapted using halftoning to reproduce colour images. Much refined, gravure printing is still widely used today.**

Right: **Magazines and books (including this one) are now printed by offset lithography. Photographs are digitized and combined on the computer screen with text and other artwork, and the finished pages are usually reproduced in cyan, magenta, yellow and black inks, with halftoning applied to images. Colour fidelity can be tightly controlled throughout the process.**

COLOUR REPRODUCTION
Printing images onto prepared photographic paper is one thing; reproducing photos on a printing press is quite another. There are three methods for printing onto passive substrates (surfaces like plain paper, which do not contain dyes waiting to be activated): intaglio, relief and planographic.

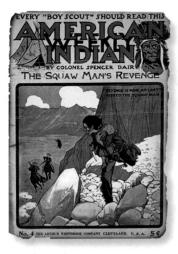

Above: Chromoxylography lacked the finesse of chromolithography, but it was cheap and made possible the garish covers of popular magazines and 'pulp fiction' at around the turn of the twentieth century. Since primary-coloured inks were used, graphical elements such as headlines and backgrounds were often red, yellow or blue, contributing to the distinctive look of the genre.

Engraving, a form of intaglio, has been used since the fifteenth century to reproduce works of art. Grooves of varying width and depth are cut into a soft metal plate; the engraver's task is to make these mimic the shading of the original image. To make a print, the plate is coated with ink, which settles into the grooves. When the plate is pressed against the paper, deeper grooves deliver darker lines. A variation is etching, in which lines are cut out of a mask placed over the plate, so that when acid is applied, it eats only into the lines.

In the photogravure process, introduced in the second half of the nineteenth century, a coating of gelatine is applied to the etching plate and exposed to light through a positive transparency of a photograph. This hardens the gelatine selectively, leaving the least exposed parts softest and most susceptible when the plate is then washed. The plate is etched through the remaining gelatine. A fine texture (aquatint or mezzotint) on the plate serves to hold ink. Photogravure is essentially a monochrome process, but printmakers could apply different inks to various areas to create plate-coloured pictures.

In the late nineteenth century, mass-produced 'story papers' (weekly newspapers that serialized romances or mysteries) often used colour pictures printed by chromoxylography, a relief process in which designs were cut into wooden blocks. In a reversal of the intaglio method, ink coated only the uncut areas. By using a different block for each of the primary colours (and sometimes additional colours), and cutting dots or stripes for lighter areas, printers could produce a full-colour illustration when the blocks were printed in turn. The results were often eye-catching but generally coarse and garish.

The invention of halftoning in the 1880s made it possible to reproduce photographs by automating the conversion of light and shade into printable patterns. A photograph was exposed through a 'screen' – a glass plate marked with a grid of evenly spaced opaque lines – that made the image resolve as a regular pattern of round dots, larger in darker areas. This could be transferred to a printing plate by the same method as in photogravure. As with chromoxylography, colour images were reproduced using multiple plates, usually red, yellow and blue. The process, known as relief halftone or typogravure, yielded characteristically subtle colours.

The offset lithographic press (*see page 176*) was invented at the turn of the twentieth century and would become the preferred option for colour halftone printing. Since it uses a planographic process, in which the difference between inked and uninked areas is chemical rather than physical, litho allows finer halftones. Cyan, magenta and yellow later replaced red, yellow and blue as the primary plates, resulting in better subtractive mixing, and a black plate became standard. In the 1990s, laser technology made it possible for plates to be created from a digital image.

Gravure methods are still used, notably where continuous print is required – in wallpaper and packaging production, for example. The design is engraved onto a cylinder, leaving no join or gap in the pattern. Flexography, a relief process using flexible plates, is commonly used to print on nonporous or three-dimensional substrates.

LIVING WITH COLOUR

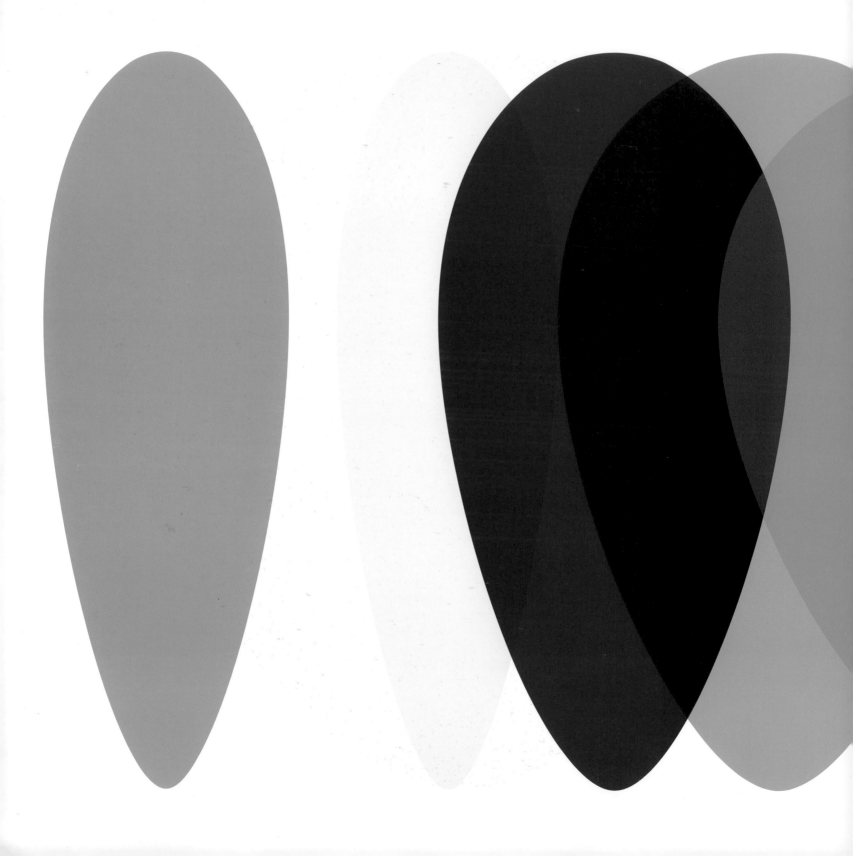

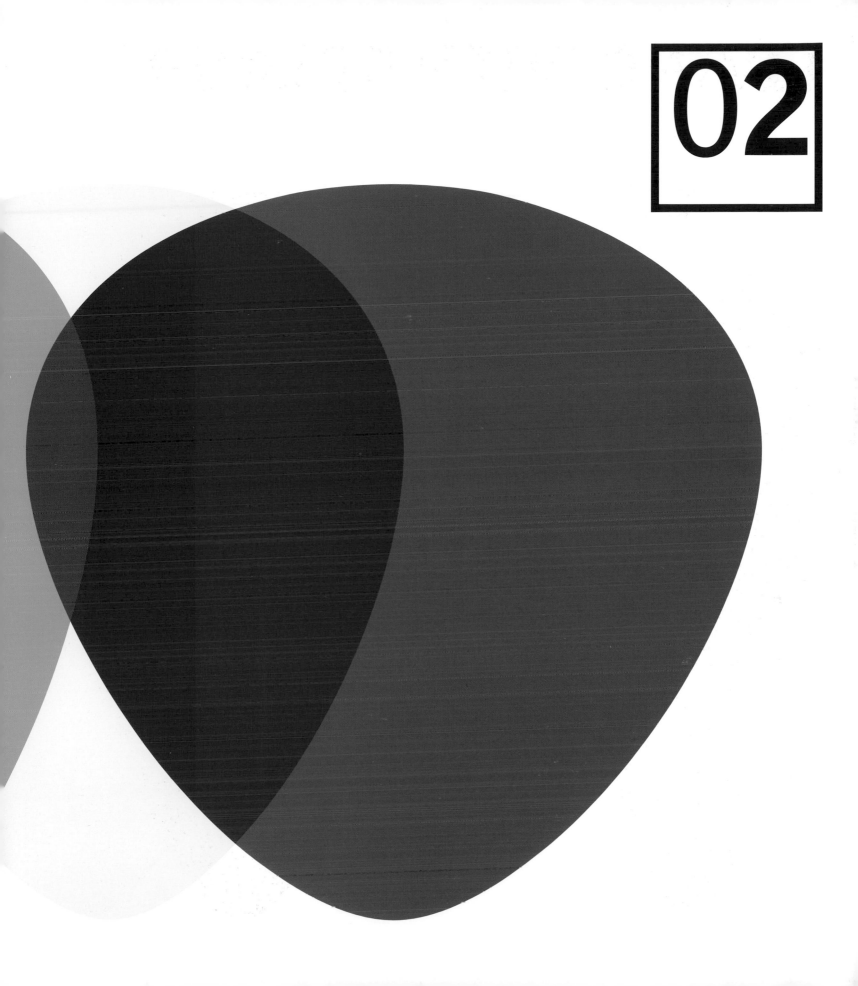

02

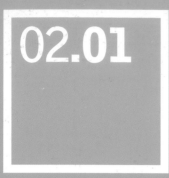

02.01

COLOUR TRENDS

Equipped with a sound understanding of the physics and psychology of colour, the designer must sooner or later decide on an actual palette for a project. Here, current trends may be as significant as universal truths. The end product not only needs to work as a colour composition within itself, it also must seem appealing and credible to the audience it targets.

The melting pot into which the designer throws all of these influences is the mood board. Mood boards are used by designers in all fields, from haute couture to home decorating. The board may be an easily portable folder or an entire wall of a studio. There may be general-purpose boards creating the feel of a season or a brand, or specific boards exploring possibilities or alternatives for a given project. A haphazardly constructed mood board developed during the initial conception stage of a project may be transformed into a polished work of art for presentation to the client.

There are no hard-and-fast rules about what can or should be included. Materials commonly found on mood boards include fabric swatches, magazine clippings, Polaroid photos of inspirational colours perhaps spotted in the street or at a design event, as well as objects found lying around the designer's home or in the office.

A mood board is not merely a repository; it's a space for experimentation. Seeing the effect of juxtaposing colours and finishes on the board, the designer will gain a better idea of whether certain elements are likely to work well together in practice. The arrangement of items may be random, but often the designer will try to reflect the way colours and textures are likely to be used. For example, an interior designer might include a large swatch intended for flooring at the foot of his or her board, with a smaller sample for accessories higher up.

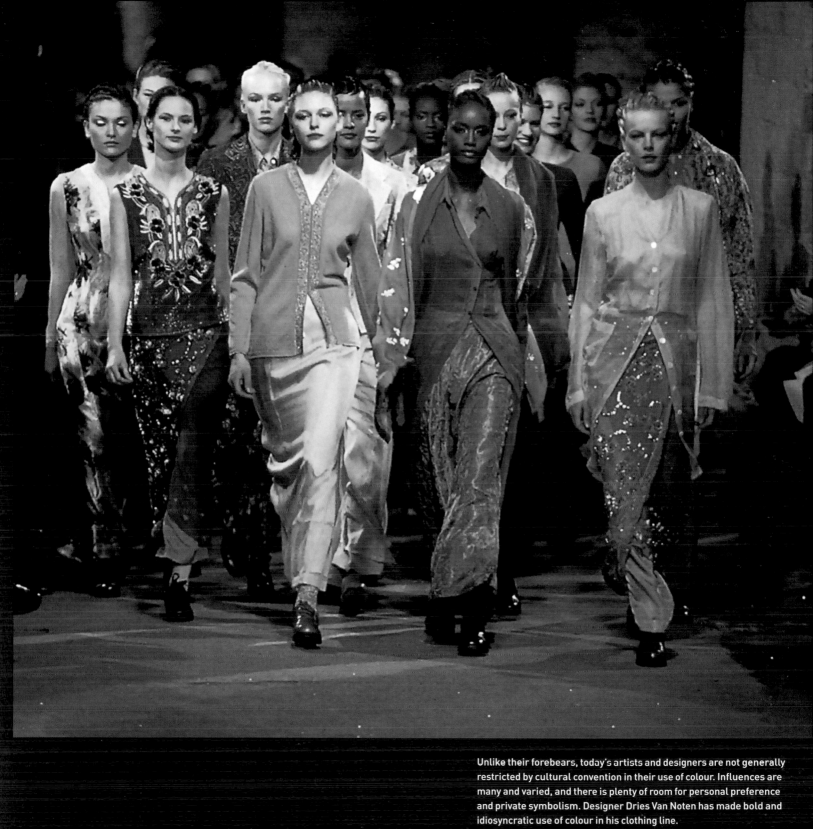

Unlike their forebears, today's artists and designers are not generally restricted by cultural convention in their use of colour. Influences are many and varied, and there is plenty of room for personal preference and private symbolism. Designer Dries Van Noten has made bold and idiosyncratic use of colour in his clothing line.

CHANGING ROOMS Until the Victorian era, the colour palettes of garment making, product design and interior decoration were, if not timeless, subject to slow and gradual development. The explosion of industrialization, global trade and travel and personal wealth resulted in a more subjective and experimental approach to these palettes.

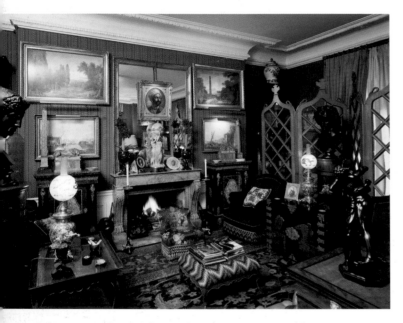

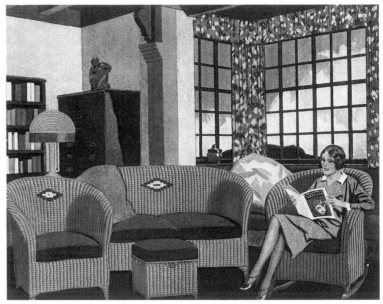

This approach, together with a new awareness of foreign cultures and a fascination with classical antiquity, led to all sorts of sartorial and architectural atrocities. Provoked by an absence of natural light in their closely packed houses (electric light had yet to become the norm) and empowered by bright new paints and dyes, the Victorians articulated their interiors in splashes and swags of sharply contrasting colours.

Order and restraint were reintroduced in the early twentieth century. Mass production, just as easily as it commodified variety, could impose uniformity: Henry Ford offered any colour as long as it was black. Colours remained bright, but, influenced by modern art, palettes and forms became simpler and more coherent. Art deco (known at the time as moderne) streamlined the reinterpretation of classicism and heralded the yet more rational International Style, guided by Bauhaus colour theory (*see page 44*).

When the 1930s brought economic depression and austerity, design entered a 'taupe age' that continued with the battleship-grey palette of the 1940s. At the same time, however, keeping up with trends became more important. Attracted to cinemas as a form of escapism, middle-class women in particular aspired to the dress and decor of their silver-screen role models. It was this period that saw the rise of the fashion magazine and the interior designer.

During the 1950s, economic resurgence and wartime breakthroughs in technology produced an optimistic era of pastel-coloured domestic appliances, outlandishly patterned textiles and surfaces and big pink frocks. As an increasingly liberal society began to value personal expression over convention, strong, bright colours re-emerged in the psychedelic clothing and interiors of the 1960s.

Above left: Victorian rooms were busy and cluttered by modern standards, with a profusion of colours. With heavy curtains and little artificial lighting, these interiors would often have been experienced in near darkness.

Above: Colour settled down in the early twentieth century, with more rational palettes complementing the increase in illumination from larger windows and ubiquitous electric lighting.

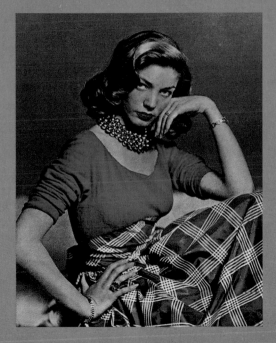

Choices that might seem highly individual, however, are often dictated nonetheless by trends. Blue denim jeans became associated in the middle of the twentieth century with individualism and rejection of authority, a reputation that still gets them banned from many schools, workplaces and even upmarket wine bars. Yet they are so commonplace, it would be hard to claim that wearing them makes much of a statement. Until recently, visitors to the communist states were well advised to pack a few spare pairs of jeans, as they could be profitably traded with locals who saw them as a symbol of Western freedom. Today, jeans are just as much an urban uniform across the former Eastern bloc.

The rejection of colour is another popular choice. More than two-thirds of consumer clothing sold in the United Kingdom and the United States in 2003 was black. This is a trend that shows no sign of abating, and while for some it may signify membership in a specific group, as with the goth look, for others it is merely a safe option. But the same could be said of choices that directly reflect short-term trends, however striking. Dressing conventionally and following fashion are both ways of avoiding the need to explore form and colour on one's own.

There may be something to be said for leaving such decisions to the experts. Home decoration has seen a recent return to the bold experimentation of the Victorians, proving that unfettered self-expression does not always lead to the most aesthetically pleasing results.

Below left: **Marianne Panton in a dining room with furniture designed by her Danish husband, Verner Panton, and manufactured by Swiss furniture manufactuer Vitra.** Designers like Verner Panton dressed the 1960s and '70s in bright colours and groundbreaking shapes. These exciting, iconoclastic interiors are now simultaneously celebrated by the design cognoscenti and satirized in 'retro' movies like the Austin Powers series.

Above: **The muted palettes of the mid-twentieth century created sophisticated looks through colour harmony.** Today, many people prefer to buy separate pieces rather than complete outfits, putting them together according to their own sense of colour.

Below right: **Minimalism pervaded the upmarket interiors of the 1990s, creating an austere kind of drama but risking an absence of humanity.** Earth tones in wood and natural fibres softened the look.

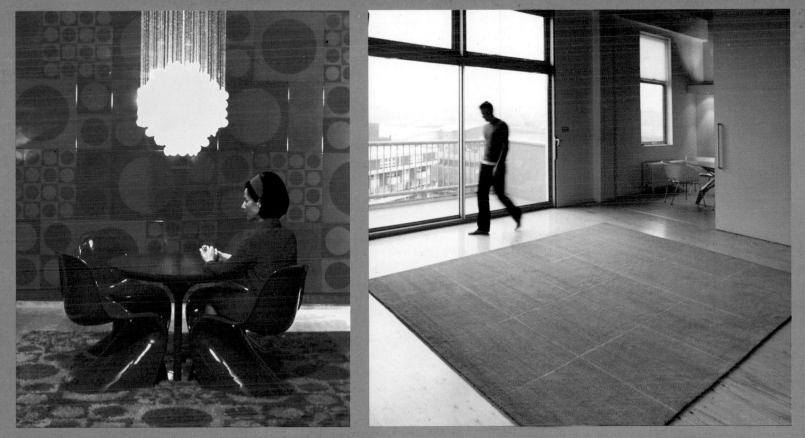

COLOUR FORECASTING Colour trends are gerenally no longer dependent on technical advances in pigment manufacture: whatever the designer wants can usually be achieved. This allows great creative freedom but makes it difficult to identify a currently fashionable palette or predict what colours will be in vogue next season – essential knowledge for industry professionals.

A number of companies offer colour forecasting services. Arguably the most influential – and probably the most expensive – is the Color Marketing Group (www.colormarketing.org), whose several hundred members are invited to contribute to its analysis of current and future colour use. CMG's Color Directions publications are divided between Consumer/Domestic and Contract/Commercial sectors, reflecting the fact that people decorating their own home, for example, may make different choices from interior design professionals.

CMG's Forecast Palettes do not so much specify exact colours as describe how certain hues will be treated. They include concepts such as Pinkle, a 'non-gender-specific, aged Pink' reminiscent of 'vintage velvets and Victorian rose gardens', and Iron Ore-ange, a 'sophisticated and mature background with ethnic undertones'. Bad puns aside, the descriptions evoke their own microcosms of colour psychology.

This highlights the unsurprising fact that colour forecasting is far from an exact science. When asked to describe their own palettes, designers invoke complex emotional, cultural and historical resonances that can be highly subjective. Interviewed by the Pantone Color Institute, another forecasting agency, Anna Sui said of a spring collection: "It is about clarity, freshness,

Below: **Paint manufacturers can no longer compete with only a basic selection of colours. While their master catalogues contain just about every possible shade, new colours are grouped and named each season, and sheens, shimmers, and glazes are offered to modify them.**

Below right: **Apple's iMac introduced colour to the computer industry, previously ruled by beige.**

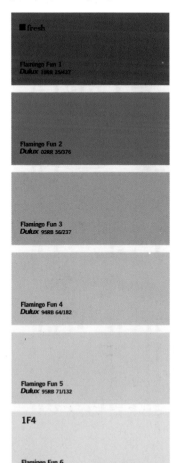

fresh

Flamingo Fun 1
Dulux 19RR 25/437

Flamingo Fun 2
Dulux 02RR 35/376

Flamingo Fun 3
Dulux 95RB 56/237

Flamingo Fun 4
Dulux 94RB 64/182

Flamingo Fun 5
Dulux 95RB 71/132

1F4

Flamingo Fun 6
Dulux 01RR 77/091

coolness—fun-in-the-sun sports, surfing, and the beach." Do the colours evoke these activities by referring to the qualities mentioned first, or vice versa? Or are we hearing more about the creative process than the product?

Despite the vagaries of the trendsetters' thought processes, colour forecasters are happy to offer specific predictions for up to two years in advance. If the cynical observer is inclined to wonder whether these are merely self-fulfilling, the practitioner might reply that this would be as good a way as any to bring some semblance of order to colour use.

Pantone is typical in taking colour directions from fashion designers and passing them on to those working in other disciplines. In general, haute couture leads, with cosmetics close behind; high-end commercial interiors follow; product design, with often longer development cycles, races to keep up; and trends finally filter through to general contract and domestic interiors, where conservatism and idiosyncrasy may slow progress. Recently, however, this

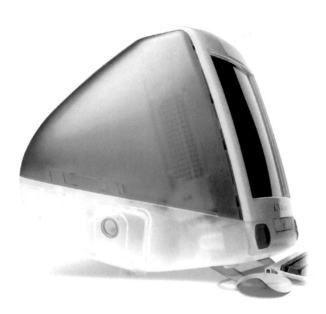

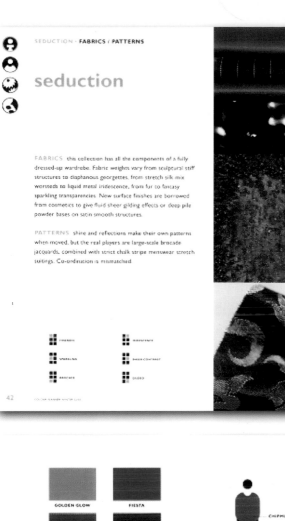

Left: Colour trends are monitored and forecasted by a number of commercial organizations. Their reports, such as this Pantone Color Institute brochure, analyse the use of colour in clothing, furnishings, and other sectors for the benefit of their subscribers. But who are the influencers, and who are the influenced?

sequence has been interrupted by the rise of independent-minded, creative product designers who have pushed ahead of clothing trends, and by the efforts of suppliers to the domestic market – such as paint manufacturers – to promote a quick turnover of new palettes.

So a fickle attitude to colour is not the preserve of fashionistas. While only a minority subscribe to forecasting services, designers in all disciplines need to keep a close eye on colour trends. When the Apple iMac was introduced, for example, its success was partly attributable to the careful choice of a signature colour, Bondi Blue. Yet only a year later, this was phased out and replaced by a set of five fruit-inspired hues. Despite industry scepticism, sales confirmed the wisdom of the decision.

With unusual hues now a dime a dozen, the next frontier is finish: pearlescent, iridescent, ultramatte and so on. Colour forecasters acknowledge that texture and sheen are becoming equally important in manipulating the perception of a product.

PART 02. LIVING WITH COLOUR

CHAPTER TWO

COLOUR INDOORS

Walk into a home decorated by a property developer for resale, and you will more than likely find all the walls painted white. Using colour effectively in a home – let alone trying to suit all tastes – is a challenge often rejected even by designers, who may resort to colour minimalism rather than risk disaster.

Like pre-Renaissance painters, we have a troubling tendency to choose colours based on prejudice and convention rather than on how they will work together. Most of us have had the experience of walking into someone else's home and being pleasantly surprised by the effect of a colour we normally dislike. Often, an aversion to a colour has a lot to do with unfortunate associations (*see page 48*) or experience of its misuse in previous decorating projects. This can prevent us taking advantage of the aesthetic and psychological benefits of colour.

Whether you believe, as some colour therapists do, that colours have their own vibrational energy capable of impinging on every cell in your body, or that they affect you in more mundane ways, colour undoubtedly has an impact on the way you live. Applying a particular colour scheme to a room can make it appear larger or smaller, more vibrant or more relaxed. Colour therapists would go further, saying that by using coloured light, bathing in coloured water and eating certain-coloured foods, you can alleviate physical or emotional illness. The way you decorate your home thus becomes more than just a matter of aesthetics.

A chaotic home with random colour can have its own appeal, especially for those influenced by the creative concerns and time pressures of bringing up children. But even small areas of studied harmony – a bathroom, perhaps, or a well-lit corner of a living room – can offer a welcome space for rest and relaxation, a sanctuary from the stresses of the world. The busier your life, the more wonderful such spaces are likely to feel.

Right: **Traditional, modern or eclectic, the feel of every home is largely dictated by the colours and textures within it. Paints, lighting, textiles and accessories contribute to the overall effect, as illustrated in this dining-room interior created by the contemporary English designer David Bentheim.**

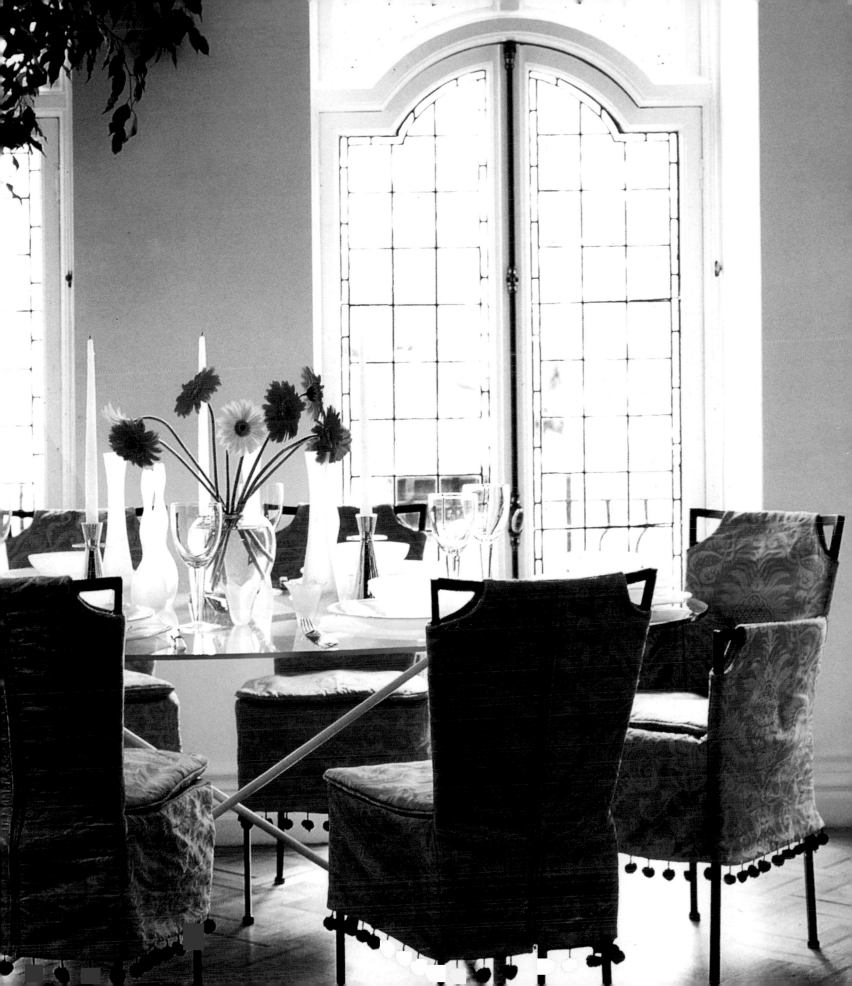

PAINTS AND LIGHTING The home decorator of the twenty-first century is surely the luckiest colourist in history. At the paint counter of many DIY shops, virtually any colour that can be perceived by the human eye can be mixed in a couple of minutes. Many shops are even equipped with a colourimeter, so they can copy the colour of any object you take along.

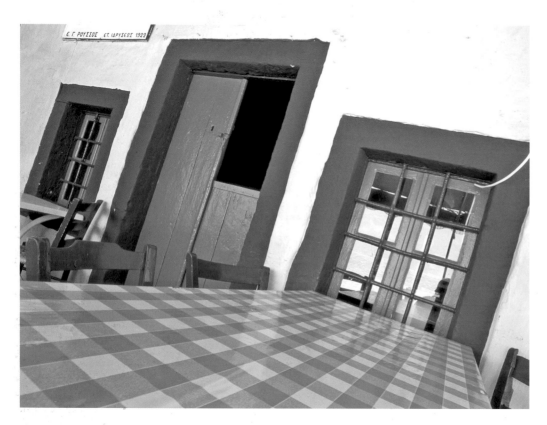

turquoise, while deep reds can prevent a large space becoming barn-like. A splash of warm colour at the end of a long corridor or open-plan room can draw the eye and give a better sense of the overall shape of the space.

Colour temperature must also be considered literally. Pale blue walls in a north-facing room will work hard to make you feel chilly, even in warmer climates, while bright yellows in a southern exposure may have you reaching for your sunglasses indoors. Light from the east and west has subtler characteristics, and it pays to work with it rather than against it, using warm tones analogous to the yellowish morning light from the east, blues to go with the evening light from the west.

The colour and mood effects you are aiming for should influence your choice of electric lighting. Most rooms will be lit by natural light during the day and by artificial light in the evening. The two are not mutually exclusive, but most people prefer their daylight undiluted. In a room short of natural light, rather than turning on lamps during the day, try painting the walls a light, pure colour and

More colours, of course, means more choices to make. But a few basic rules can help. The principle of complementarity and the colour harmony schemes described on page 42 will guide you towards pleasing combinations. A colour wheel based on afterimage complements, such as Munsell's, is most appropriate when planning large fields of colour. One important difference in painting a three-dimensional space rather than a canvas is that colour fields can reflect light onto each other: a single colour applied to every wall in the room will be reinforced, while complements will mute each other.

Warm or dark colours tend to advance while cool or light colours tend to recede (*see page 120*). This makes obvious sense in interiors – after all, warmth generally comes from enclosure and cold from exposure. A small room can be opened out by using a light, cool colour such as a pale

Above: **The bright blue paintwork and furniture used in this Greek taverna reflect the blue seas and skies of the Mediterranean. The whitewashed walls are both a psychological and practical way of keeping customers cool in the hot, Greek summer sunshine.**

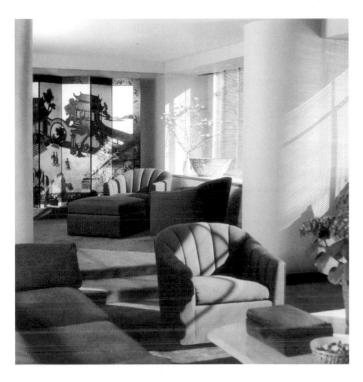

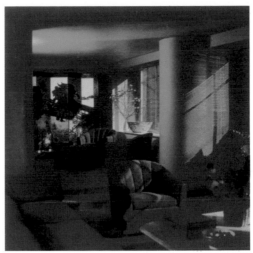

Left: The same room can look very different depending on the lighting. The time of day will affect the colour of natural light entering through the windows, the way light strikes objects and the relative brightness of areas within the space. Artificial lighting will create another feel again.

Below. While minimalism is often associated with monochrome interiors, colour can play a part even in the most austere styles. In this interior by David Bentheim, a strong warm colour applied to one surface infuses the whole stairwell, offsetting the coldness of a brilliant white spotlight.

hanging mirrors. Lamps with colour filters and even automated colour changing systems can be used to paint with light, changing the mood of a room at the flick of a switch. Natural light can be filtered by stained glass: a simple pattern in just one window can achieve a tremendous effect.

Texture is also important to the overall colour effect. The tradition of using matte, water-based paint for walls and solvent-based gloss or eggshell for woodwork is now often subverted; hard-wearing and washable matte paints remove the practical barriers to experimentation. Although strongly textured paint finishes have largely fallen out of favour in domestic interiors, subtle stipples and sheens are being introduced into many manufacturers' ranges.

Flat areas of colour are not the only option. Techniques such as sponging and rag-rolling can introduce partitive mixing effects. Or, using masking tape or stencils, you can create stripes and motifs as a personal alternative to mass-produced wallpapers

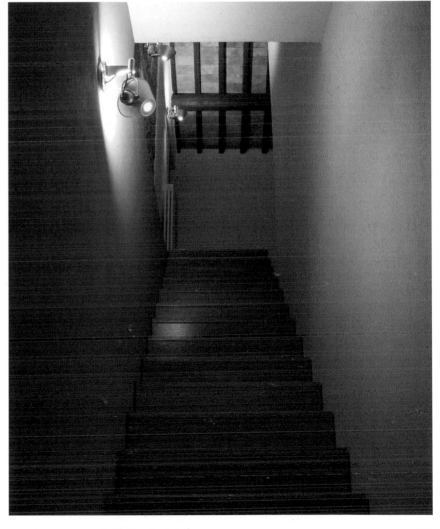

TEXTILES AND FLOORING If choosing paint is a risky business, choosing the wrong wall covering can be as close to a fatal mistake as you can get in interior design. Some wallpapers are surely designed to inflict cardiac arrest; and even those that seem wonderful in the shop may look awful once hung. Colour, texture and pattern must all be carefully considered.

Below: However wide the range of paint colours available to the interior decorator, it can never match the variety of colour, texture and pattern offered by textiles. Whether used for curtains, cushions, tablecloths or other strategically placed accessories, fabrics can bring an extra dimension to a room. Chintzy prints (top left) have suffered a long decline, but they are now newly fashionable as an antidote to excessively spartan interiors. Coarser weaves (top right), popular in the 1970s, are now used mainly in neutral colours to add natural texture. Checks, ginghams and plaids (bottom right) add a country feel to more traditional rooms.

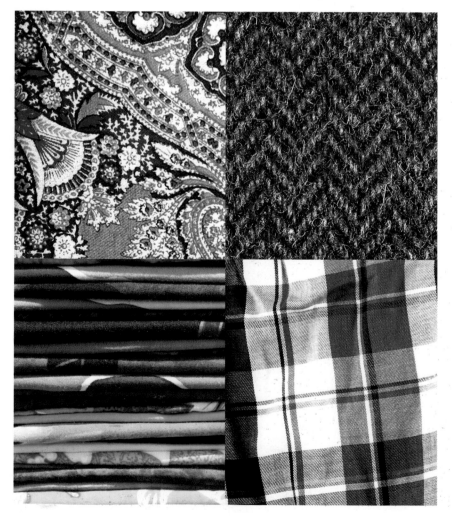

As in all fields of graphic design (*see chapter 03.01–03.05*), colour composition in wallpaper patterns may be harmonious and soothing or garish and jarring. Strong patterns have come back into fashion in recent years – at least with interior designers, if not the general public – and can be used to dramatic effect, often on just one wall of a room. But repetitive designs can also be surprisingly calming and grounding. Never discount textures and patterns solely because of their period associations, or because you have to struggle to think of an example you have seen that works well.

A coloured pattern on the walls will make it more difficult to introduce additional elements into a room. Once you have chosen a 'signature print' – the one that is likely to dominate your design – a standard policy is to select one colour from the pattern and apply it throughout two-thirds of the room, using the remaining colours on accessories and other details. Coordinated fabrics, which reproduce the pattern of a wall covering, may overload the senses if the design is a colourful or fussy pattern, but those with large motifs in muted colours can work well, creating either traditional or pop art effects. They are often available in a complement or reverse of the pattern.

Fabrics offer an extraordinary range of possibilities for interior decoration. The way you use them will depend as much on their qualities when stretched, pleated, draped or hung as on their colour and texture. Blinds and curtains may block out light completely for nighttime blackout, or filter it, softening the atmosphere of a room and providing daytime privacy. The effect achieved may depend as much on what is behind the fabric as on its own colour, and textiles are particularly prone to metamerism, in which two colour samples appear to match under one condition but not another. Keep swatches of colour in the room where you plan to use them for several days, and see how they behave.

Carpeting can also introduce colour and pattern to a room. Although the multicoloured maelstroms found in so many postwar homes are probably best forgotten, both wall-to-wall carpets and rugs are available in designs ranging from traditional geometric patterns to Afghan rugs commemorating the conflict with Russia in Kalashnikov motifs.

For obvious reasons, earth tones are popular in floor coverings. The simplest way to introduce them is to find an existing wooden board or parquet floor and repair, sand and seal it. Modern homes are often floored with unattractive materials that can be overlaid with wood or manmade products. Laminates, vinyls, ceramic tiles and linoleum provide an endless choice of colour, texture and pattern. You can use flooring as a supporting surface – either neutral in colour or drawing together the different elements of your colour scheme – or as a bold statement. The main limitations are practical: a pale, deep pile rug may scatter light attractively around a room, but it won't look so hot after the dog runs over it a few times.

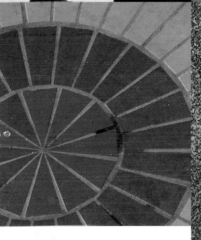

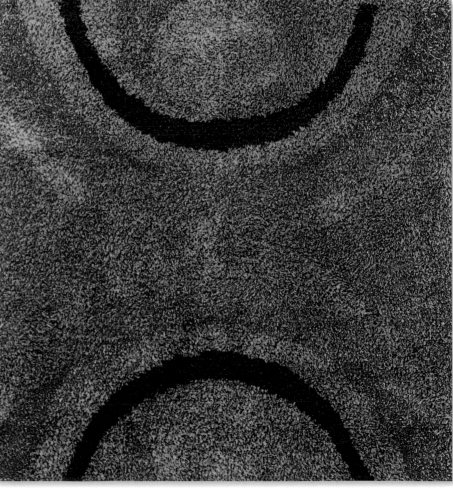

Above and right: **Wall-to-wall carpeting became popular after the Second World War, but it now faces stiff competition. Wood and wood-effect laminates are installable by the DIY enthusiast. Vinyl and linoleum have shed their utilitarian image and gained new colours and patterns. Ceramic tiles are increasingly seen outside the bathroom. And for warmth underfoot, rugs are available in striking modern designs.**

ACCESSORIES AND APPLIANCES
The objects in a room can have as great an impact on its appearance as the way it is decorated and furnished. And the number of objects we consider essential in our homes is constantly increasing. Many of us seem to function in relation to a set of objects in predefined positions: a TV set in the corner of the living room, for instance.

When labour-saving household devices first became commonplace in the late nineteenth century, they were marketed for what they could do rather than the way they looked. By the 1930s, however, designers such as Raymond Loewy were turning domestic appliances into style statements. Loewy favoured chrome – which, besides fitting his ethos of industrial streamlining, had the advantage of reflecting any colour scheme rather than clashing. But he also used primary colours like scarlet to evoke feelings of forward-looking optimism.

If Loewy designed the space age, new looks were required for the digital era. Memphis, a movement led in the 1980s by the Milanese designer Ettore Sottsass, was characterized by bright colours, rectilinear forms and a deliberate flouting of established rules. Among Sottsass's designs (many predating Memphis) were typewriters and other office machines for the Italian manufacturer Olivetti, which influenced the shapes of electronic business machines for decades. Sottsass's use of bold colour, however, was not so widely adopted. Personal computers were uniformly beige until the late 1990s.

Apple Computer's bulbous, translucent iMac, launched in 1998, typified a widespread move away from hard-edged shapes towards more organic forms. This appealed to a softer, less aggressive, more introspective mood in Western society, perhaps in reaction to the thrusting 1980s and anticipation of the forthcoming millennium. The movement was facilitated by new computer-aided design (CAD) techniques that made it much easier to work with irregular, curvaceous forms.

This trend in turn is now giving way to new ideas. Apple's latest products have moved on to a palette of white and bare metal. If the choice of white seems conservative, consider how many more connotations it has than beige. The exclusive cachet of the brand is further enhanced by unusual textures, the soft, rubbery finish of the iPod music player contributes to its appeal as a handheld device. Combinations of white and stainless steel are among the currently popular choices in the kitchens of design-conscious homes; perhaps there is a common factor in the triangle of function, pleasure and status symbol.

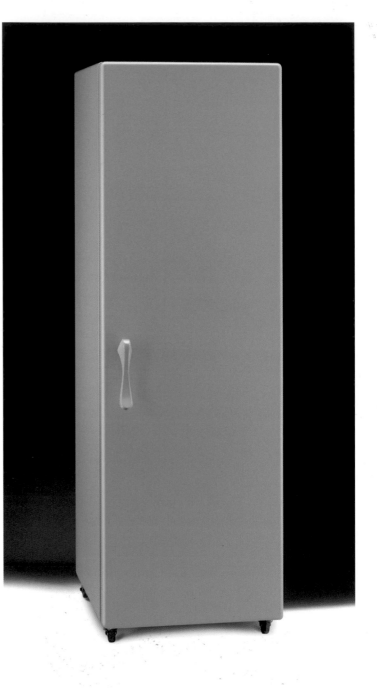

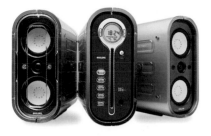

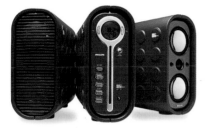

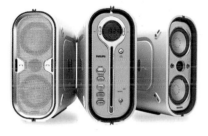

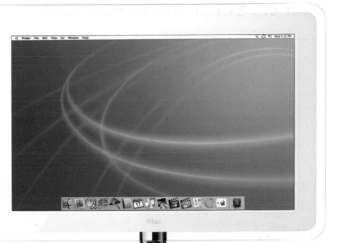

Left to right (from opposite page):
While most home appliances come in self-effacing white, this fridge is available in several bold colours. The three versions of Philips's Emotive Micro music system offer different textures as well as colours. The Dyson vacuum cleaner, a supremely functional object, nonetheless gains many sales from its distinctive shape and colour scheme. Apple's latest flat-screen iMac comes only in pure white – a new generation of appliance?

Humbler machines have also had designer makeovers. The now-familiar Dyson vacuum cleaner recalls Memphis in its harsh forms and distinctive colours, although British designer James Dyson firmly stresses that its appearance derives from functional rather than aesthetic concerns. A postmodern approach – borrowing here and there from tradition, but eschewing convention – can also be found in other upmarket appliances, such as the fridge designed for Italian manufacturer Smeg by the architect Renzo Piano.

Recorded music plays a regular part in the ambience of most modern homes, and hi-fi equipment comes in a bewildering variety of shapes and sizes influenced by every aspect of design trends and popular culture. While boom boxes destined to be carried around and shown off by teenagers often flaunt their wattage with overblown styling, household units are typically compact and restrained in design. Philips's Emotive Micro, an innovative range of systems introduced in 2002, offers a choice of cool green, aggressive red and minimalist metal housings, encouraging buyers to make colour choices that reflect their attitude as well as their decor.

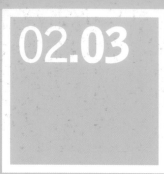

02.03

COLOUR IN ARCHITECTURE

Colour does not feature prominently in many recent accounts of architecture. In fact, a glance through any archive of images representing the most highly regarded buildings of the twentieth century will show the extent to which colour slipped out of the language of architecture. Only in the first years of the new millennium has it resurfaced as an issue powerful enough to draw the interest of individuals like Rem Koolhaas (b. 1944), Sir Norman Foster (b. 1935) and Alessandro Mendini (b. 1931). Their book *Colors* (Princeton Architectural Press, 2001) is devoted exclusively to the subject.

At the beginning of the twentieth century, when architects like Adolf Loos (1870–1933) and Le Corbusier (1887–1965) began to create buildings that became emblematic of the modern movement, there was no place for colour for two reasons. First, the architects of the modern movement wanted to distance themselves from what they saw as the misuse of colour. Second, the form of many modern buildings could be emphasized through using white alone.

It was not that colour itself was rejected, more that the decoration of buildings had started to become inappropriate – and this was not a new concern. As Gerhard Mack points out in his introduction to *Colors*, as early as the first century BC, the Roman architect Marcus Vitruvius (c. 70–25 BC) articulated his frustration at seeing buildings being painted in ways that bore no relation to their structural nature:

> For columns reeds are substituted; for pediments the stalks, leaves and tendrils of plants; candelabra are made to support the representations of small buildings ... similar forms never did, do, nor can exist in nature ...

De architectura, Vitruvius's ten-volume work on city planning and architecture, was regarded as a key text throughout Europe until well into the Renaissance, when similar opinions were voiced by the Italian architect Leon Baptista Alberti in his *De re aedificatoria* (1485).

Architects working in the modernist tradition did not want to outlaw colour; just to see it used sympathetically. Le Corbusier's *Vers une architecture* (1923) may not have devoted a single line to colour, but he used it in his buildings and went on in 1930–31 to isolate the forty-three colour tones he relied on to affect spatial relationships in his work.

Fortunately, the principles of modernist architecture have correspondingly developed and thawed enough for contemporary architects to experiment with colour. Developments in building materials, meanwhile, continue to expand the palettes available.

Colour took a back seat in most of the high architecture of the twentieth century, but it is now central to the work of respected architects such as Rem Koolhaas, as illustrated in The McCormick Tribune Campus Center at Illinois Institute of Technology. Such architects believe buildings should respond to their cultural as well as geographical environment, and colour can play as large a part in this as form.

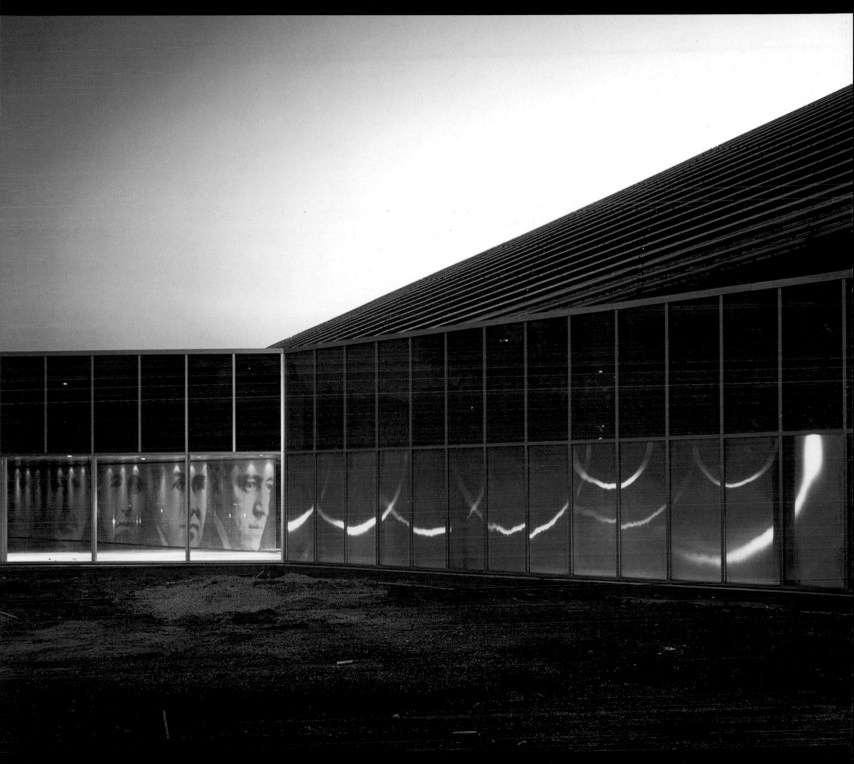

Below and right: **From dusk onwards,** neon lighting is often the predominant feature of modern city streets. Buildings merge into a glaring haze, defying any overall impression of harmony and logic, regardless of their structural forms. Making sense of all this is a challenge to the urban architect.

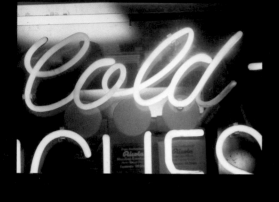

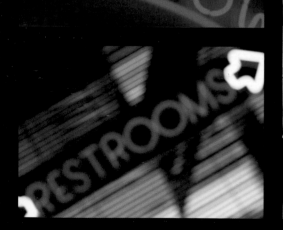

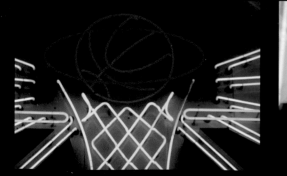

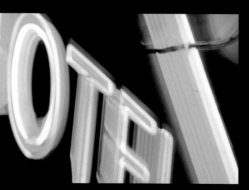

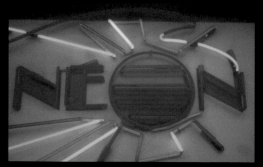

COLOUR IN THE CITY Many contemporary architects use colour as a reflection of the use or immediate environment of a building, or to make connections between it and broader cultural themes and expectations. Architect Rem Koolhaas believes that the use of colour must be guided by our changing perception of it.

Koolhaas was one of the founders of the Office of Metropolitan Architecture (OMA), an organization set up to define new theoretical and practical relationships for architecture within contemporary culture. Examining the options architects have for using colour, he traces a trajectory from the modernist position through the 'exuberance' of the 1960s and 1970s to the minimalism of the 1990s, with its emphasis on the colours of actual materials.

Alongside this, he identifies other ways in which we have been exposed to colour, such as the enhanced, luminous world of TV and computer screens, which he describes as "more glamorous than any real colour on real surfaces…. Colour, paint, coatings, in comparison somehow became matte and dull." Computer-based designers, comparing the vast RGB colour space on their screens with the limitations of reflective colour in the surfaces they create, will immediately know what he means.

Koolhaas mentions that when people working at OMA were asked to suggest which colours they would like to use, only ten chose a single colour. The others saw their colours as a treatment that was "not simply a layer of colour but a more subtle conditioning, a layer that alters the state of the painted wall of an object, a colour that would interfere with the status of the painted object."

Ultimately, Koolhaas's vision of colour is one that fully engages with the contemporary urban environment: "It is only logical that, with the incredible sensorial onslaught that bombards us every day and the artificial intensities that we encounter in the virtual world, the nature of colour should change, no longer just a thin layer of change, but something that genuinely alters perception. In this sense, the future of colours is looking bright."

While Koolhaas ponders an ordered response to today's ambient colour stimuli, most major cities are plunged after dark into a riot of coloured light that can be thoroughly overwhelming. Whereas an architect may use colour to reflect function or status, to clarify spatial relationships, or to provide orientation, illuminated shop signs rarely bear any relation to the facades of the buildings to which they are fixed. Instead, each points inwardly towards the world of its corporate affiliation. The purpose of each is to attract more attention than its neighbours, and the result can be disorienting. When you need a pharmacy, you may spot its symbol from halfway down a street, ignoring other signs. But driving through a city at night, trying to locate a particular building, demands an exhausting mental effort to register and then reject all of the irrelevant illuminations.

This process of destabilizing city space – of colour damage – seems as irreversible as it is sinister. As urban spaces are annexed by chain stores retailing the same goods from the same manufacturers, they begin to adopt similar patterns of signage. The streets of London and New York orient consumers towards a single vision of fixed brands and corporate superiority. How fixed that template will become remains to be seen.

Below: High-energy lighting screams a thousand messages at once to the rear lamps of the passing traffic. Even the stars are blotted out by 'light pollution'. The cumulative effect can be exciting, but is this the way we want all our cities to turn out?

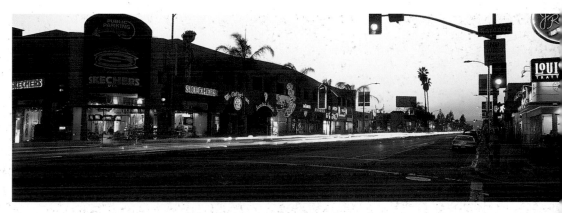

COLOUR IN PRACTICE If modern architecture is predominantly colourless, or at least monochrome, this only serves to accentuate the impact of buildings that make strong use of colour. On the following pages we briefly tour some of the more intriguing recent applications of colour in architecture.

Right: Architectural colour need not be reflected from surfaces but can be created by light. The recently built Laban Dance Centre in London has a skin of translucent plastic through which the interior is partially visible. By night, light from inside is projected outwards, turning the riverside building into a beacon that seems symbolic of its contribution to the regeneration of the urban environment around it. To design the colour scheme, Swiss architects Herzog and de Meuron worked with British artist Michael Craig-Martin, known for his brightly coloured paintings of everyday objects.

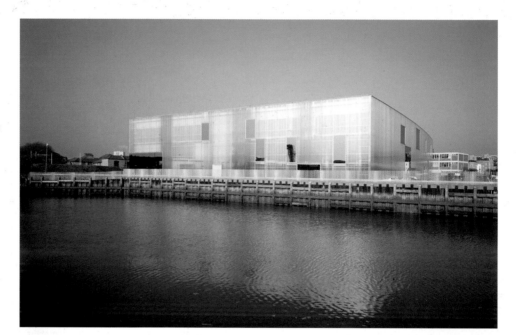

Right: Mexican architect Ricardo Legorreta (b. 1931) has said that he 'can't live without colour'. Like his library at San Antonio, Texas – known locally as the 'red enchilada' – British designer Zandra Rhodes's Fashion and Textile Museum, London, makes emphatic use of a single hue. In this case an existing building was reworked. While architectural changes transformed it functionally from a wholesaler's into a museum, colour transformed it visually. Founder Zandra Rhodes (b. 1940) is also known for her bold use of colour.

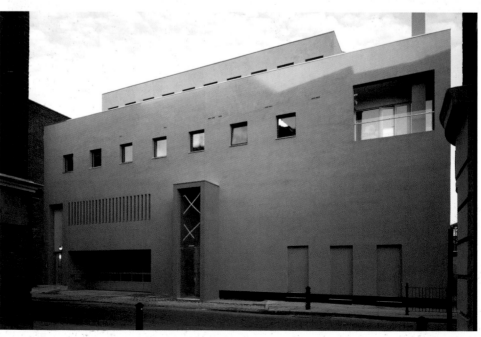

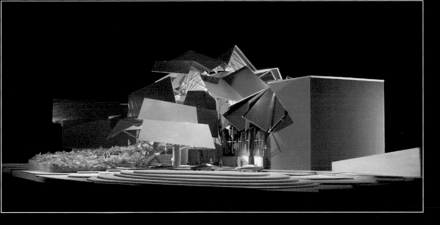

Left: **Frank Gehry, one of the most respected contemporary American architects, historically is best known for monochromatic buildings such as the Guggenheim Museum in Bilbao, northern Spain. His latest project, however, explodes with vibrant, primary colours. The Puente de Vida (Bridge of Life), a new national museum for Panama, was founded to educate the public about the importance of biodiversity. Gehry, however, has little interest in the current trend for environmentally friendly building methods and has not focused on incorporating ecological principles such as energy efficiency and recyclability into his design. From an aesthetic point of view, however, the building clearly responds to its location and to the ethos it represents. Bright colours inspired by local flora and fauna are applied to an irregular arrangement of geometric forms, joyously evoking a teeming mass of life.**

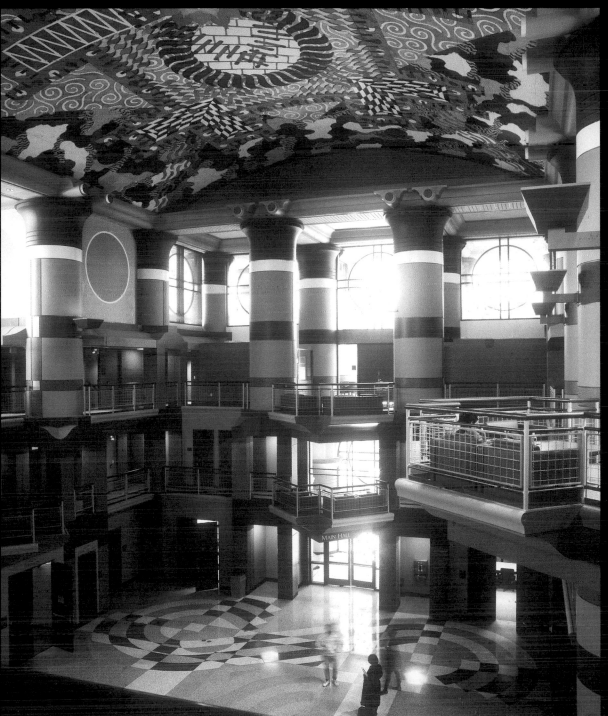

Left: **Designed by John Outram, well known for his provocative use of colour, the Computational Engineering Building (1997) at Texas's Rice University was created to house individuals from many different backgrounds, brought together to apply computing skills to engineering. In the extraordinary postmodern interior colour covers every available surface. Each colour was selected for its symbolism. Above all, there was a desire to make the building a stimulating environment for creative thinking.**

Left: Designers are increasingly willing to experiment with colour in surfaces and lighting, and the range of products available to specifiers has grown enormously in recent years. This interior at Powder, a New York club, uses an unusual colour scheme, distinctive textures and bold forms to create a unique ambience. Modern lighting installations are often highly controllable, governed by electronic switchboards that can store complex patterns and play them back in timed sequences.

Left: Public and semi-public spaces allow more dramatic colour and lighting effects than would be appropriate in a domestic setting. The unique interior of the Morimoto restaurant, Philadelphia, is the work of Karim Rashid, the prolific designer previously noted for his use of form and colour in furniture, accessories and consumer products. Conventional tungsten lighting incorporated into the wavy, organic forms of the walls is complemented by LEDs (light-emitting diodes) in the table dividers, creating a shifting and pulsating colour ambience.

Right: While many architects shun colour, it is commonplace in vernacular building design and decoration. Brightly coloured nineteenth-century houses known as Painted Ladies are a distinctive feature of the San Francisco urban landscape. These elegantly proportioned houses were originally more sombre in appearance but gained their colour in the 1960s and 1970s, when they were renovated by hippie-era residents. Similar treatments of period houses can be seen in many European cities, and the effect has been reproduced in modern housing developments. In Disney's artificially created community of Celebration, Florida, period-style homes feature many splashes of bright colour – but the palette is strictly controlled, with no provision for self-expression.

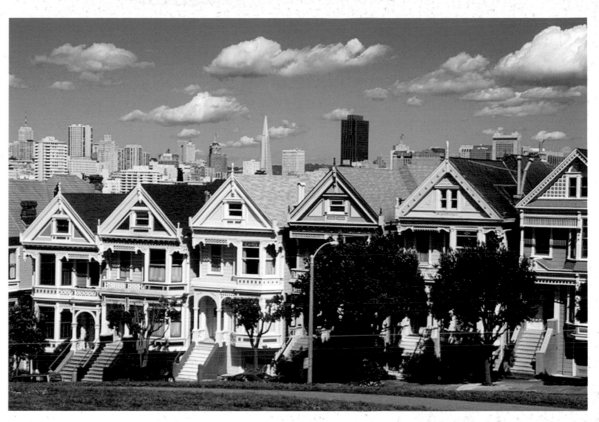

Right: Computer-aided design is integral to the practise of many contemporary architects, and 3-D modelling systems not only assist with planning the structure of a building but also offer a preview of the finished product. Historically, the architect would have developed colour schemes in drawings, using his or her knowledge and experience to predict how surfaces and spaces would appear in reality. Today, it is possible to 'walk through' (or around) a building constructed on screen, with light and shadow calculated for a given time of day or year. Complex artificial lighting setups can also be simulated.

The detail and accuracy with which still or moving images can be 'rendered' is limited only by the time and effort required of the software operator to define forms, surfaces and light sources with the required degree of precision. But the subjective effects of colour and light remain elusive: the true 'feel' of a building can be experienced only in reality, or in the mind of the architect.

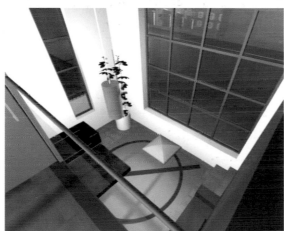

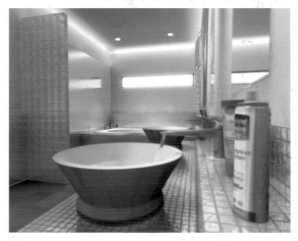

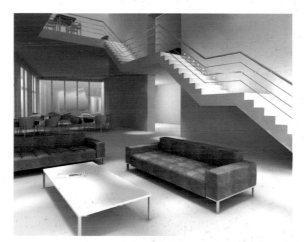

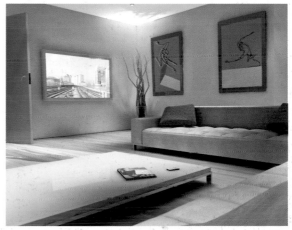

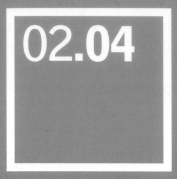

02.04

COLOUR IN PHOTOGRAPHY

The person credited with creating the very first form of colour photographic reproduction is James Clerk Maxwell (1831–79). In 1861, Maxwell experimented with colour filters and monochrome emulsions, using the filters to transmit different light wavelengths to the light-sensitive medium, a crude form of colour separation. He then projected each image simultaneously using three projection 'lanterns', each fitted with the appropriate filter. The result was a moderate success. Maxwell reproduced his subject – a tartan ribbon – in colour, following a complex process that required three projectors working at once. He used the additive principle of colour (*see page 26*), in which primary colours of light are combined in projection to produce intermediate hues, the brightness and colour varying according to the different strengths of light transmitted through the monochrome photographs by each projector.

The Lumière brothers (Auguste, 1862–1954, and Louis, 1865–1947) developed the first properly viable colour photographic process in 1907. They called their process Autochrome, and it was in effect an application of the ideas Maxwell had demonstrated more than forty years earlier. The colour filters were built into the film as a layer of tiny starch grains dyed with three different colours. When exposed to light, the starch grains acted as colour filters, restricting the light according to the wavelengths each minuscule grain would allow to pass. When the film was developed correctly and then shown with the appropriate screen, a real colour photograph resulted. The images tended to be relatively dark, and the colours tended towards the pastel, but the process remained the only workable solution until the mid-1930s, when Kodak created a film that worked on the subtractive process.

The subtractive process (soon named Kodachrome) used three layers of light-sensitive, dyed emulsion, each sensitive to just one section of the colour spectrum. When processed as film positives, the result was a colour photographic slide ready for viewing. From then until the development of digital photography, film developments have, by and large, been refinements and advances on the Kodachrome process. It is interesting to note that the idea of using dyed emulsions to create subtractive colour photographs was first suggested in 1869, just a few years after Maxwell's additive colour experiments, by French scientist Louis Ducas du Hauron (1837–1920). However, the limitations of photographic emulsions at the time prevented subtractive colour photography from being more than a theoretical proposal for another sixty years.

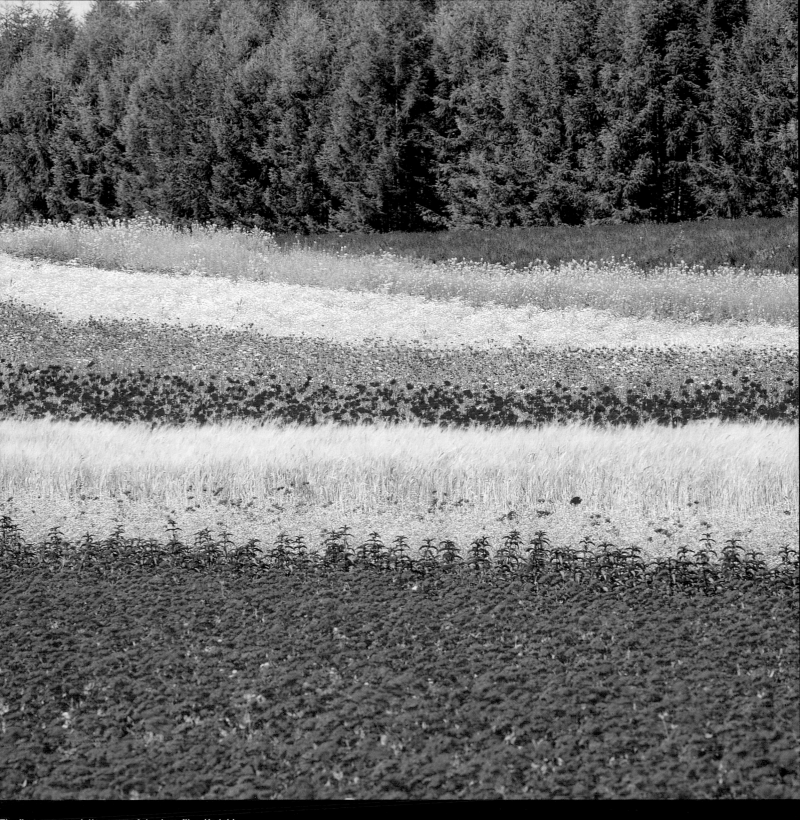

The first commercially successful colour film, Kodak's
Kodachrome, was introduced in 1935. Film speeds and
quality have improved, but the basic principle, layers of
light-sensitive dyed emulsions, remains the same.

RECORDING LIGHT Photography is all about recording light, so different light sources will have dramatically varied effects on the look of a photograph. Our eyes are marvellously adaptable; in a sense, they provide natural white-balance adjustment, so we are rarely aware of the various colour balances of different sources of light. Photography, however, records faithfully without providing automatic correction.

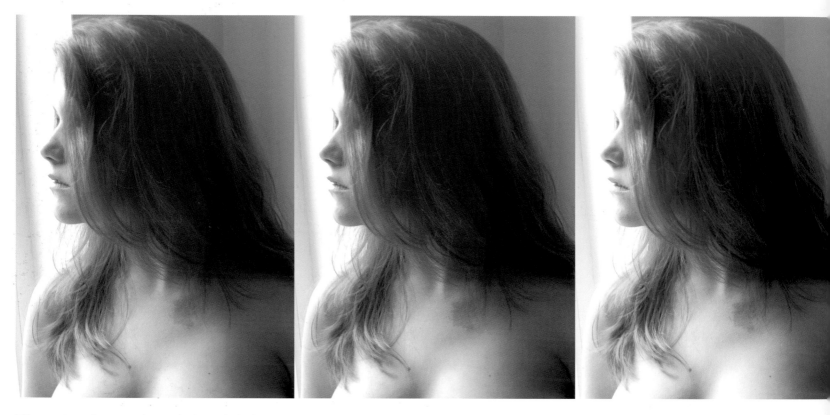

The result is photographs in which the light looks 'wrong' – too red, too green or whatever. We have to adjust for this at some point in the photographic process, whether by using filters, employing digital white-balance features in the camera or applying colour correction steps in Photoshop.

The wavelength composition of sunlight varies greatly during the day; in early morning and late afternoon, light is warmer than in the middle of the day, simply because sunlight hits us obliquely through the atmosphere. This acts as a filter on the shorter wavelengths, allowing a greater proportion of the red end of the colour spectrum through. During the middle of the day, sunlight hits us more directly, resulting in a shorter trip through the atmosphere and less-filtered light. Compared with dawn and dusk photographs, the colour bias of images taken at this time of day will be less

White balance settings can have a significant effect on your images. Here we've deliberately tricked the camera to expose for the wrong lighting to show this effect.
Above left: The excess of blue indicates a picture taken in daylight with the camera set to compensate for tungsten (sometimes called incandescent) lighting.
Above centre: This image was shot under tungsten lighting with the camera set to daylight.
Above right: Finally, shot under fluorescent lighting with the camera set to tungsten.

warm; the light contains an even balance throughout the spectrum, thus appearing whiter, or cooler.

Although the colour variation of natural light throughout the day can vary, our eyes are conditioned to accept low-lying light sources and reddish casts with evening images. However, the colour casts of artificial lighting are much more extreme. For example, tungsten lighting – standard lightbulbs, also known as incandescent – produces far more light in the red end of the spectrum than anything else. The result is images with orange-tinted whites and muted greens and blues. One way around this is to use a colour filter designed to correct the strong reddish bias. However, tungsten light is often not particularly bright in photographic terms and can demand slow shutter speeds, so filtering out more light is not going to help matters.

Another problem is fluorescent lighting. This kind of source produces light with a greenish balance, and its effect on skin tone can make people look unwell in photographs. Obviously this is rarely desirable, so you will need to counter it in some way. A colour filter can help, but the variations found with fluorescent lighting mean that you should turn first to the white-balance controls in your camera.

Things can become very complicated when shooting scenes with multiple light sources. Interiors lit with tungsten lights but with daylight coming through windows are difficult to photograph if you want an even-coloured look to your photographs. You may be able to use studio lighting with coloured gel filters to introduce blue-biased light to counteract the tungsten, but you may be forced to resort to selective colour corrections after the fact in Photoshop. One possible approach is to shoot two versions of the scene, one white-balanced for interior lights and one balanced for daylight. You could then combine the shots in Photoshop, picking the areas you want from each one.

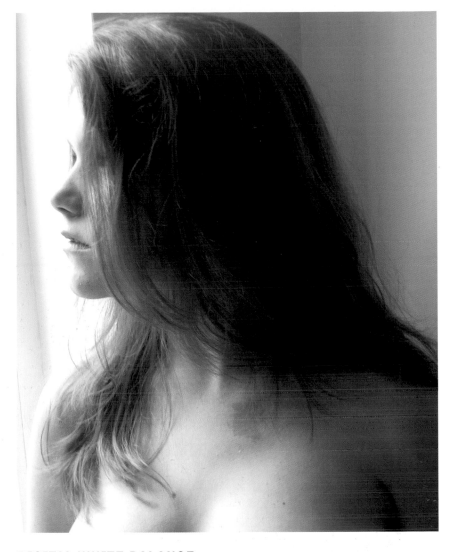

DIGITAL WHITE BALANCE

Some digital cameras may attempt to perform a measure of white-balance correction automatically, but that is not a particularly professional way to work. Good digital cameras include a feature for setting a 'digital white balance' yourself, effectively telling the camera what should be white, so that it can work out what to do to neutralize any colour cast that may exist, then apply that neutralizing process to subsequent photos. The process is normally very simple to do. For example, setting a manual white balance in many makes of digital cameras involves shooting a well-lit white card or similar flat white object and then assigning that as the white-balance target. As with the above image, photos taken from then on will be appropriately balanced.

When you use digital white-balance features, remember to reset the camera as you move to different lighting conditions, either by using a new white-balance source or by setting the camera back to normal. If you fail to reset your camera, it will incorrectly 'correct' your images as you work.

CREATIVE USE OF COLOUR

Using colour creatively is as much a matter of looking carefully as it is about using technical trickery. However, there are many features in Photoshop that offer excellent colour control to the digital photographer, from Levels and Hue/Saturation to the Adjustment Layers and Variations.

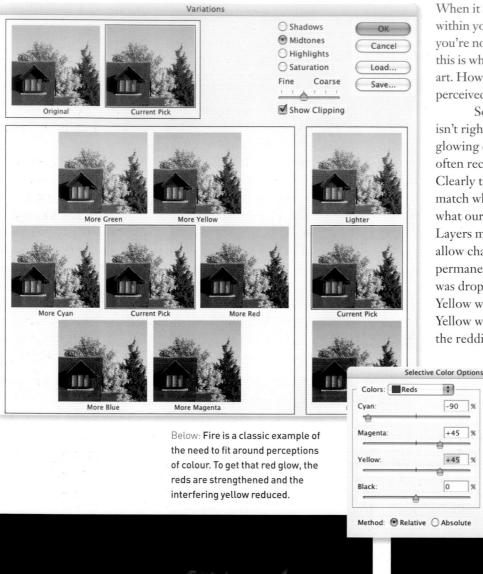

When it comes to creative colour usage, you're completely within your rights to throw the rulebook out of the window. If you're not concerned with realistic colour, this is fine. In fact, this is where digital photography can become a real free-form art. However, if you're trying to make images look closer to perceived reality, you'll need to proceed a little more carefully.

Sometimes you just know when the colour in a picture isn't right. Photographs of fire often have this problem; glowing embers look a rich orange to our eyes, yet they are often recorded as pinky-yellows and whites in photographs. Clearly this sort of image is in need of adjustment to make it match what we see. This example has been altered to reflect what our eyes perceive. Choose Adjustment Layer in the Layers menu and pick Selective Color. Adjustment Layers allow changes to be made without altering the image permanently. With Reds selected in the Color menu, the Cyan was dropped down to minus 90%, and both Magenta and Yellow were set to +45%. Then, with Yellows selected, the Yellow was dropped to -80% and Magenta to -30% to counter the reddish-yellow cast in the ironwork.

Below: **Fire is a classic example of the need to fit around perceptions of colour. To get that red glow, the reds are strengthened and the interfering yellow reduced.**

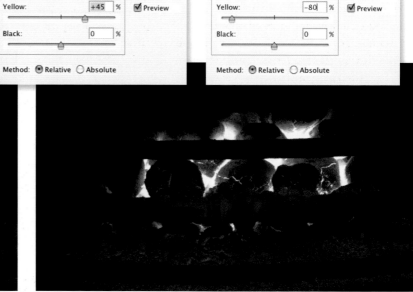

part 02. living with colour

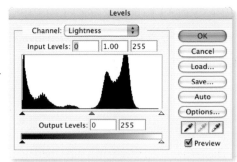

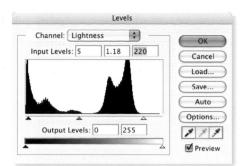

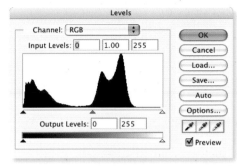

Above, left, and below: **Adjusting levels can lead to posterization, which can been seen as gaps in the lower left histogram. This problem can be avoided using the Lab colour mode, and only editing the Lightness channel. This preserves subtleties of hue while still allowing contrast improvements. The resulting histogram (lower right) shows significantly less damage.**

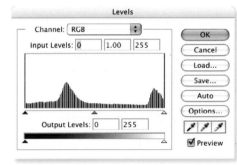

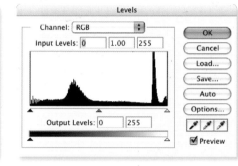

stretching out what's left to fill from the darkest to the lightest points, heavy-handed use can lead to posterizing in once subtly varying tones. It will also have an effect on colour, to an extent: adjusting levels the normal way – to the RGB channels – stretches colour values as well as brightness and contrast.

To avoid this, and also to moderate the effects of losing subtleties, you should switch the image mode to Lab instead of RGB, at least for this process. This mode devotes one of the three image channels entirely to brightness and contrast data, while the other two define colour using two axes. The Levels dialog now defaults to working on just the Lightness channel; tweaking this leaves the colour values untouched, so when you switch back to RGB, there's less damage done to the image. The two 'after' Levels illustrations to the left demonstrate the difference.

The temptation to boost the saturation of your shots as a matter of course may be strong, but don't get carried away. Although the impact you're after may be muted by weak sunshine, you may find it best to boost just a few aspects of the image rather than all colours wholesale. One method is to use Photoshop's Hue/Saturation controls, found in the Adjustments section of the Image menu. In the example below, the editing has been restricted to just reds, with a very small tweak to yellows. The result is an image that looks like it was taken with stronger sunlight: more saturated, but not overall and not unrealistically so.

If you're not sure about what to alter, the Variations feature, found in the Adjustments list in the Image menu, provides a way to experiment with pushing different colour strengths around in an image. Add more cyan and yellow to the highlights, make the midtones lighter or darker, all with simple clicks. This is a bit of a quick-fix feature, but it can still be useful – particularly if you protect areas you don't want changed.

The Levels feature in Photoshop is an excellent tool for finding out about the extremities of an image's range, whether it contains true blacks and whites or whether the brightest and darkest points are a bit dull. It also provides the tools for tweaking these as well as for adjusting the tonal midpoint, both excellent for bumping an image up from tonal obscurity. Be warned that changing the levels in an image can create problems. Because it involves throwing image data away and

Below: **Increasing the saturation of your image can have a dramatically enriching effect. The best results are achieved by targeting specific colours rather than applying a blanket colour correction.**

COLOUR MANAGEMENT OF DIGITAL PHOTOGRAPHY As explained on page 164, colour management is based on International Color Consortium (ICC) profiles that are used to translate the colour values read or required by specific devices into or from a universal, device-independent colour space, International Commission on Illumination (CIE) Lab. In the digital camera workflow, this means converting the raw data from the camera into CIE Lab colour values and then into a working colour space for subsequent manipulation and, through a further transformation to a particular print device's colour space, eventual printed output.

As we saw, it is very difficult to create a profile for a digital camera because lighting conditions affect its colour behavior. That said, creating such a profile can be done for cameras that will be used in controlled lighting conditions (studio work), and some of the more professional-level digital cameras do ship with supplied colour profiles.

With a calibrated monitor, it is possible to test colour profiles by eye. In Adobe Photoshop, you can preview the effect of assigning any colour profile to an image to see which produces the best result. One possibility is to use sRGB (the 's' stands for 'standard'), at least to start with. Although this profile was developed to represent a 'typical' PC monitor, it also happens to be a fairly good match to the colour gamut (range of detectable colours) of many digital cameras. But unless the image is destined only for display on such monitors, it is a good idea to convert from sRGB to a working space with a larger gamut, such as Adobe RGB (1998), because some colours (saturated yellows/oranges and green/cyans offset print, and good quality ink-jet printers can reproduce but which are outside the sRGB gamut.

Once the image has been assigned a suitable input profile and converted to the working space, image editing can proceed as desired. It is advisable to do this in RGB, even if the ultimate destination for the image is CMYK print. This is because most RGB colour spaces are bigger than CMYK ones, so if the image might also be used for an on-screen medium, the most colour information will be preserved in RGB. An RGB working space is also linear (equal amounts of R, G and B always make a grey, something not true in output spaces like CMYK), and perhaps most important, you cannot exceed ink limits (the total amount of ink a press can put onto paper) while working in RGB. Too much ink can cause drying and set off problems, or even cause the paper to tear on the press. Working in RGB and then converting to CMYK using an

appropriate output profile is the best way to avoid this, as ink limits are respected in any conversion to CMYK.

You can preview the effect of the conversion to CMYK using Adobe Photoshop, and even simulate the final printed result with a profiled inkjet through a process called cross-rendering (see below). RGB is also the right colour space for inkjet printers that do not have a separate RIP (raster image processor) – all consumer-level products fall into this category – and for photographic-paper printers used in some professional labs.

Below: Photoshop's Print Preview dialog shows an array of colour-management options. Notice that when printing, it's possible to select either the document's colour space, or your predefined proofing colour space. The latter will simulate the named device using your printer. You will also need to select a profile for your device (the print space) or choose the printer's own management.

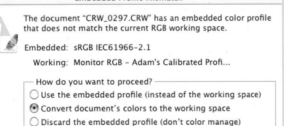

Canon EOS 300D: CRW_0297.CRW (ISO 100, 1/200, f/10, 27 mm)

OK
Cancel

○ Basic   ○ Advanced

Settings: Custom

Adjust | Detail

White Balance: Custom

Temperature   5400
Tint   +7

Exposure   +2.95
Shadows   0
Brightness   50
Contrast   +25
Saturation   0

20.3%   ☑ Preview   R: ---- G: ---- B: ----

Space: sRGB IEC61966-1   Size: 4096 by 2731 (+)
Depth: 16 Bits/Channel   Resolution: 480 pixels/inch

Left: Following the workflow from start to finish, we start with a source image from a digital camera, in the sRGB colour space. Here the raw image is shown in the Photoshop CS Raw Image Importer. Once OK is clicked, the image progresses into Photoshop itself, where we are invited to convert to the working space, in this case one set up for the user's monitor. This is a sensible step if it is a larger space, and now the image can be worked on.

Embedded Profile Mismatch

The document "CRW_0297.CRW" has an embedded color profile that does not match the current RGB working space.

Embedded: sRGB IEC61966-2.1

Working: Monitor RGB – Adam's Calibrated Profi...

How do you want to proceed?
○ Use the embedded profile (instead of the working space)
● Convert document's colors to the working space
○ Discard the embedded profile (don't color manage)

Cancel   OK

Below: After the editing stage, colour profiles play an important part in proofing and output. If you are outputting to CMYK, for example, you can select a working space that will be used in the conversion of the image. The custom profile settings (available from the CMYK space drop-down menu) allow you to define exactly how colours are converted from RGB to CMYK.

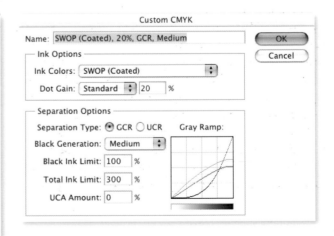

Color Settings

Settings: Custom

☐ Advanced Mode

Working Spaces
RGB: Monitor RGB – Adam's Calibrated Profile
CMYK: ColorSync CMYK – Generic CMYK Profile
Gray: Dot Gain 20%
Spot: Dot Gain 20%

Color Management Policies
RGB: Off
CMYK: Off
Gray: Off

Profile Mismatches: ☑ Ask When Opening ☐ Ask When Pasting
Missing Profiles: ☐ Ask When Opening

Description

OK
Cancel
Load...
Save...
☑ Preview

Custom CMYK

Name: SWOP (Coated), 20%, GCR, Medium

Ink Options
Ink Colors: SWOP (Coated)
Dot Gain: Standard 20 %

Separation Options
Separation Type: ● GCR ○ UCR   Gray Ramp:
Black Generation: Medium
Black Ink Limit: 100 %
Total Ink Limit: 300 %
UCA Amount: 0 %

OK
Cancel

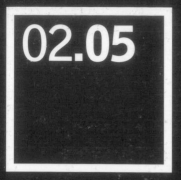

COLOUR IN THE MOVING IMAGE

Movies gained colour before they gained sound. Georges Méliès (1861–1938), who pioneered narrative cinema in the late nineteenth century, made the first colour film, *Le manoir du diable*, by hand-tinting individual frames. This technique was widely used even up to the 1930s, and the fact that filmmakers considered it worthwhile to paint up to six colours onto hundreds of thousands of frames indicates just how powerful an attraction colour must have been to early audiences.

More cheaply, a tint to indicate mood could be applied to a whole film or to sections. As an interesting example of the subjectivity of colour, Western films were tinted blue to indicate nighttime, since our eyes detect mostly blue wavelengths in low light, but orange served the same function in Japan. About the Far East, presumably in reference to the warm evening light there.

It was recognized that, as with still photography, a true colour process was needed to capture natural colour on film. Efforts to design such a process, however, were beset by problems, and the first successful colour cinematographic system ended up using only two colours. Kinemacolor, invented by US motion-picture pioneers Charles Urban (1867–1942) and G. Albert Smith

(1864–1959) in 1906, used two colour filters mounted on a rapidly turning wheel. Images were recorded on successive frames of black and white film through a colour filter, with alternating frames being exposed and filtered for colour using a projector with similar filters. The red and green components, fused in motion, created the impression of a full-colour image on screen.

The Technicolor camera developed around 1932 by the film making company used three different filters, currently the three-strip process, used one strip for the red and green components as well as [...] [...] red, green and blue films simultaneously. [...] final product [...] developed, [...] filters [...] richly saturated colour in films [...] show [...] when a film [...] on [...] that produced [...] reproduce a full colour range [...]

[...] most [...] colour process was difficult [...] fully [...] [...] long to shoot [...] colour [...] [...] imagination [...] colour films [...] world [...] *Le third colour*. [...] in 1935, the three-strip Technicolor appeared finally [...] on the screen [...]

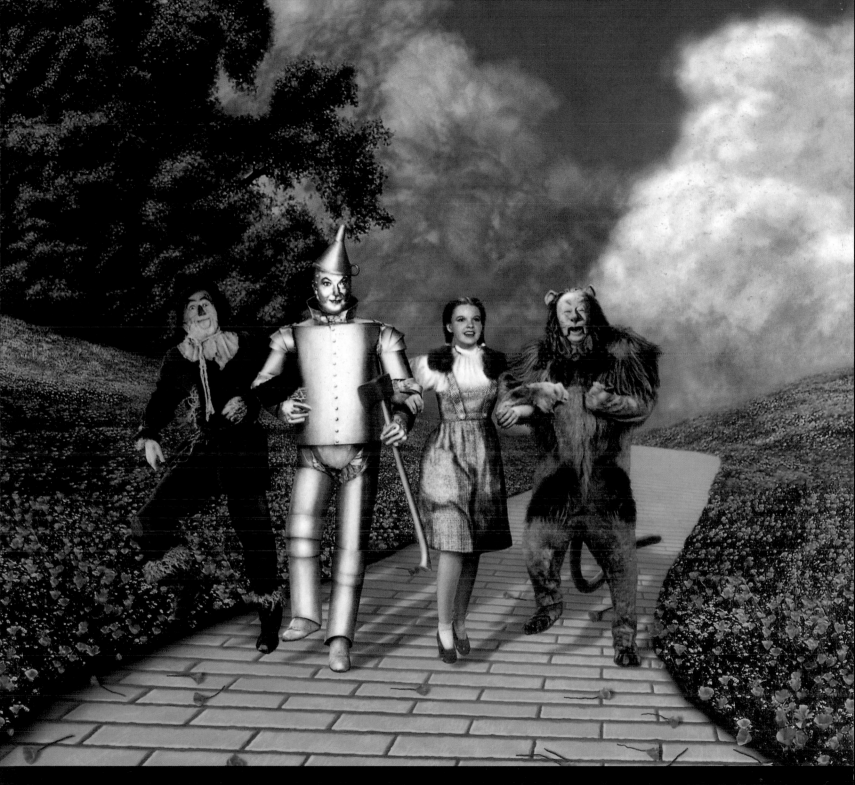

Technicolour added a new dimension to feature films like *The Wizard of Oz* (1939). Studios soon discovered that colour attracted larger audiences, and directors were quick to exploit new possibilities for artistic and symbolic uses of colour in their work. Colour correction,

COLOUR IN FEATURE FILMS
The age of 'glorious Technicolor' lasted only two decades, from the 1930s to the 1950s. *Becky Sharp* (1935), an adaptation of the William Makepeace Thackeray novel *Vanity Fair*, was the world's first full-colour feature film. Some critics complained that the film featured too much blue.

Adding at least 50 percent to the cost of making a movie, colour was an expensive luxury, and many productions could afford to use it only in brief segments. RKO's Fred Astaire/Ginger Rogers vehicle *Carefree* (1938), for example, was to have had a colour sequence for a song-and-dance number, but to keep costs down, the studio changed its mind. The song, by Irving Berlin, was 'I Used to Be Color Blind'.

The fact that Technicolor required multiple strips of films in the camera meant that it remained somewhat unwieldy, and it was overtaken in the early 1950s by Kodak's Eastman Color, which captures all three colours in light-sensitive dyes layered on a single negative. Sadly, the layer that absorbed blue light has turned out to be chemically unstable, causing visible deterioration over time. Some Eastman stock was transferred to monochrome three-strip sets as a backup when first printed, but in other cases, restorers have had to work hard to recover the original colours.

Today, the very existence of film is threatened by the rise of digital video cameras capable of shooting movie-quality footage. Only a few directors have so far been persuaded to switch, but the potential for huge cost savings has not escaped the studios' attention. Currently, footage shot on film is routinely transferred to digital as an 'intermediate' for computer-based editing, then returned to film for projection.

Although colour is now the norm, black-and-white film is still widely used for specific purposes. David Lynch used monochrome to create the grotesque, nauseous atmosphere of *Eraserhead* (1976) and to lend a historical feel to *The Elephant Man* (1980) before turning to deliberately heightened colour in the dark, disturbing *Blue Velvet* (1986), which paradoxically recalls the cheerful innocence of the Technicolor era. Steven Spielberg memorably used only one colour, red, in *Schindler's List* (1993), to striking and moving effect.

Red is also a key colour in Nicolas Roeg's *Don't Look Now* (1973), with the tension and fear in the film built around a child's red coat. Roeg is cited as an influence by Francis Ford Coppola, whose *Rumble Fish* (1983) tells the story of two brothers, one of whom is colour-blind as well as hearing impaired. The film is presented in black and white, switching to colour at the end to highlight a central motif of brightly coloured tropical fish.

In Gary Ross's *Pleasantville* (1998), the use of colour becomes a plot device as two teenagers from the full-colour present are transported into the monochromic world of a 1950s TV sitcom, gradually painting it with colour – both literal and metaphorical – as the story progresses. The special effects required for this were achieved digitally. 'Digital colorists', skilled in manipulating colour balance either subtly or dramatically, have also contributed significantly to the look and mood of films such as the *Lord of the Rings* trilogy.

Below: While many high-budget, lavishly presented movies had been made before the invention of Technicolor, their sumptuous sets and costumes had only ever been seen in monochrome. *Becky Sharp* (1935), starring Miriam Hopkins as the tragic heroine, was the first shot in full colour, albeit with rather exaggerated tones.

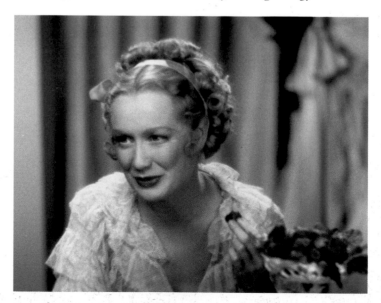

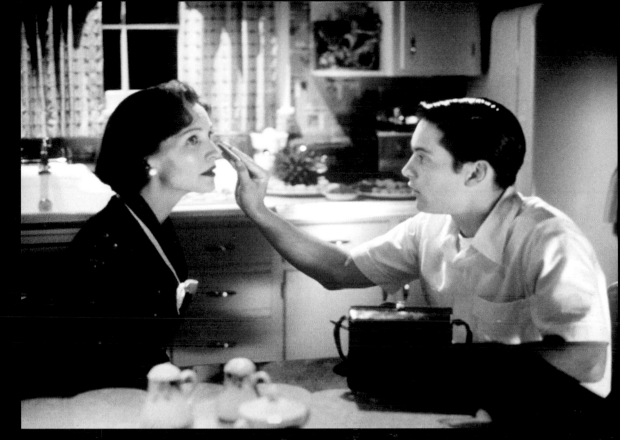

Right: *Pleasantville* (1998) features colour and black-and-white characters and objects occupying the same scenes, a trick that could only have been pulled off successfully with newly available digital editing technology.

Right: The diminutive figure in *Don't Look Now* (1973) turns out not to be quite what it appears. If the title wasn't enough to warn us that a shock was in store, the symbolism of the character's red hooded coat should be enough to tip us off.

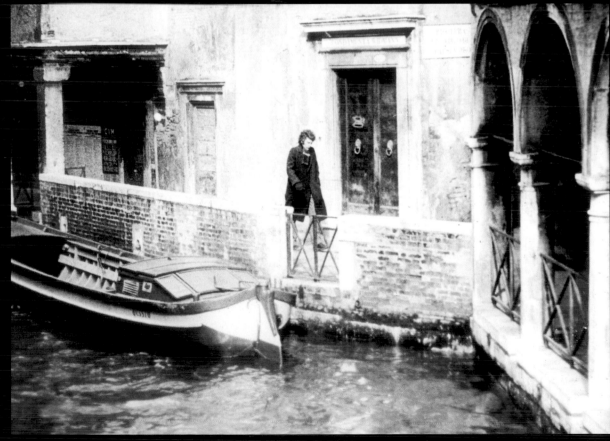

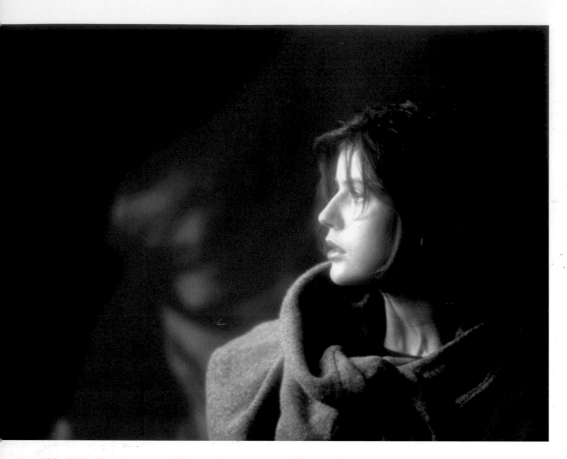

Alfred Hitchcock once said that a director should keep a film as simple as possible to avoid confusing the audience. This was somewhat disingenuous, considering the amount of symbolism he used in his own work. Whether a film is a full-length Hollywood feature, a lipstick advertisement or an art-house short, it is likely to be a multilayered text, with colour representing a significant layer of meaning.

The director (and sometimes the writer) will normally decide and control what is conveyed by colour, although the effects will be realized by the art director and director of photography. Which colours will be identified with characters, like Madeleine's green in Hitchcock's *Vertigo*? Which will be emphasized in landscapes, backgrounds and interiors? And what about those small details? Even the colour of a salt shaker may be imbued with meaning. Nothing in a film is there by accident – although a flash of a red Coke can may indicate paid product placement rather than symbolism. Look at the work of filmmakers such as Michael Powell, Peter Greenaway and Stanley Kubrick to see how everything in a scene is significant.

Colour symbolism is fundamental to the conception of Krzysztof Kieslowski's critically acclaimed *Three Colors* trilogy. The colours are those of the French flag, symbolizing liberty (blue), equality (white) and fraternity (red). Kieslowski used three different cinematographers to give each film a distinctive palette dominated by its eponymous colour.

Above: **In Krzysztof Kieslowski's *Three Colors: Red* (1994), the colour represents fraternity, and we find characters in search of intimacy and love. As might be expected, the movie is full of symbolic red objects, including ribbon, clothes, a dog's lead, traffic lights and a giant red hoarding.**

Right: **Alfred Hitchcock used many kinds of symbolism. The central theme of *Vertigo* (1958) is a man's obsession with a woman, Judy, who resembles his dead lover, Madeleine. Green symbolizes death in the film. Judy first appears dressed in green, and when (after much persuasion) she dresses herself as Madeleine, she is illuminated by a green neon sign.**

Warren Beatty's screen adaptation of *Dick Tracy* (1990) was critically panned for its wooden performances and uninvolving story, but acclaimed for its use of colour, which mimicked the cartoon strip genre on which it was based. Cinematographer Vittorio Storaro, who also worked on Coppola's *Apocalypse Now*, believes colours have specific meanings that are transmitted to the viewer as vibrations of energy. Whether or not audiences understood the meanings he was trying to convey, they were struck by the film's palette of strong primary colours.

Red is a powerful and ambiguous colour in movie symbolism. In Michael Powell and Emeric Pressburger's *The Red Shoes* (1948), the heroine's shoes represent a changed lifestyle, artistic fulfillment, coming of age and sexual awakening. As in the rather disturbing Hans Christian Andersen fairy tale that inspired the film, however, there are also undertones of danger. Dorothy in *The Wizard of Oz* (1939) – another movie combining colour and monochromic sequences – wears red shoes, although they are silver in the novel on which the film was based. This may have been a way of introducing symbolism to echo *The Red Shoes*, or may even have been meant as an allegory about communism. More likely, Dorothy's red shoes were just a better exploitation of Technicolor.

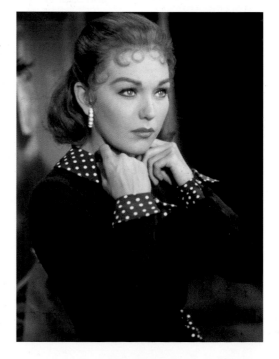

Clockwise from below left: **David Lynch's** *Blue Velvet* (1986) uses colour symbolism from the title onwards. Red curtains recur in his work, representing a mysterious and dangerous unknown. This film opens and closes with an image of red roses. In *American Beauty*, (1999) the roses are reduced to petals showering the teenage object of the protagonist's fantasies. Tropical fish feature in a switch from monochrome to colour that Francis Ford Coppola, director of *Rumble Fish* (1983), thought viewers might not even notice if they were sufficiently engrossed in the story. Warren Beatty's *Dick Tracy* (1990) inhabits a colour-coded world.

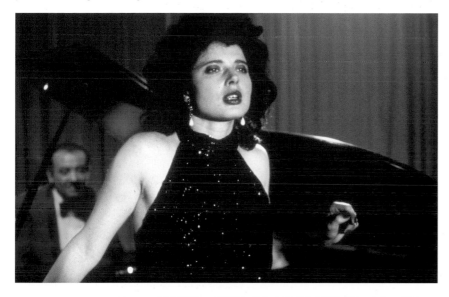

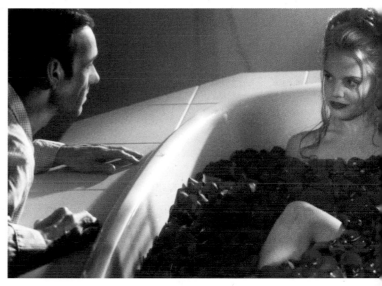

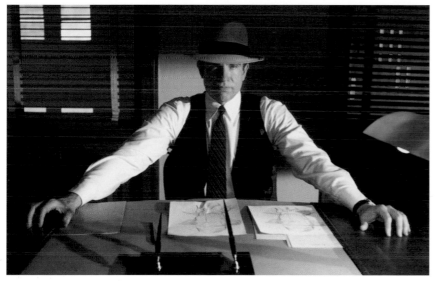

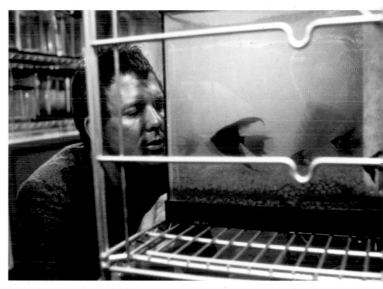

In *American Beauty* (1999), directed by Sam Mendes, red rose petals (of the flower variety that gives the film its name) descend from the sky to cover nubile teenager Angela in the dreams of middle-aged Lester Burnham. Here, some meanings are shared and some divided between the characters: Angela is on the cusp of sexual maturity; both characters yearn for a different life. Both are revealed to be emotionally vulnerable, but it is Lester who faces the most tangible danger in the film.

Here are some other examples of colour symbolism in film to look out for and ponder:
the green key lime pie in *Natural Born Killers*
the red fire imagery in *Wild at Heart*
the yellow clothing in *Basquiat*
the green filter in *The Matrix*
the blue box in *Mulholland Drive*
the white rabbits in *Donnie Darko*

COLOUR IN ANIMATION
Classical colour animation, of the sort used in the original Walt Disney films, was created by photographing cels. 'Cel' is short for celluloid acetate. A sheet of this clear material is hand-painted, and placed over a background, and photographed to create each frame.

The process begins with a pencil drawing of the outline of a character for each frame. After a test animation is mocked up from the drawings and approved, the lines are inked onto each cel by hand. From 1958, the xerographic process enabled the pencil lines to be photocopied onto the cel, saving much money and time. Colour fills are then hand-painted onto the back of the cel. Between twelve and twenty-four frames created this way are required for one second of film, making this an intensive process.

Colour xerography allowed the use of coloured lines as well as black, so that the outline of a dark-coloured character could be lightened to read better, and phenomena such as fire could be outlined more realistically in complementary or analogous colours. This technique was resurrected for the film *The Secret of NIMH* (1982), made by ex-Disney animator Don Bluth with a relatively small team of a dozen animators. Cels were still painted by hand from a specially defined palette of six hundred colours.

Below: **Colouring cels by hand accounts for a significant proportion of the enormous labour involved in producing a feature-length animated movie.** *The Secret of NIMH* **(1982) pared down methods as much as possible but still required a palette of 600 colours for its characters.**

The palette of classical animation typically favours somewhat muted colours, but it covers the full spectrum. Other animators have taken different approaches to colour. The influential Czech surrealist filmmaker Jan Svankmajer (b.1934) works in a characteristically dull, often brownish palette reminiscent of baroque painting, creating the distinctive and macabre atmosphere of works such as *Alice*, his version of Lewis Carroll's *Alice's Adventures in Wonderland*.

Rather than animating drawings, Svankmajer films three-dimensional objects using stop motion. A character model is posed, a single frame of film is shot, then the model is adjusted slightly. Realistic motion is built up by calculating a series of adjustments over a number of frames. The same technique is the basis of mainstream features such as Aardman Animations' *Chicken Run* (2000). Art direction, set design and lighting are as important here as in live-action filming, the main difference being that the camera shutter can remain open longer, so the extremely intense lighting used on film sets is not required.

The first fully computer-generated cartoon, *Toy Story* (1995), was modelled and rendered in 3-D graphics software. Produced by Pixar and released by Disney, the film uses a bright and saturated colour palette, as do *Chicken Run* and other recent animated features, including Pixar's *Finding Nemo* (2003). Drawn animation can be produced using 'digital ink and paint' techniques, in which pencil drawings are scanned into a computer to be digitally coloured and output. Examples include Disney's *The Lion King* and television shows like *Futurama*.

A fast-growing genre is 2-D computer-based animation. US Animation, a very efficient software package from Toon Boom Technologies, provides a complete production solution: lines are either drawn on screen or are scanned, and can then be digitally painted and animated. It has been used in recent full-length features such as Klasky-Csupo's *The Wild Thornberrys* (2002) and the art-house hit *Les Triplettes de Belleville* (2003). A simplified version, Toon Boom Studio, has enabled thousands of amateur, student and low-budget animators to produce professional-quality work for distribution through the Internet.

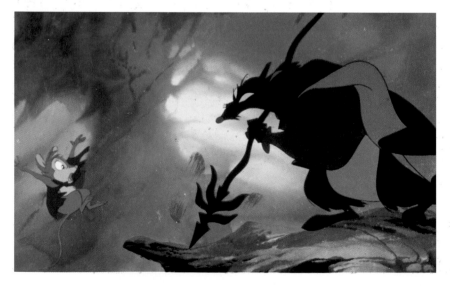

part 02. living with colour

Right: *Toy Story* (1995) was the first full-length digitally produced movie. All the characters were created as highly detailed digital models and animated within three-dimensional computer environments, combining the creativity of hand-drawn animation with the cinematic scope of live action. Colours and lighting were under the complete control of the filmmakers.

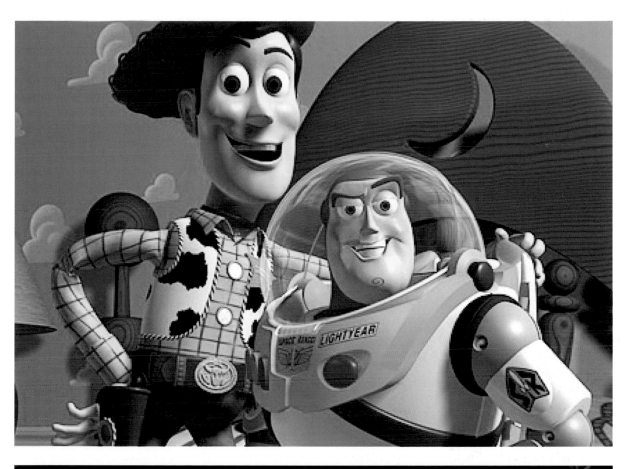

Right: Aardman Animations' popular animated movies may look similar to *Toy Story* at a glance, but their production methods could hardly be more different. In the claymation technique, characters are constructed from modelling clay and painstakingly posed for each frame. Scenes are lit with scaled-down versions of live-action lighting setups and are shot on colour film.

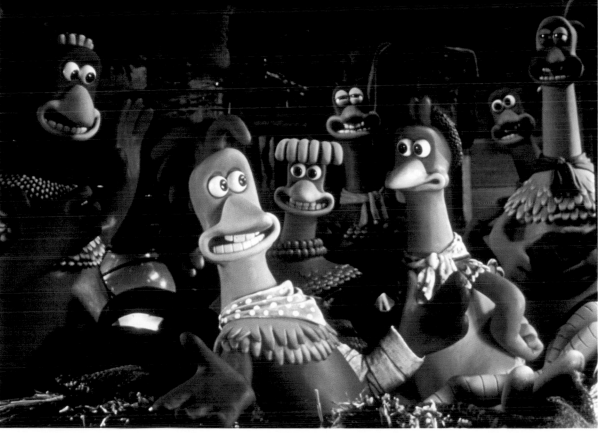

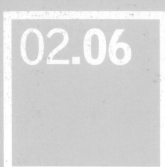

02.06

PART 02. LIVING WITH COLOUR

CHAPTER SIX

COLOUR IN ART

Human beings have always created art as a way of communicating messages about their environments, rituals, beliefs and feelings – or simply for decoration. Art has been made in many media for thousands of years. The earliest known examples of painting are those found on the walls of caves; wall paintings were widespread during the Greek and Roman empires, and found across Asia.

Murals dating from 600–900 at Chichén Itzá in Yucatán, Mexico, feature an incredibly vivid pigment known as Maya blue. In 1996, scientists using an electron microscope discovered that this pigment contained extremely small particles of iron, manganese, chromium and titanium. When the painted surface is illuminated, a quantum effect causes the nanoparticles to vibrate at the same wavelength as the scattered light, thus creating the brilliant colour.

Mural painting reached an artistic peak during the Renaissance, but muralists were never able to reverse the tendency of the art to fade, wash or crumble off surfaces. The recent restoration of the Vatican's Sistine Chapel, including the famous ceiling frescoes painted by Michelangelo (1475–1564), took about twice as many years as the original painting to complete, and nobody can be truly sure that the colours are as they would have originally appeared.

Mosaics are an alternative way to decorate walls, floors and ceilings. Again, these were commonplace in classical times, and although early designs were fairly primitive, gradations of colour later began to appear. By the late Middle Ages, mosaicists were discovering optical mixing and exploiting simultaneous contrast.

Another medium that was perfected in medieval times was stained glass, which by the tenth century could be seen in churches across Europe. Though they lacked any real understanding of the physics of light, medieval window-makers evidently knew how light would shine through their compositions. Aware that blue is the colour that will strike the eye most strongly as daylight fades, they used blue to emphasize important figures.

We have already outlined the impact of pigments and colour techniques on medieval, Renaissance and baroque painting (*see chapter 01.04*). The more recent history of art is one of dramatic development in the understanding and exploitation of colour and media. In this brief section, we look at some of the major figures in art from the impressionist movement to the present day. It is by no means an exhaustive listing. However, it provides some insight into how our understanding of colour has had an impact on the visual arts.

The origins of our use of colour are lost in prehistory. The oldest known cave paintings were made about 30,000 years ago, but in 2000 archaeologists in Zambia discovered what are believed to be pigments and painting tools estimated to be 350 to 400,000 years old, predating *Homo sapiens*. The canvas of the first artists was probably the human body.

IMPRESSIONISM AND BEYOND When you think of colour in art, the painting that springs first to mind may well be impressionist or postimpressionist. The impressionist movement developed in France in the 1860s as a reaction to the mannered style, which featured a muted brownish palette, then a norm enforced by the politically powerful French Academy.

The impressionists (including Claude Monet, Pierre-Auguste Renoir, Camille Pissarro and Paul Cézanne) wanted to record what they experienced when looking at the real world, not create an idealized image. Rather than adding black or white to 'model' objects in light and shade, they used dabs of brilliant colour to build up an impression of a scene. While other painters stayed indoors constructing formal compositions, they worked outside, painting from life. Their work was lighter and more spontaneous.

One of the influences on the movement was the artist J. M.W. Turner (1775–1851), who had ruffled feathers in the English art establishment with his own use of colour. Although Turner had begun working only a few years before, it was his earlier phase that appealed to the impressionists. He later allocated colours (chiefly red, yellow and blue, to which he attached symbolic meanings) to areas of a canvas before deciding

Below: Turner's highly individual use of colour, as demonstrated in *The Hero of a Hundred Flights* (1800–10), was influenced by seventeenth-century Dutch masters. Turner's often symbolic use of colour was scorned in his own lifetime, but it is now regarded as a turning point in European painting.

what objects would be represented by them. He would commonly introduce superfluous items into a scene purely to introduce colours.

This was anathema to Monet (1840–1926), who believed in painting what he saw. The way he saw it, of course, was unique. "If I can someday see M. Claude Monet's garden," wrote Marcel Proust in *Le Figaro*, June 15, 1907, "I feel sure that I shall see something that is not so much a garden of flowers as of colours and tones." Monet did in fact bring his artists' skills to bear directly on his garden in Giverny, France, as well as his paintings of it. For example, he planted red tulips with blue forget-me-nots to create an impression of violet. Many garden designers are wise to such effects and use afterimaging to manipulate transitions between one part of a garden and another.

After the impressionists came an explosion of painting styles that took colour experimentation further. The fauves, led by Henri Matisse (1869–1954), used non-naturalistic colour, often applying paint to the canvas straight from the tube to create vibrant images more analytical of emotional than visual responses.

The fauves were influenced by Vincent van Gogh (1853–1890), the Dutch artist whose use of colour was a law unto itself. His paintings, some of the most reproduced in

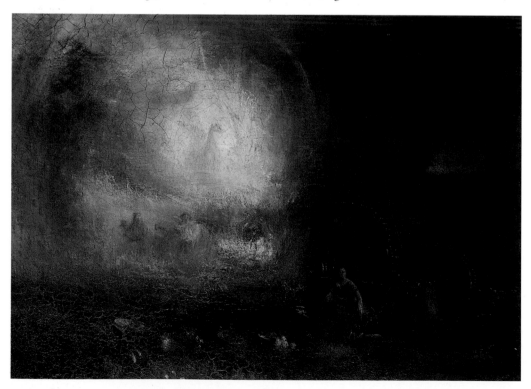

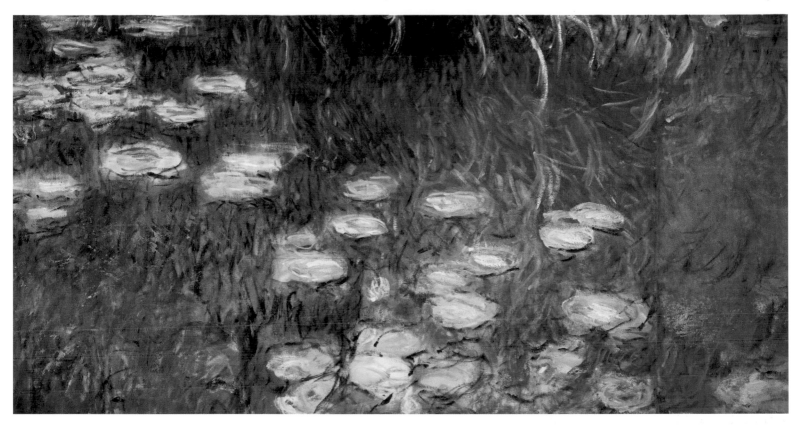

history, reflect in thick swirls of colour the inner turmoil that would ultimately destroy him. Van Gogh's technique was inspired by artists he met when visiting his art-dealer brother, Theo, in Paris, including Pissarro and Paul Gauguin (1848–1903). Like many of the impressionists, he favoured partitive colour mixing, using stippling methods reminiscent of Seurat (*see page 32*).

Paul Gauguin came to painting late in life, after working as a sailor and a stockbroker. His initial figurative style became, like the fauves', more 'primitive', in the sense that real-world objects were less precisely depicted. By 1886, his work involved large areas of flat colour without obvious brush marks, and curious colour schemes that seemed to imply a certain otherworldliness. He called this technique 'synthetism' and professed a hope that art would focus on exploring the 'interior life of human beings'.

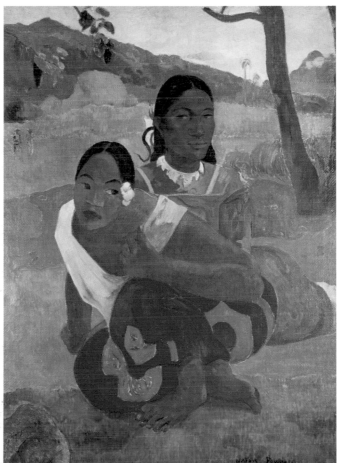

Above: **Claude Monet's** *Water lilies, morning* (1918). Although influenced by Turner, Monet rejected Turner's formalism in favour of a subjective response to the colours he saw in landscapes. For Monet and the other impressionists painting was all about seeing colour rather than form.

Left: **Paul Gauguin's** *Nafea Faaipoipo (When Are You Getting Married?)* (1892). Gauguin spent the last decade of his life in the South Pacific, where he developed a new style of painting using fields of intense colour. Expressionistic in feel, critics described Gauguin's use of colour 'barbaric', a term Gauguin accepted readily as he felt it complemented the unspoilt peoples and nature of Tahiti.

MODERNIST MOVEMENTS

Along with fauvism, a number of movements originating in Europe in the early twentieth century laid the foundations of modernism in art. Bold use of colour was a common theme. In Italy, futurism rejected 'worm-ridden' artistic snobbery and emphasized the speed, energy and power of the machine and the restlessness of industrialized life.

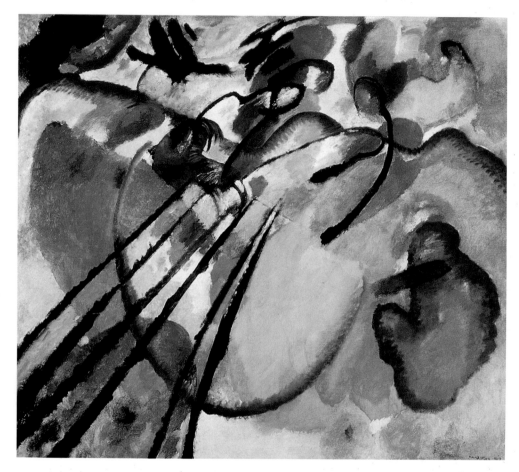

The Technical Manifesto of Futurist Painting (1910) thundered: "Brown tints have never coursed beneath our skin; it will be discovered that yellow shines forth in our flesh, that red blazes, and that green, blue and violet dance upon it...."

In Germany, expressionism strove to project an inner emotional state through colour. The Russian-born abstract artist Wassily Kandinsky (1866–1944), who lived in Munich, had a condition known as synaesthesia (*see page 44*) that enabled him to 'see' colours in musical sounds and notes. Works like *The Angel of the Last Judgment* (1911) paid homage to Goethe's colour theories (*see page 48*) and embodied the ideas in Kandinsky's book *Concerning the Spiritual in Art* (1912).

Paul Klee (1879–1940), born in Switzerland, met Kandinsky and other expressionists in Munich. After a 1914 visit to Tunisia, he wrote: "Colour has taken possession of me; no longer do I have to chase after it.... Colour and I are one."

Above: **Wassily Kandinsky's** *Improvisation #26* (1912). Kandinsky's unique approach to colour was partly rooted in synaesthesia, a confusion between the senses. For him, musical notes were coloured; other people can name the colours of smells, tastes or days of the week.

He created breathtaking compositions of coloured squares inspired by his travels, of which the watercolour *Red and White Domes* (1914) is particularly evocative. Klee and Kandinsky would later teach at the Bauhaus (*see page 44*).

Cubism was arguably the most influential movement in modern art. It included not only painters and sculptors, but also architects, musicians and poets. The cubists, including Pablo Picasso (1881–1973) and Georges Braque (1882–1963), believed that "true reality lay in the essential idea and not in its reflection in the material world." Whereas the impressionists had rejected shading in favour of suggesting the general play of light, the cubists made no attempt to depict 'coherent' lighting, instead using shading and colour to give objects volume in ways unconstrained by realism. Often several aspects of one subject are shown simultaneously.

Surrealism arose out of the psychoanalytic idea of the subconscious. Paintings by the surrealists, including Salvador Dalí (1904–89), René Magritte (1898–1967) and Max Ernst (1891–1976), combine seemingly unconnected images rendered in a precise, metarealistic style. The intention was to mildly derange the senses, provoking the viewer to question social and artistic norms. Dalí (1904–1989) borrowed colour techniques from other periods of art history, using heavily symbolic colour schemes and the cubist technique of noncoherent lighting. Many of his paintings seem to be set outside and yet have a feeling of the indoors, mirroring the anxiety that occurs between conscious and unconscious states.

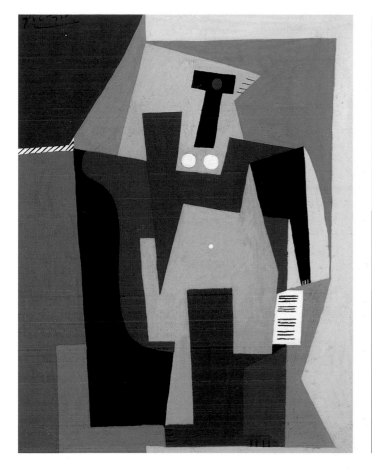

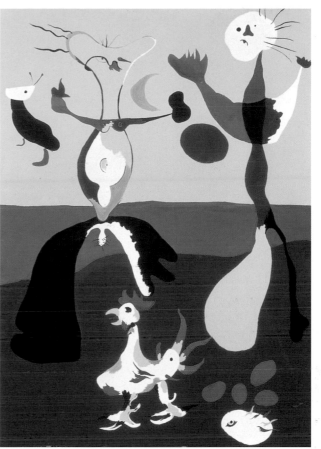

Above, above right and below: Ambiguity and hyperreality link these three famous colour compositions. Pablo Picasso's shades and tints of primary colours in his *Composition* (1923) (above) create a harmony defying natural visual interpretation (*see pages 116–19*). Salvador Dalí's *Swans Reflecting Elephants* (1937) (below) reveals naturalistic colours, which, when combined with illogical shading, only heighten the unreality of his scene. Finally, the primary colours in Joan Miró's *The Farmer and His Wife* (1936) (above right) serve the composition more than the depiction of its elements. The colours are clashing rather than playful, reflecting his war-torn country.

Frida Kahlo (1907–1954) was regarded as a surrealist by the surrealists, though she did not consider herself to be one. Born near Mexico City, she suffered an accident at the age of eighteen that injured her spine, pelvis and foot. In her self-portraits, body parts are often replaced with objects. Kahlo's work is deeply symbolic and uses dream imagery, folk art and Mexican motifs in jarring colours.

The work of Joan Miró (1893–1983) has a wonderful childlike quality, though it often deals with dark and complex themes. He experimented with media and colour reproduction, often combining different techniques in one work. In *Parchment Série III* (1952–53), he printed a central grey field from an etched plate onto an irregularly shaped piece of parchment; he then added colour in gouache.

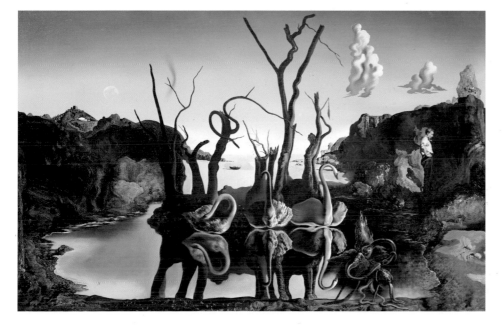

AMERICAN REALISM From around the time of the First World War, certain American painters set out to find new artistic identities of their own, distinct from the European schools. This was achieved through experimentation with all aspects of theme and technique, including colour.

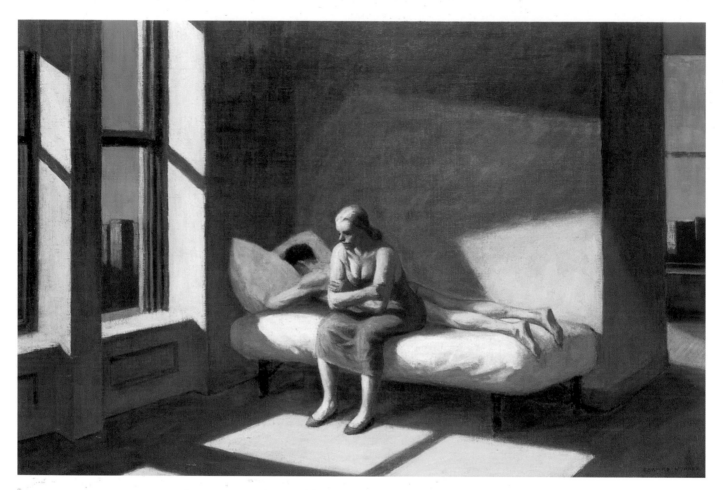

The Armory Show (1913), which an estimated half million people attended, was a landmark event in early twentieth-century North American art. The exhibition not only showcased European impressionism and modernism, but it catalyzed a surge in interest in modern American artists. Besides the Armory Show, one figure, Alfred Stieglitz (1864–1946), was also central to the development of modern art in the United States. Married to Georgia O'Keeffe (1887–1986), Stieglitz was associated with a significant number of young artists, as well as being a recognized modern photographer in his own right.

Another towering figure in the history of American art is Edward Hopper (1882–1967). Hopper trained as an illustrator and attended the New York School of Art before

going to Europe in 1906, where he was unimpressed by modernism, drawing inspiration instead from the Old Masters in museums. On his return, a conspicuous lack of interest in his European-themed paintings provoked a switch to American subjects and the bleak yet nostalgic style for which he is now remembered. The skilful use of light and colour is integral to Hopper's rich evocation of place and atmosphere.

A contemporary of Hopper's was Georgia O'Keeffe. O'Keeffe's work represents a link between realism and expressionism. She

Above: **As with many of Edward Hopper's urban paintings, *Summer in the City* (1950) conveys a powerful sense of alienation and isolation. His use of light and shade together with the now famous muted colour palette, and in particular the dusk-blue sky, help to reinforce the sense of loneliness.**

trained and practiced as a realist painter and produced a number of well-received works until 1908, when she apparently decided that she would never achieve greatness in this style. Influenced by the teachings of Arthur Wesley Dow (1857–1922), who believed in the expression of personal ideas and feelings through the use of line, colour, light and shade, she later began to produce striking semi-abstract paintings, including large-scale close-ups of flowers. O'Keeffe's use of shading varies from the meticulously realistic to the highly stylized, but with oddly similar effect. She seems to have perceived form and colour separately. She once described a process of seeing shapes that she would use in a painting once she found a colour for them. The colour would unlock an emotion crucial to the work.

Perhaps the most celebrated comtemporary American artist is Andrew Wyeth (b. 1917). Wyeth, who was taught traditional principles of drawing by his father, the noted illustrator N.C. Wyeth (1882– 1944), works mainly in pencil and watercolour. The realistic depiction of sunlight is a key element in his exterior scenes. Like many of the great painters, he uses a generally subdued palette, allowing colour interactions and the occasional touch of bolder shadow and highlight to produce the illusion of intense light and colour.

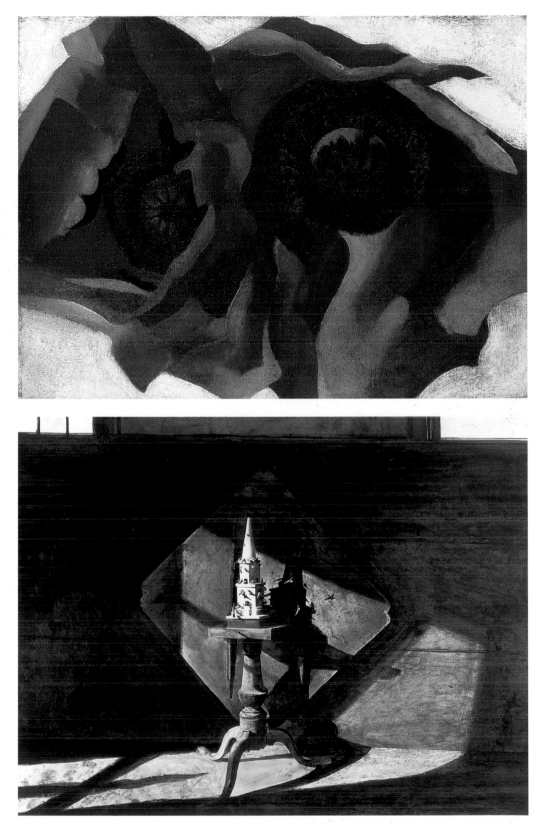

Above right: **As demonstrated in** *Poppies* (1927), **Georgia O'Keeffe chose colours not only to represent the real or even subjective appearance of the objects she painted, but to convey emotional states. In both form and colour, many of her works teeter between figurative and abstract.**

Right: **Andrew Wyeth's** *The Belfry* (1978). **Wyeth's work is notable for its technical prowess. Yet he has said: "A purely technical experience [is] going to be very short-lived. Both technical and emotional have got to be on even terms to be good."**

ABSTRACT EXPRESSIONISM In the 1940s, a group of painters based in New York reacted against social realism in American art, developing new styles to address grander themes. Believing fervently in the spontaneous expression of subjective feelings and responses, they produced striking works – often on a large scale – that shredded conventional ideas of form and colour.

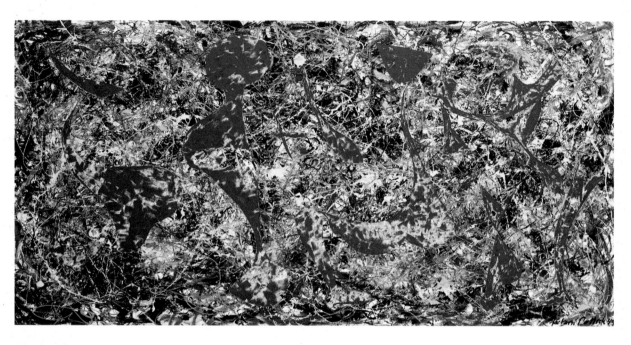

Right: Jackson Pollock's *Out of the Web: Number 7* (1949) is an example from Pollock's famous action painting period, which was sympathetic to the surrealist theory of automatism. The apparent random use of colour was a way by which an artist could express his or her unconscious.

The best known of the movement's exponents are Jackson Pollock (1912–56) and Mark Rothko (1903–1970), who are briefly profiled here. But not all work associated with the genre was either entirely abstract or obviously expressionistic. The paintings of Willem de Kooning (1904–1997) are mostly figurative, though vigorously gestural. His use of colour was bold and idiosyncratic: the Canadian critic Robert Fulford has written of his ability to take "the most unlikely combinations ever seen in one picture – wild pinks, liver-like shades, an amazing variety of oranges, intense pastels borrowed from mass culture – and by a private alchemy make them work."

By contrast, Barnett Newman (1905–1970) developed a stripped-down style based on vertical bands of colour that he called 'zips', painted very plainly on vast canvases, with few vestiges of brushwork. His influence encouraged Frank Stella (b.1936) to reject expressive painting in favour of geometric colour compositions that, like Newman's, often had jarringly expressive titles, such as *Hyena Stomp* (1962). Stella was among the founders of the minimalist movement in art and sculpture with which Ellsworth Kelly (*see page 112*) is also associated.

The most dramatic incarnation of abstract expressionism was Jackson Pollock's 'action painting' technique, which literally translated the artist's emotion – through the action of his mind on the muscles of his body – to the canvas in huge sweeps and splatters of colour. He worked mainly in commercial 'enamel' (nitrocellulose-based) house paint, which was more fluid than artists' oils but stable and available in a wide range of colours.

Rothko has in common with Barnett Newman the search for a sense of the sublime through the perception of colour. His mature style is typified by canvases almost filled with soft-edged colour fields, created by layering oil- and egg-based paints in thin washes. The hue, value, saturation, translucency, and texture of Rothko's colours are all integral to the mood created. While he rejected any representational interpretation of his paintings as landscapes, it is hard to resist seeing a horizon in the divisions between colour fields, and this may affect the meanings and sensations we attach to the colours above and below. For many viewers, the darkest and most saturated canvases are the most compelling, powerfully fulfilling Rothko's aim of conveying something 'intimate'.

Left: Rothko's colour compositions, such as *(untitled) Red* (1958), provide an almost immersive visual experience, encouraging and rewarding extended viewing.

POP ART Perhaps the last great art movement of the twentieth century was pop art. Here, the epic was replaced with the mundane, and the mass-produced was awarded the same significance as the unique. The British critic Lawrence Allowa first used the term in a 1958 issue of *Architectural Digest* to describe primarily US and British art that was inspired by popular culture and consumerism.

The term has since been used to describe paintings that draw attention to postwar consumerism, defy the form of abstract expressionism, and deal with 'low' forms of visual culture – advertisements, product packaging, comics and mass-produced decorative objects – that people experience in 'ordinary' life. The movement's origins can be seen in the 1950s in the work of Richard Hamilton (b. 1922) in the United Kingdom and Jasper Johns (b. 1930) and Robert Rauschenberg (b. 1925) in the United States. Common influences included the Bauhaus and Dada.

Below: Warhol's manipulation of this originally red-and-white soup can, from a series of posters he made in the early 1960s, generates disorienting colour constancy effects; not just the can but its surroundings begin to look false.

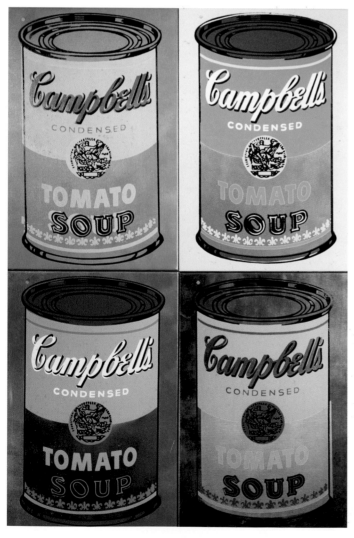

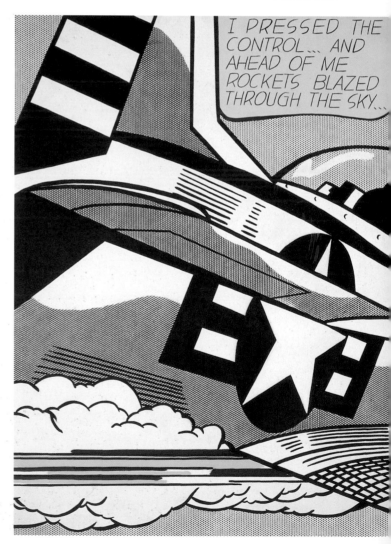

The Dadaist Marcel Duchamp (1887–1968) had exhibited 'readymades', common objects, like a snow shovel and a urinal, that he declared to be art. The pop artists added a reproductive element to this recontextualization of the everyday. Hamilton's *Just What Is It That Makes Today's Homes So Different, So Appealing?* (1956), widely regarded as the first work of pop art, was executed as a collage that included photos cut from cheap magazines.

Perhaps the greatest pop artist, the one whose style has inspired so much subsequent art, was Andy Warhol (1928–87). After working as a commercial artist for fashion magazines, starting in 1962 he took familiar images, such as the Campbell's Soup can, and presented them in garish screen prints, often juxtaposing versions with different colour schemes. His use of colour may have initially appeared vulgar and overdone, but today his technique has become iconic. The use of printing, rather than painting, reflected the industrial, impersonal ethos Warhol claimed to espouse – "I'd like to be a machine, wouldn't you?" – yet much of his work was deeply nostalgic. It is often forgotten that his famous Marilyn Monroe images were created after her death.

Warhol's use of colour is often said to represent the changing face of America. Writing about a recent Warhol retrospective, art critic Richard Dorment commented that "we travel from the exuberance and optimism of the Kennedy and early Johnson years, reflected in the clear, hard-edged, red-white-and-blue simplicity of the Brillo Boxes, to the fuzzy, out-of-focus oranges and turquoises of the Ford and Carter eras, ending up with saturated reds, blacks, and silvers of the mink-coated Reagan years." You can experiment with colour in a Warhol print yourself at webexhibits.org/colorart/marilyns.

Another key pop artist was Roy Lichtenstein (b. 1923). His painting *Whaam!* (1963) borrows heavily from comic-strip imagery and colour, but it makes a more complex point about technology and war, best appreciated when the work is seen at its original size (nearly three by two metres).

Below: Lichtenstein's *Whaam!* (1963) shows how the artist deconstructed the process of colour reproduction by hand-painting hugely enlarged pastiches of mass-produced images.

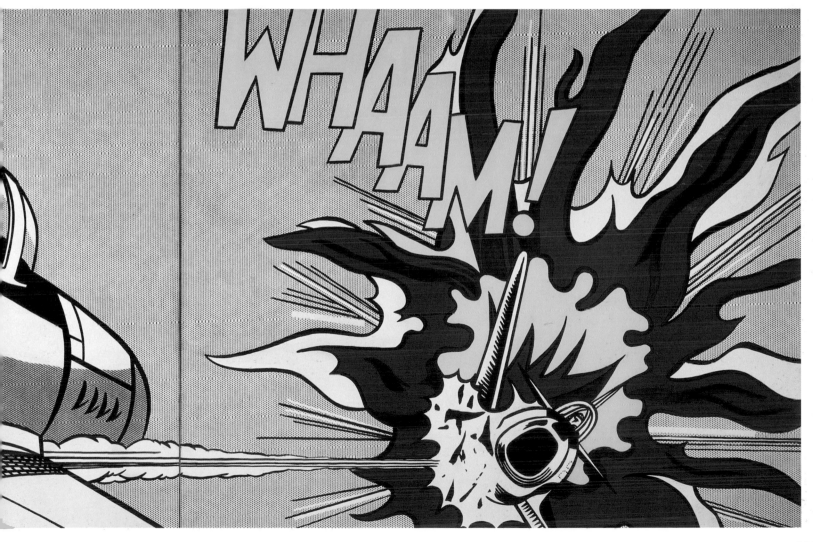

GEOMETRIC ART Some artists have striven to reduce colour and form to their essences, such as those discussed here. In 1915, Kazimir Malevich (1878–1935) launched suprematism, which rejected any depiction of the external world in favour of 'the supremacy of pure sensation'. He painted exclusively with circles and polygons of primary and secondary colours, deliberately avoiding any sense of depth, gravity or horizon.

The suprematist movement significantly influenced other schools, notably constructivism, whose adherents defined the progressive art, architecture, design and typography of post-revolutionary Russia. The constructivist László Moholy-Nagy (1895–1946), who went on to teach at the Bauhaus (*see page 44*) and in the United States, was a leading figure in the early development of graphic design.

Another key figure in geometric abstract art was Piet Mondrian (1872–1944). Mondrian found his own route to geometric abstraction. The compositions of coloured rectangles and black lines for which he is best known represented the crystallization of his thinking, articulated in the magazine *De Stijl*. Mondrian recognized that every artist pursued universal truths in 'the relationships between lines, colours, and planes', but he wanted to do so 'only in the strongest way'.

HARD EDGE

Following the abstract expressionists emerged a group of artists who were later to become famous for a style of painting that was given the name 'hard edge'. A major exponent was Ellsworth Kelly (b. 1923). This American artist has worked for half a century with fields of mostly primary colour. *Broadway* (1958), a red parallelogram on a white background, presents a simple figure-ground relationship (*see page 120*) that becomes less certain as it is viewed. Other works are divided into multiple canvases, each painted a single colour. Kelly's perfect, featureless 'masses' of pigment seek to isolate colours from their symbolic and emotional associations, yet his project is ultimately sensual rather than conceptual.

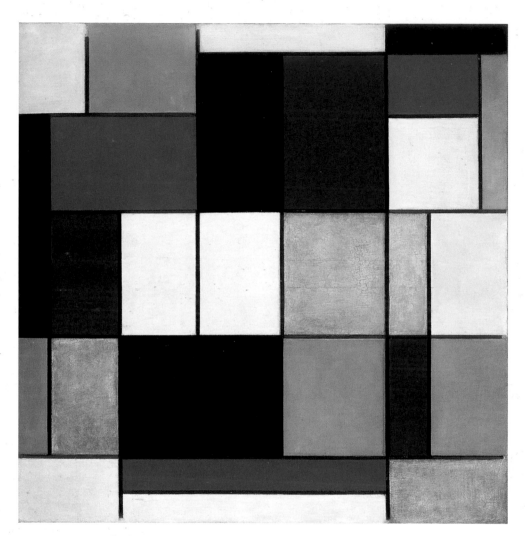

Above: Piet Mondrian's *Grand Composition A*, like all his 'compositions', uses grids of primary colours. 'The primary colour that is as pure as possible realizes this abstraction of natural colour', he wrote. Mondrian's work expresses his concept of 'pure plasticity', in which he brought art to its bare essentials, with even the curve banished from his work.

BRIDGET RILEY (b.1931)

Riley's first abstract paintings were monochrome works of sophisticated optical illusion. From 1967 she moved into colour, and has since developed an abstract language in which colour and form generate a range of visual sensations, often involving light and movement. She cites Paul Klee (*see page 104*) as a major influence. Riley's work is not driven by academic study of optics or colour, but her own principles are shown in such statements as: 'A colour in painting is no longer the colour of something but a hue and a tone either contrasting with other hues and tones or related in shades and gradations', ('Making Visible', in Kudielka, *R. Paul Klee: The Nature of Creation*, London: Hayward Gallery, 2002). The power of her compositions is undeniable.

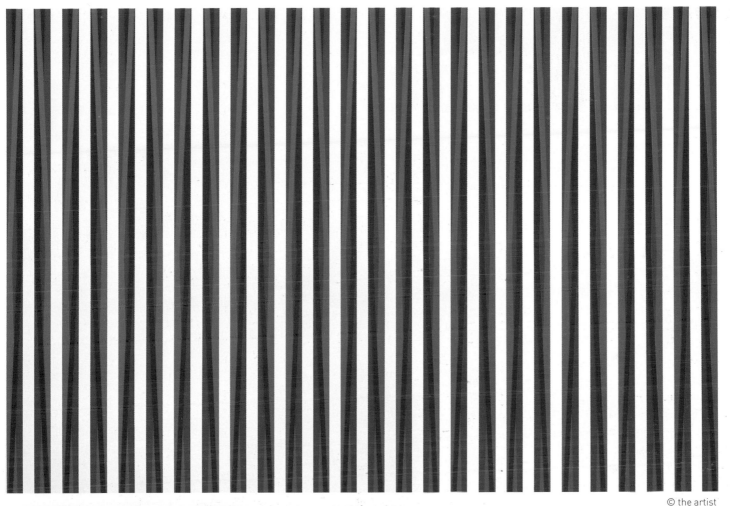

Top: **Bridget Riley's** compositions, such as *Firebird* (1971), often seem to defy viewing, confusing the eye with carefully calculated repetition and contrast.

Above: **Dan Flavin** limited himself to an incredibly narrow range of colours and forms, as can be seen in *Untitled (to Agrati)*, yet he created dramatic and evocative work.

DAN FLAVIN (1933–96)

Flavin worked almost exclusively with fluorescent lighting tubes. Some of his pieces took the form of artworks that could be exhibited in galleries, while others were specific to sites, including New York's Grand Central Station. Only nine colours and two shapes (line and circle) were available in his chosen medium, but he found ways of arranging them to varied and powerful effect. Like those of other minimalists, his compositions were at once arbitrarily formal and yet laced with symbols, almost to the point of mysticism.

JAMES TURRELL (b.1943)

Turrell began working with light and space in the 1960s. He sees a place for the sublime in everyday life and aims to generate in the viewer something like 'the wordless thought that comes from looking in a fire'. Many of his works use low levels of coloured light within a dark space and must be experienced over a period of several minutes. Others create architectural spaces in which the sky becomes the art. Turrell's most ambitious project, the conversion of a crater in Arizona into a light-based artwork, has been in progress since 1972.

DESIGNING
WITH COLOUR

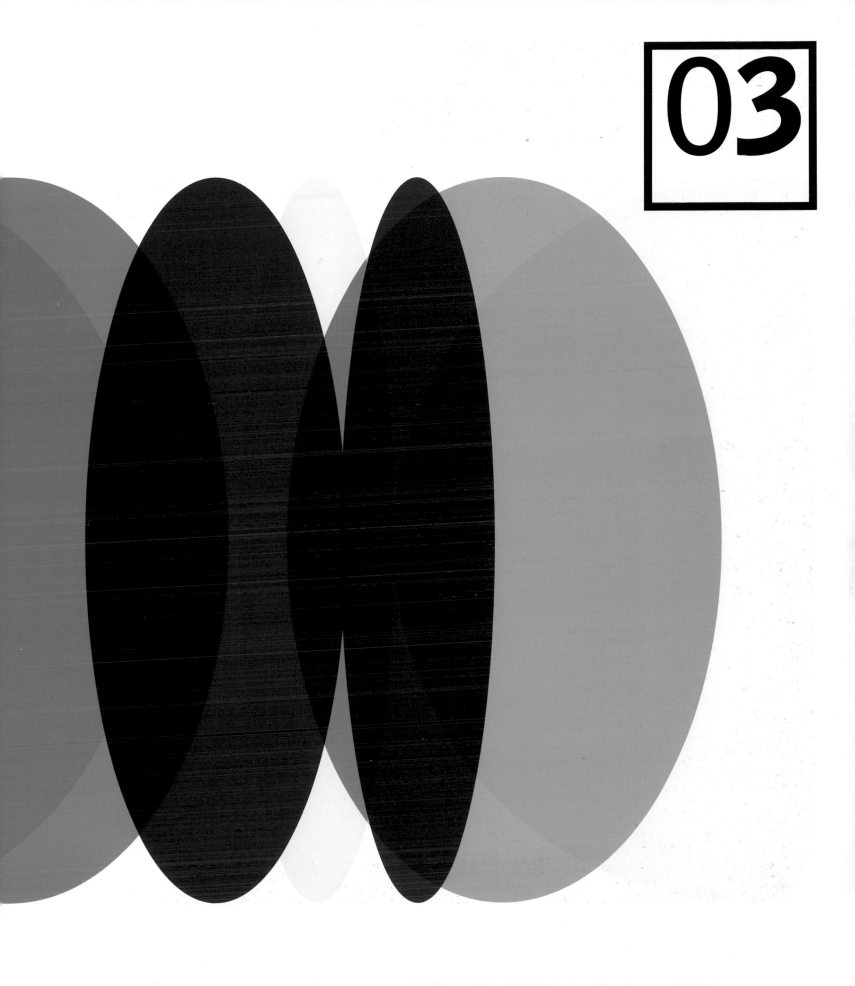

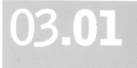

03.01

COLOUR COMPOSITION

There are many conventions governing composition and layout, and all will interact with colour to produce an overall impression. The principles outlined in the following pages are not presented so that you can follow them slavishly – most are too vague for that anyway – but to provide a framework that you can bend and twist to a point where it may be close to snapping.

Perhaps that seems a little melodramatic, but once you get into the swing of designing according to certain rules, whether learned or developed intuitively, it is all too easy to fall into a rut. This is especially true if you are working on a publication or in an environment where style is set rigidly, welded into templates that rarely shift. In such circumstances, it is worth remembering that the smallest changes can lead to exciting results.

One of the benefits of computer-based design – contrary to prejudice – is that the computer has no fixed ideas. When you sketch a layout on a pad, your brain and hand will tend to guide elements into conventional positions. On the monitor, your mouse hand can whiz objects around much more randomly and generate new possibilities. Having produced a happy accident, you can always use your knowledge of conventions to analyse why something looks good and develop it rationally.

Negative space should perhaps be mentioned first. In page layouts, white space radically influences a reader's perception of text and images. Opening up the leading between lines of type or surrounding a block of text with generous margins can allow a page to breathe. In graphics and photos, negative space (not necessarily white) can add drama and influence an interpretation of the visual content. For example, in cropped photos, extra space is conventionally left at the side the subject is facing; cropping the opposite way allows political editors to show a figure with nowhere to go and a dangerously exposed rear.

Right: This 1930s magazine cover provides a classic example of colour composition. Both colour and form are carefully balanced. The vein of the leaf, which is depicted in flat colour fields, provides an opposing diagonal to the figure, shaded three-dimensionally in monochrome. Yellow, being a stronger colour than red, is tempered by a larger neighbouring area of blue.

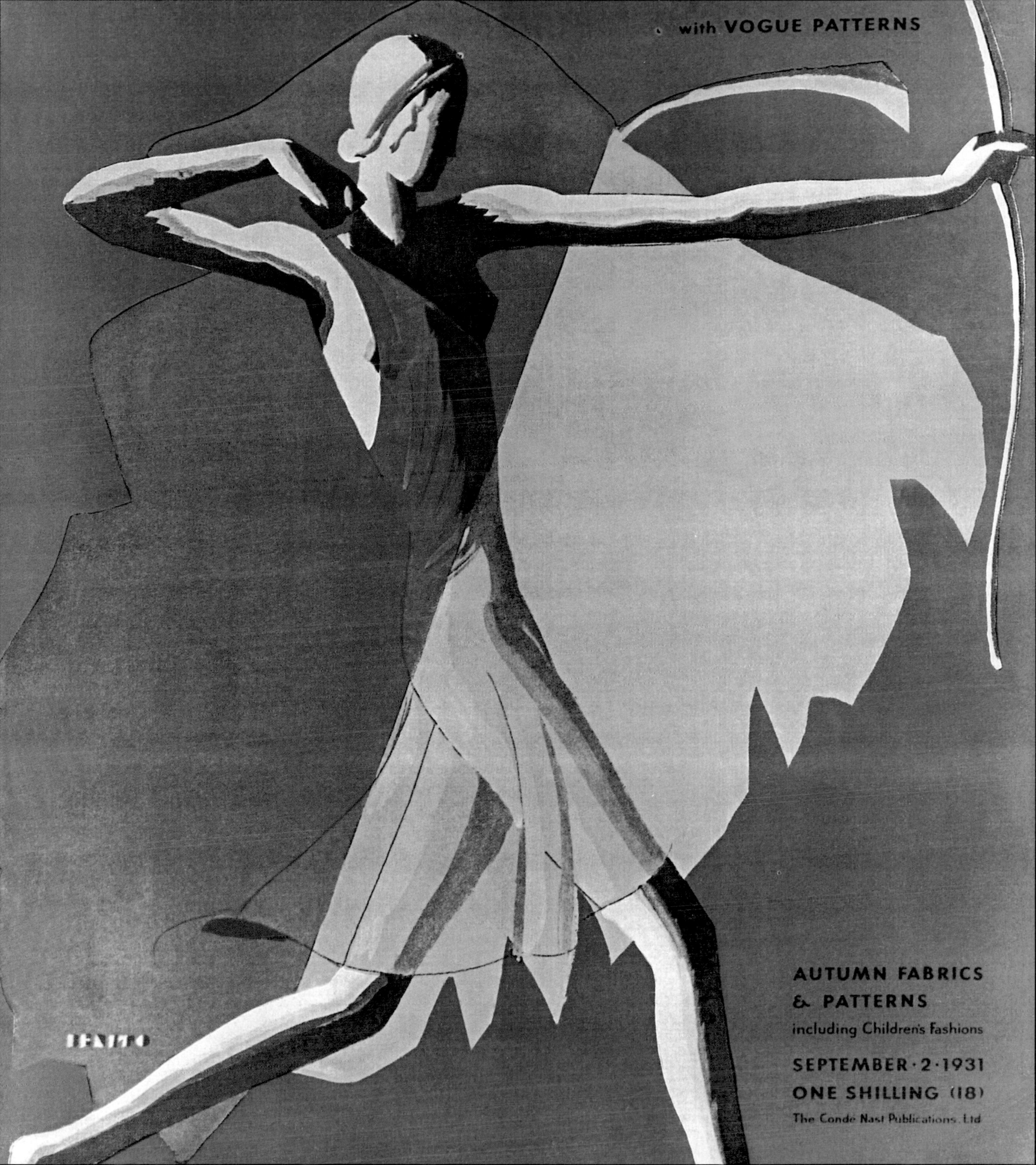

with VOGUE PATTERNS

BENITO

AUTUMN FABRICS
& PATTERNS
including Children's Fashions

SEPTEMBER · 2 · 1931
ONE SHILLING (18)
The Condé Nast Publications Ltd

BASICS OF COMPOSITION The way we take in a composition is rooted both in the evolution of our eyes and brains and in our cultural experience of reading texts and looking at pictures. Although it is impossible to predict how random individuals will respond to a given arrangement of elements, some useful rules of thumb are widely accepted.

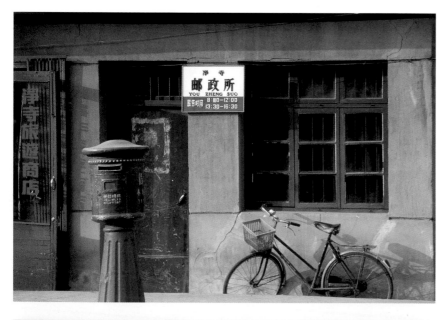

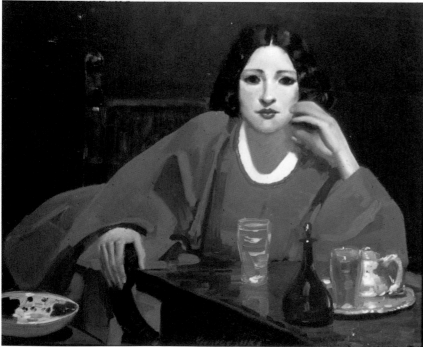

The place where the viewer's eye will land first is the 'focal point'. Before we begin influencing the eye with colours and forms, there are certain natural focal points on a page or canvas. One is near the centre, but a little higher, and can be slightly to one side. Others are found in a square surrounding this and can be located either by dividing the canvas into nine equal squares (the 'rule of three' or 'thirds'), or by drawing diagonal lines between the corners of the canvas and bisecting them.

Try placing two or three elements of different sizes and colour values at focal points, or working out from just one focal point. You can use a focal point indirectly or negatively: forms may surround it, or lines may lead the eye to it. Of course, you can ignore the conventional focal points altogether, as long as your composition makes some kind of visual sense. Key elements are often arranged to form a triangle, or within an imaginary circle. All of these principles can be scaled to govern smaller areas within a composition.

When laying out two-dimensional static artwork, we need to remember that our brains evolved to interpret activity in a three-dimensional scene. This has a number of consequences. Because moving objects are of more immediate significance in the real world than still ones, we instinctively look for movement in a scene. Movement can be defined as consecutive sightings of a similar form in different positions. But even simultaneous instances can trigger a sense of movement.

Above left: **This photo is more artful than it might seem. The window and the mailbox centre on diagonally opposite focal points. Horizontal lines draw the eye outwards: what is through the door? Around the corner?**
Left: **Compare this monochromic composition with the focal point diagram opposite, top left. The small highlight on the chair back is essential to the painting.**

A sequence of shapes scattered across a page can suggest motion, with the assumed direction being left to right or top to bottom. (There is some uncertainty about whether this differs in cultures that do not write text this way.) The shapes need not be identical, or even very similar; colour is one of the cues that can encourage us to associate them. If the shapes vary consistently in size, from large to small, there will also be an impression of perspective, with smaller forms receding into the distance.

Lines often serve the functional purpose of dividing an area, but they can also be used to lead the eye. When our attention is attracted by a figure that consists of a line, we tend to follow it, again in the conventional directions. Lines or shapes radiating from a point give the impression of moving towards that point, and draw the eye to it. A similar effect occurs wherever lines cross, while parallel lines reinforce each other. Horizontal lines make the page appear wider and give an impression of calm and expansiveness. Verticals can be elegant and imposing, but they may feel restricting. Diagonal lines appear dynamic.

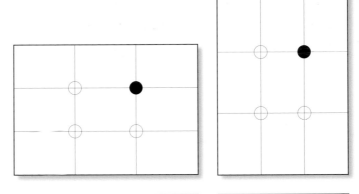

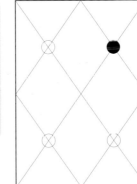

Left: These diagrams show two ways to fix the conventional focal points within a rectangular composition. Clockwise from top left:

Rule of 3 in horizontal (landscape) format: a photographer's favourite, also suitable for paintings and graphical compositions.

Rule of 3 in vertical (portrait) format: supremely elegant (it's no coincidence that the diagram is reminiscent of a Georgian window), but can feel pinched.

Bisected diagonals in portrait format: the focal points move outwards horizontally compared to the rule of 3, expanding the composition within the canvas.

Bisected diagonals in landscape format: again feels more expansive than the rule of 3, but risks a lack of interest at the centre.

Below: We instinctively interpret colour and form as if they are part of a real-world scene. The photo on the left shows an interior receding into the distance. Reduced to a few simple colour fields (right), the image gives a similar impression of perspective and recession. Such effects play a part in how we 'read' any graphical composition, whether or not it aims to depict reality.

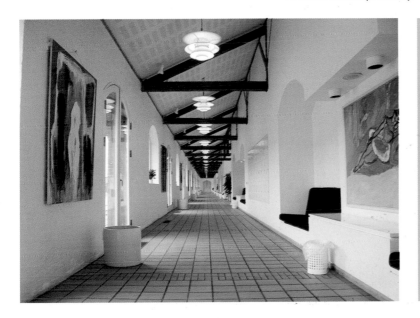

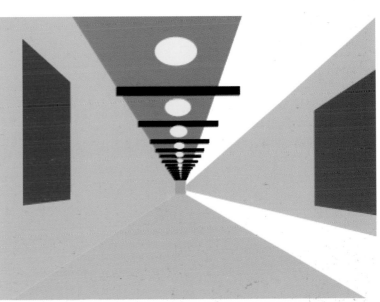

COMPOSING WITH COLOUR Within a scene, we tend to see relatively large, plain elements as a backdrop to smaller, more distinct ones. The latter catch our attention first and seem closer. This principle is known as 'figure and ground' and is important for several reasons. First, it contradicts the assumption that smaller items will necessarily seem less significant: in fact, they may well dominate. Second, it tells us that a composition in which figure and ground are not immediately distinguishable may seem lifeless and uninvolving. Elements should be differentiated by size and colour.

Third, the principle of figure and ground combines with our knowledge of colour theory to help us understand the impressions created by colour within a composition. Warm hues (in the red part of the colour wheel) tend to advance towards the viewer, while cool (blue) hues recede. Therefore, applying a warm colour to a figure will accentuate its tendency to jump out, and cool colours will encourage a ground to recede; reversing this will tend to negate the effect, giving a more balanced and less striking impression. A small splash of warm colour on a cool background will be more pleasing than the reverse.

It might be assumed that figure elements should also be brighter than grounds, but in fact dark figures against a bright ground are much more acceptable to the human eye. We write in black on a white background, despite having long had the technology to do the reverse, because it seems more natural. Changing the value (lightness) of the ground can have a strong effect on an image as a whole, especially in graphical compositions made up of uniform colour fields. Light figures on a dark ground seem to emerge from shadows or darkness, making them seem luminous and often mysterious or foreboding, an effect that was fully exploited in Renaissance painting.

A midtoned background either forces figure colours into a narrower range of values (all lighter or all darker than the ground), resulting in a muted or hazy effect, or, by allowing some figures to be lighter and others darker than the ground, prevents the composition being interpreted in terms of spatial recession, an effect that is visually disorienting but can be graphically rewarding.

Elements that differ most in value from the background will always draw the eye first, almost regardless of differences in hue. As we have seen (*see chapter 03.01*), colours are intensified by being placed on a very dark or very light ground, but their temperature and tendency to advance or recede may also be affected: blue on white can advance, while red always advances against black, even in extremely dark shades, as is powerfully demonstrated in the well-known paintings by Mark Rothko.

Below: **This carefully judged composition sets warm, advancing earth tones against cool, receding blues to give an immediate impression of scale and distance despite comprising only simple forms. Note the use of repetition and leading lines.** Agent: Digital Vision; Artist: Nigel Sandor

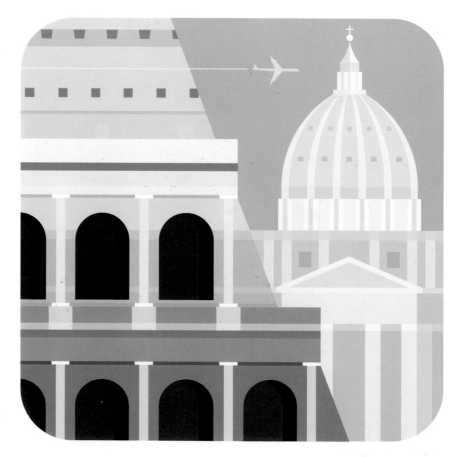

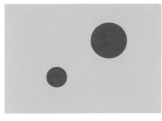
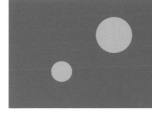
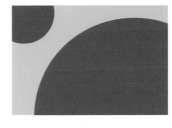

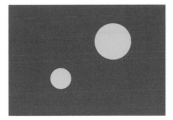
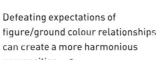
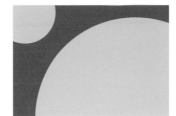

Repetition, or rhythm, is an important feature of many compositions. The use of colour can contribute to the effects of repeating lines and shapes: graduation of lightness and/or saturation can tell us which way movement is going, or reinforce the impression of forms fading off into the distance. More distant objects appear lighter, less saturated, and less distinct, an effect that can be created by blurring or 'feathering' elements or reducing the detail with which they are drawn.

Progressive sequences of colour lead the eye and make the composition more dynamic, while repetitive sequences give a sense of order and balance. We also know (*see chapter 01.02*) that closely spaced repetition of hues creates optical mixing, giving the overall effect of a continuously coloured surface. Similarly, exact repetition of lines, shapes or colour fields – pattern – can allow an area to appear uniform even though it may contain a large amount of detail.

Top: A natural figure/ground relationship. A large field of cool hue is interrupted by darker, smaller fields of warm hue.
Bottom: With the colours reversed, the cool figures are equally well distinguished but more numinous.

Defeating expectations of figure/ground colour relationships can create a more harmonious composition.
Top: Normal temperature relationship, reversed value relationship.
Bottom: Normal value relationship, reversed temperature relationship.

Playing with proportional relationships.
Top: Because the large shapes are more regular, darker and warmer than the negative space, they tend to appear as figures in front of a ground.
Bottom: With figure/ground cues now thoroughly confused, we flip between seeing blue discs and a red arch.

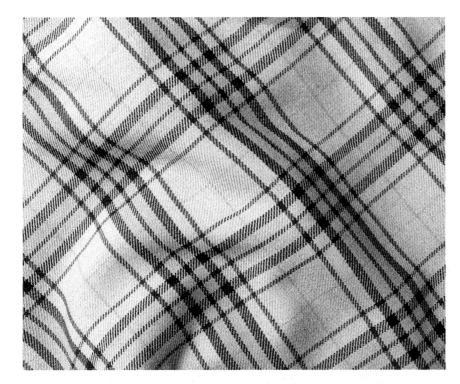

Above: The repetition of colour and form within patterns such as this tartan creates a sense of order and balance which prevents them seeming garish or distracting.

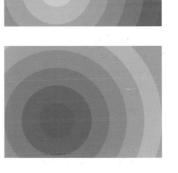

Progressive colour sequences are dynamic, suggesting motion or depth.
Top: Increasing values lead the eye towards the centre of the composition.
Bottom: Deprived of a contrasting ground, the dark central figure appears to recede into shadow. The lighter rings at the outside also recede, giving a less dynamic effect than above.

Repetitive colour sequences are static, discouraging the eye from travelling in any direction.
Top: Contrasting shades preserve some of the depth effect created by the rings. (Note the slight optical illusion of a spiral, which occurs when rings are broken or partly concealed.)
Bottom: Complementary colours further reduce any dynamic effect.

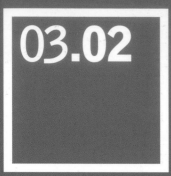

03.02

COLOUR IN PUBLICATIONS

Colour can define the nature of a printed publication at a glance. The physical size of a newspaper is no longer a reliable indicator of its nature, but use of colour is telling: the more garish the front page, the further down-market the content. Some of the loftiest titles still restrain the use of colour, or eschew it altogether, for fear of looking too populist.

The same principles apply to magazines. When visiting a foreign country, we have little difficulty in distinguishing the local *Vogue* rival from that of *Cosmopolitan*. On its cover, the former will feature a model shot under crisp, dramatic lighting, overlaid with text in no more than two colours, one of them black. The latter will present softer, brighter photography and text in at least three colours, one of them white.

Colour is recognized as a major factor in the selling power of covers. Exactly which colours will generate the highest sales, however, is sadly impossible to pin down. You would expect warm colours to sell best, but in fact blues are often successful, while many publishers shun yellow. On the crowded newsstand anything that stands out can work: a cover blocked in a single colour is always a sure seller if you can find an excuse to do it.

Colour is a functional element of page design. Many publications use colour-coded bars, or 'slugs', at the top of each page to differentiate editorial sections, helping readers 'navigate' through the issue. Coloured icons may be used to flag content on a running theme. Tints separate boxes and sidebars from the body of a page and blocks of colour overlaid with type are commonly used for 'teasers', drawing the reader's attention to content elsewhere in the issue.

Visual hierarchy is essential to printed pages. A field of similar objects is a psychological turnoff. Outside the tabloid press, giant headlines are a no-no, so often the lead story on a newspaper spread will be distinguished by having the biggest picture. In magazines, a feature article will run over several spreads, with the start often flagged by a dramatic composition of form and colour that may integrate type and imagery.

Right: **Faber & Faber is one of Europe's most important publishers of poetry. This latest redesign of its poetry covers, by Justus Oehler at Pentagram, was inspired by an earlier series by Berthold Wolpe. Bold colour combinations, taking the place of graphics, were chosen to express the mood of each book.**

John Berryman 77 Dream Songs	Wallace Stevens Harmonium	Wendy Cope Making Cocoa for Kingsley Amis	Seamus Heaney North	Ted Hughes New Selected Poems 1957–1994
Seamus Heaney Station Island	Philip Larkin Collected Poems	Michael Hofmann Acrimony	Ted Hughes Crow From the Life and Songs of the Crow	Seamus Heaney Sweeney Astray
Simon Armitage Selected Poems	T. S. Eliot Four Quartets	James Joyce Poems and shorter writings	Paul Muldoon Quoof	Ezra Pound Personae Collected Shorter Poems
Robert Lowell Life Studies	Mark Ford Soft Sift	Philip Larkin The Whitsun Weddings	Louis MacNeice The Burning Perch	Christopher Reid Katerina Brac

COVER STORIES From the first blossoming of the magazine market during the interwar period, publishers have been well aware of the power of colour to transform a cover into a visual sales pitch. Although photography has largely taken over from graphical compositions in mass-market titles, bold use of colour remains a powerful tool.

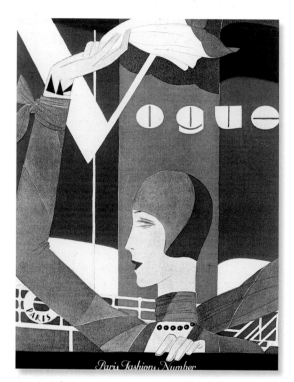

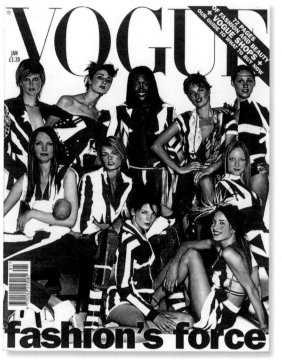

Left: *Vogue*'s early covers were typical examples of art deco style, comprising simple, rational arrangements of shapes in strong but muted colours. Today, content usually wins over form, but bright colours, clean lines and rich flesh tones compensate for lost graphical dynamism.

Below: For twenty-first-century lifestyle magazines such as the internationally successful *wallpaper**, avant-garde graphics are part of the package. The reader is challenged not to find them challenging.

Below left: Subtlety may not be the watchword of *FHM*, a top-selling men's magazine, but its covers follow a proven formula in which key colours play a vital role.

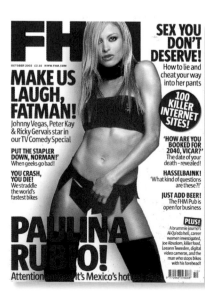

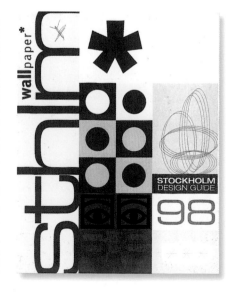

Left: Designed by Neville Brody, *The Face* was a pop-culture icon in 1980s Britain. Coinciding with the desktop publishing revolution, it applied post-punk attitudes to graphic design.

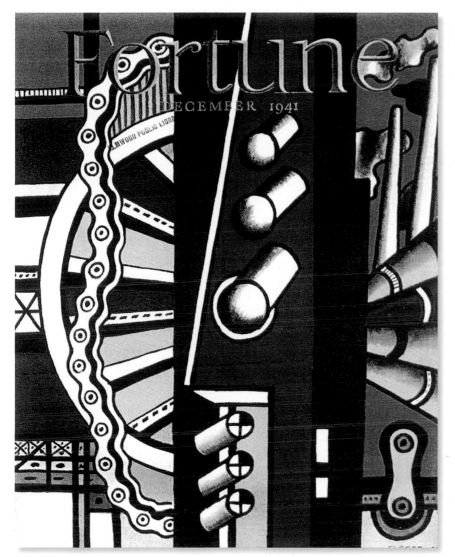

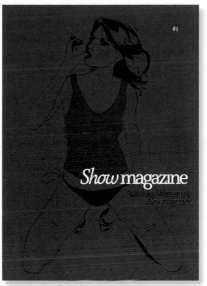

Left: This cover of *Fortune* magazine was designed by prominent artist Fernand Léger in a style he had developed in printmaking. The influence of Picasso and Braque is evident, as are elements reminiscent of Miró and Mondrian.

Below left: A perennially eye-catching style combines simple lines and psychedelic colours with the graduated tints or 'vignettes' once characteristic of airbrushing and now of computer graphics.

Above: This cover, by Jeremy Leslie at John Brown Citrus Publishing, teases with a low-contrast image. A small splash of warm colour stands out.

Below: The foreground graphic on this cover features clean lines set against a cloudy background and is coloured in broken tints to create harmony. In today's harder-headed market, a solid background and primary colours would more likely be used.

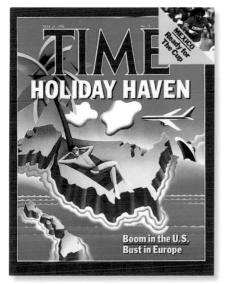

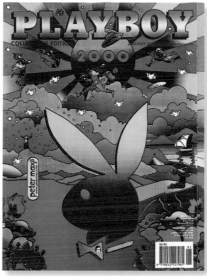

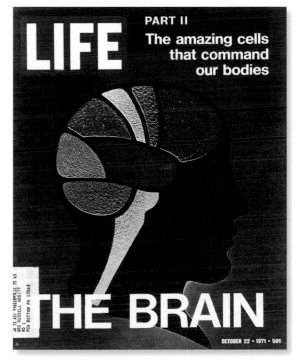

STANDING OUT AND BLENDING IN Whether thanks to the desktop-publishing revolution, strong economies or a genuine public appetite for ever more printed materials, the world seems to be increasingly crammed with publications, both desirable and unsolicited. One way to make yours stand out from the crowd is by using colour in ways nobody else has thought of.

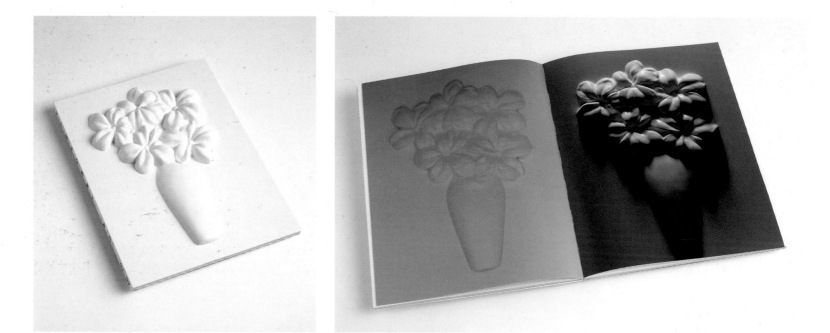

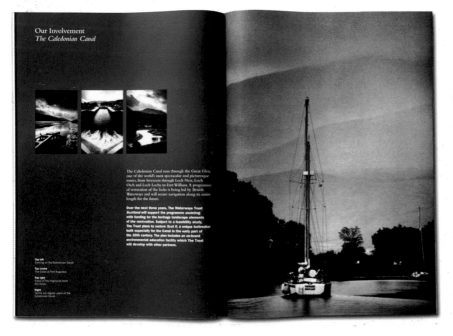

Left: The Waterways Trust was formed to help realize the potential of Britain's historic canal network. Its corporate identity, created by Pentagram partner John Rushworth, combines a nature-themed logo with evocative black-and-white photography by Phil Sayer. The restrained palette is as effective here as a riot of colour might be for an organization with a different image to project.

Above: Making company annual reports look interesting is a classic design challenge. This one was produced for Zumtobel, a leading lighting manufacturer, by the studio of graphic designer Stefan Sagmeister. The cover features a bas-relief image of a vase of flowers in heat-moulded plastic. For the inside pages, this has been photographed under various coloured lights, showing the power of the company's products to transform.

NEW COMMUNICATORS

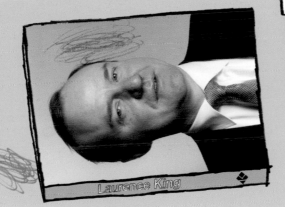

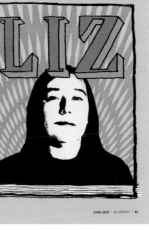

Illustration: Billie Jean

Above: This spread for leading British design and architecture magazine *Blueprint* breaks almost all the rules, but it respects colour proportions, splashing a small amount of warm orange on a field of recessive blue.

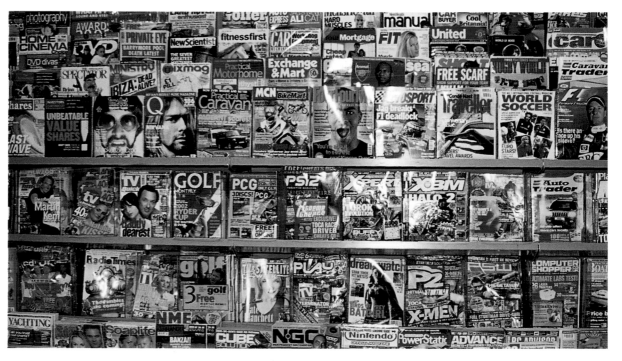

Right: On the newsstand, no one can hear you scream. The brightest of colours won't get you noticed unless you use it well. See which of these covers catches your eye. Among the first will be *Golf*, with its high-impact red-and-white diagonal stripes, and *Q*, which draws attention to itself by being more self-effacing than the norm.

BUY THE BOOK Book publishers, too, must attract attention to their products. Just as successive editions of a magazine must have enough in common visually to be recognizable to loyal readers, books in the same imprint or by the same author are often designed as a coherent series. Each book is complete in itself, though, and some flavour of its content must be conveyed.

Below: 'Story papers' were first produced on steam-driven presses in the mid-nineteenth century, but they were revitalized by the addition of colour. Hugo Gernsback's titles, such as *Wonder Stories* and *Amazing Stories*, contributed to the rise of the science fiction genre, with covers evoking the marvels to be found within.

Right: Colour is essential to the thrill of pulp fiction. These early examples are among the more restrained. As themes became racier towards the 1960s, palettes followed suit. Only the most garish of covers would suitably complement a title like *How Cheap Can You Get?* or *Fast, Loose and Lovely*.

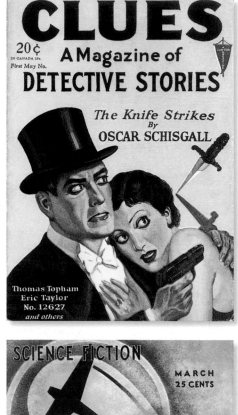

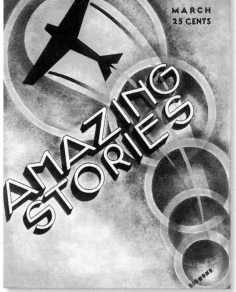

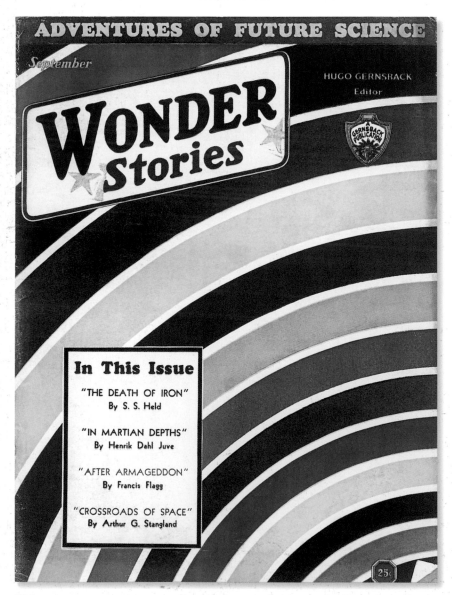

Ⓛ

Las palabras
JEAN - PAUL SARTRE

LOSADA

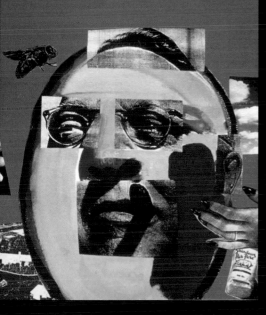

Peter Carey
The Fat Man in History
by the author of
Oscar and Lucinda

ff

Left: **Called upon to redesign the back catalogue of Spanish-language publishing house Losada, Fernando Gutiérrez placed illustrations by Marion Deuchars on solid blocks of colour.**

Left, below: **Pentagram's redesign of Faber & Faber's covers in the late 1980s provided a model for many other publishers. It was updated in 1994 by John McConnell using black, white and primary colours to achieve 'maximum on-shelf impact'.**

Below: **When an author has achieved recognition and popularity, it pays to give his or her books a distinctive look. Pentagram partner Justus Oehler designed this Faber & Faber series of Banana Yoshimoto's fiction using Japanese characters on background colours appropriate to each work.** *Asleep* **(top right) is suitably quiet in tone.**

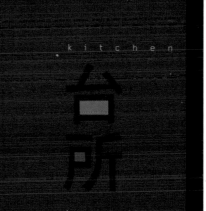

k i t c h e n

台所

banana yoshimoto
The international bestseller

ff

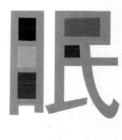

a s l e e p

眠

banana yoshimoto
translated by michael emmerich

'Enchanting, compact and
understated, this is a gorgeous
collection.' **Time Out**

ff

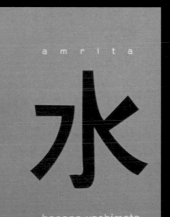

a m r i t a

水

banana yoshimoto
'The voice of young Japan.'
Independent on Sunday

ff

l i z a r d

蜥
蜴

banana yoshimoto
by the bestselling author
of **Kitchen**

ff

DIFFERENT COLOURS Books are not the only products that can be visually dominated by colour. The scheme used for a range of items can manipulate our perceptions of it subtly or aggressively. Whether the application of colour to each product is meaningful or purely differentiating, the overall effect may be to invite, excite or merely reassure.

FULL TIME COURSE
& PART TIME COURSE

One year full time and three year part-time course is a positive response to the growing need for high qualified design professionals who are able to show how design can be used to improve organisational performance. More simply this means using design, innovation and creativity effectively.

Design & Branding

DEPARTMENT OF DESIGN
Runnymede Campus

FULL TIME COURSE
& PART TIME COURSE

One year full time and three year part-time course is a positive response to the growing need for high qualified design professionals who are able to show how design can be used to improve organisational performance. More simply this means using design, innovation and creativity effectively.

Design

DEPARTMENT OF DESIGN
Runnymede Campus

Above: **Design is of special importance when communicating with designers. These brochures by Heard Design for Brunel University in London aimed to attract the right calibre of applicants for postgraduate design courses. Each degree gets its own signature colour, which then interacts with other colours in the oversized lettering of its title.**

130   **part 03. designing with colour**

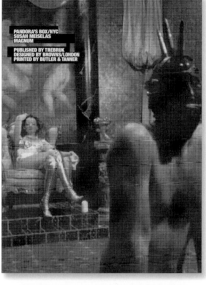

PANDORA'S BOX/NYC
SUSAN MEISELAS
MAGNUM

PUBLISHED BY TREBRUK
DESIGNED BY BROWNS/LONDON
PRINTED BY BUTLER & TANNER

Above and right: **These posters**
were created to promote a book
by American Magnum photographer
Susan Meiselas (b. 1948). The posters
were screen-printed in black on the
reverse side of coloured translucent
photographic filter gels, hinting at
the tactile qualities of the book itself.
The perceived mood of each scene is
dictated as much by the colour as by
the content of the image.
Posters and book designed by Browns
Published by Trebruk
Printed by Butler and Tanner

PANDORA'S BOX/NYC
SUSAN MEISELAS
MAGNUM

PUBLISHED BY TREBRUK
DESIGNED BY BROWNS/LONDON
PRINTED BY BUTLER & TANNER

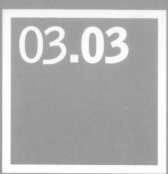

03.03

COLOUR AT THE POINT OF SALE

Walk into any store and you face a two-pronged assault on the senses: product manufacturers package their goods to maximize their appeal, and merchandisers display them to ensure they catch the eye. The disciplines of packaging and retail design thus go hand in hand, although they are characterized by different concerns and approaches.

Packaging design is a branch of graphic design, and it is all about creating a feel or ambience around a product. Very often, the packaging effectively is the product: what is inside the box may differ only marginally from rival offerings, but its outwards appearance bespeaks unique qualities and values that are calculated to entice a target audience. To achieve this psychological persuasion, more colours, textures and special effects – such as metallic foil blocking and holographic patterns – are used in packaging than in any other print sector.

Retail design is a branch of interior design. Within the store, the retail designer must encourage traffic flow to all areas, draw special attention where required, and create an overall visual environment that is coherent, inviting and conducive to purchasing. Lighting and signage are key components. As with newspapers and magazines, the colour palette at the front will tell us what kind of outfit we are dealing with, and if we proceed inside, colour should help us find our way around. Packaging and retail design come together in the creation of retail marketing units (RMUs), display stands – sometimes amounting to minishops in their own right – that present a product range within a store or shopping centre.

Merchandising in particular provides perhaps the most direct feedback of any marketing exercise. Many stores now have electronic stock control systems that track and analyse sales continually. The effect of redesigning a product display can be seen immediately in the figures. With production facilities such as large-format digital printing now widely available on fast turnaround, the enterprising retailer can implement and evaluate a new idea within days. The pressure is on the designer to deliver solutions that not only look good but deliver results.

Right: **This basket of goods from Boots, demonstrates how colour can be used both to differentiate products and to connect them. Each item has a distinctive appearance, but all share the blue logo and other elements derived from this, such as matching blue backgrounds. In only one case is the product itself visible to the purchaser.**

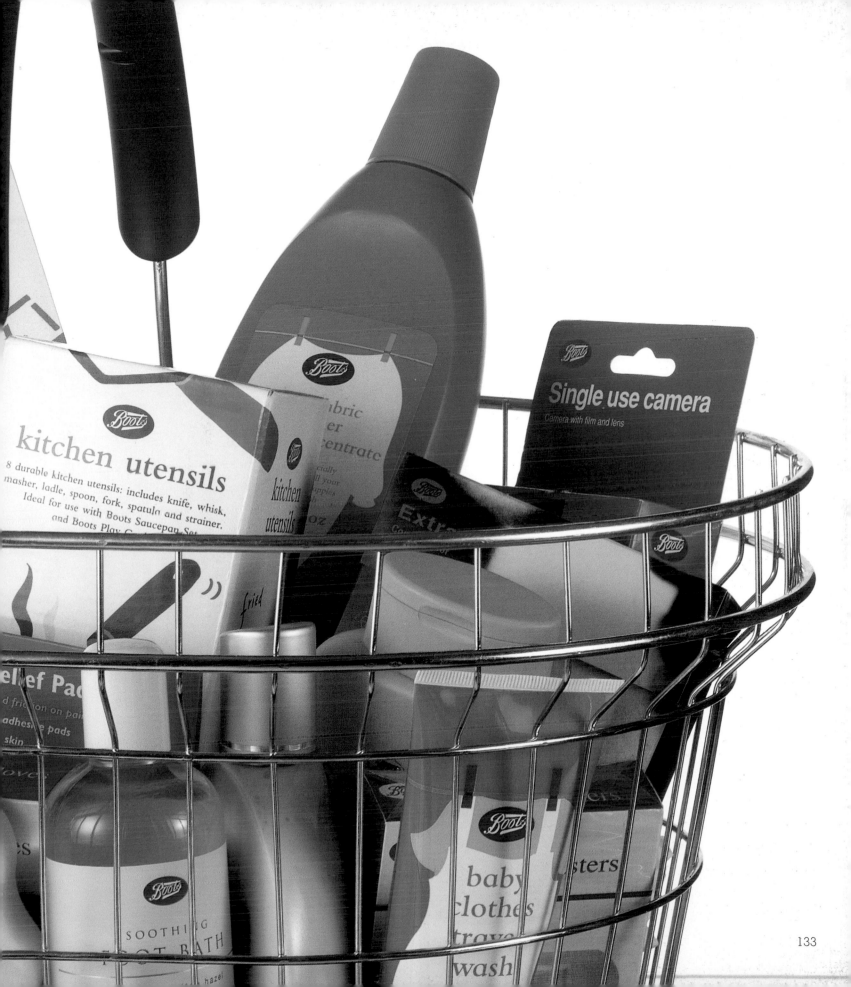

kitchen utensils

8 durable kitchen utensils: includes knife, whisk,
masher, ladle, spoon, fork, spatula and strainer.
Ideal for use with Boots Saucepan Set
and Boots Play C

Single use camera

Camera with film and lens

baby
clothes
trav
wash

SOOTHING
FOOT BATH

133

JUST ADD COLOUR Today's products don't just need unique selling points, they need 'shelf presence'. Carefully considered use of colour can help ensure that they not only grab the attention of the customer, but get the right message across. And, in an ever more sophisticated retail environment, the same goes for the shelves themselves.

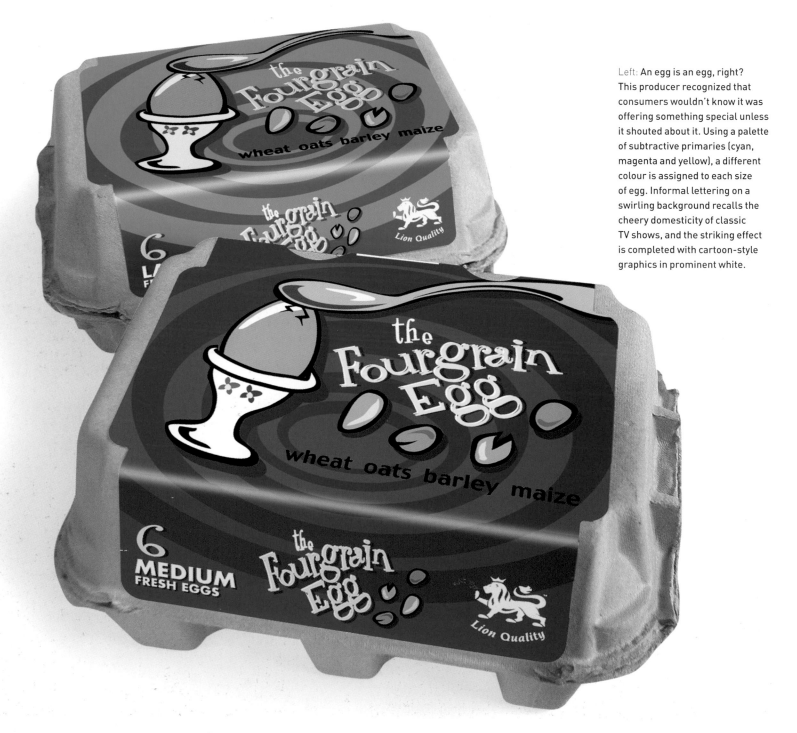

Left: An egg is an egg, right? This producer recognized that consumers wouldn't know it was offering something special unless it shouted about it. Using a palette of subtractive primaries (cyan, magenta and yellow), a different colour is assigned to each size of egg. Informal lettering on a swirling background recalls the cheery domesticity of classic TV shows, and the striking effect is completed with cartoon-style graphics in prominent white.

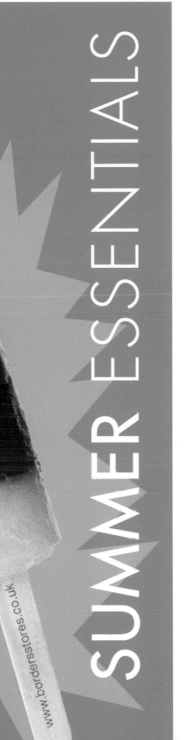

SUMMER ESSENTIALS

www.bordersstores.co.uk

BORDERS®
www.bordersstores.co.uk

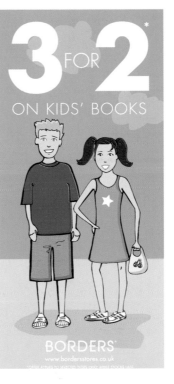

3 FOR 2*
ON KIDS' BOOKS

BORDERS®
www.bordersstores.co.uk

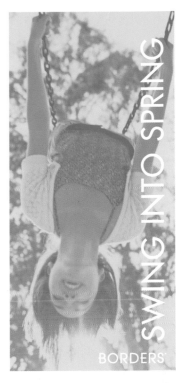

SWING INTO SPRING

BORDERS

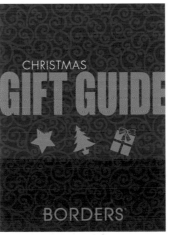

CHRISTMAS
GIFT GUIDE

BORDERS®

Above, left, and below: **Hard to believe that bookshops used to be dull and dusty. Spurred by increasingly fierce competition, bookshops such as Borders must get the customers in and send them out full-bagged and empty-pocketed. This brightly coloured signage helps, drawing attention to cut-price offers and seasonal specials. Repetition hammers the point home.**

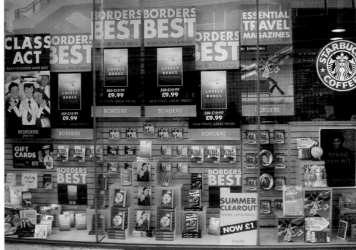

PACKAGE DEALS Our ancestors warned us not to buy a pig in a poke, but retailers know we're still more than happy to oblige. The less we can see of what's in the box, the more our expectations can be manipulated. And if we can see it, why, a little FD&C Blue No. 1 will make it look that much more luxurious. Packaging design may not seem as glamorous as creating glossy fashion magazines, but it has a more direct influence on our behaviour as consumers.

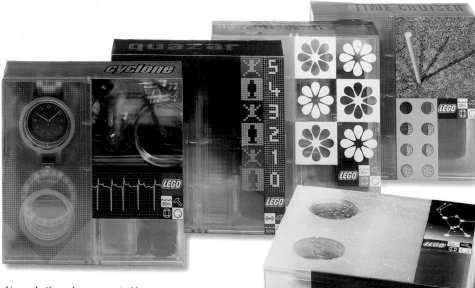

Below: Hovis applied some lateral thinking to make its basic bread range more attractive to shoppers. Depicting what you might enjoy eating with a slice, its bags suggest fresh, healthy food. We're not invited to judge the relative wholesomeness of the product itself: it's entirely invisible. Without reading, can you guess which bags contain white bread and which brown?

Above: In these boxes created by Pentagram for toy manufacturer Lego, the product is visible but subtly modified by the translucent plastic surrounding it. Unlike traditional jeweller's boxes, which tend to be somewhat crude in form and colour, this packaging is light and bright. Colours such as green and orange work with a mixture of abstract patterns and imagery to link the product to the natural world and everyday activities, rather than to high-tech ideals of clinical precision.

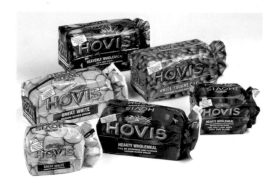

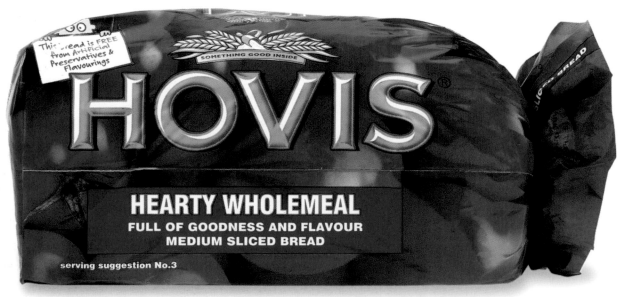

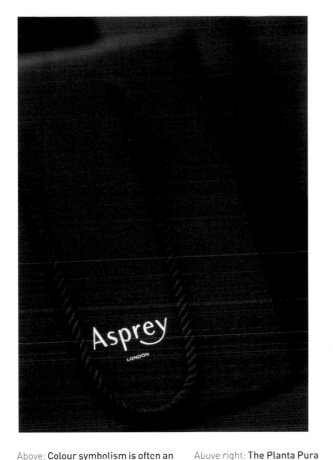

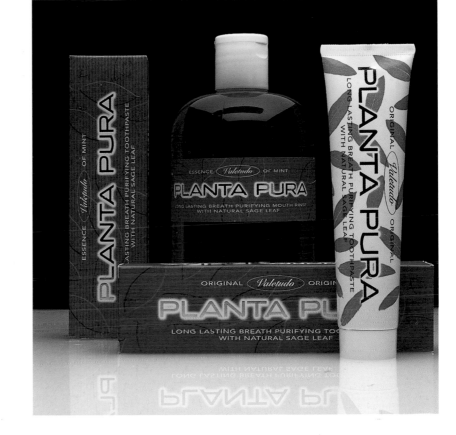

Above: Colour symbolism is often an elusive business, but to almost all of us, purple and gold mean luxury. Pentagram's Angus Hyland chose this 'sumptuous, almost regal' palette for the relaunch of British jeweller Asprey. Foil blocking provides the final touch of class.

Above right: The Planta Pura range of upmarket toothpastes and related products proves that packaging doesn't have to be predictable. While some items here use a green colour scheme and leaf motif to refer to natural ingredients, others are bright blue. The use of a single colour is enough to imply purity.

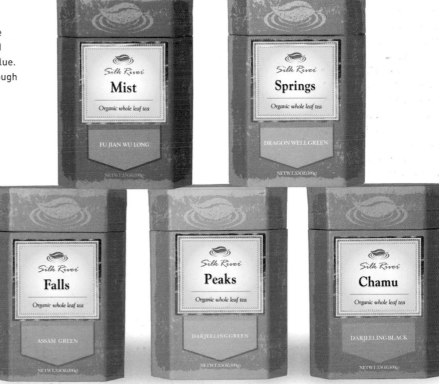

Right: Conceived by LeVesque Design, New York, this packaging for Silk River teas uses pastel colours to impart a reassuringly old-fashioned look with clean, modern touches. Each tea's prominently displayed name and unique box hue make it distinguishable at a glance.

WHAT'S IN STORE In the self-service age, products don't come to us, so their vendors need to make sure we can find our way to them. Every supermarket and department store is a small country with its own roads, maps and signs. They're presented in their own language, of which colour is part of the grammar. But will we understand, or shake our heads and head back over the border?

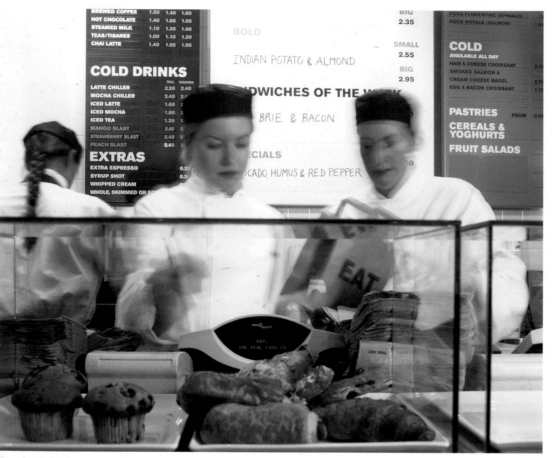

Left: The counter of a deli or sandwich shop not only has to look mouthwatering, it must be instantly comprehensible. Angus Hyland's designs for London café chain EAT fulfill both criteria. The packaging and menu boards all feature warm, natural, brown tones set off with splashes of vibrant colour.

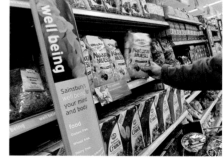

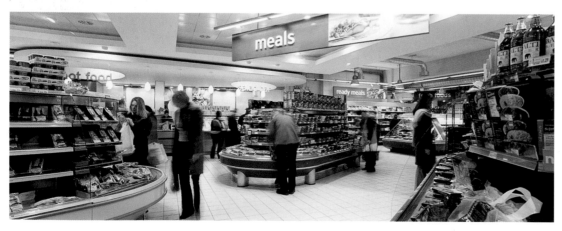

Above and left: **The quality of the signage tells you a lot about a supermarket. Sainsbury's has combined images with short phrases and a cheerful orange theme to create a feel-good shopping experience. Sticking with the corporate colour ensures the store feels like a coherent whole, but it does mean navigation is unaided by colour-coding.**

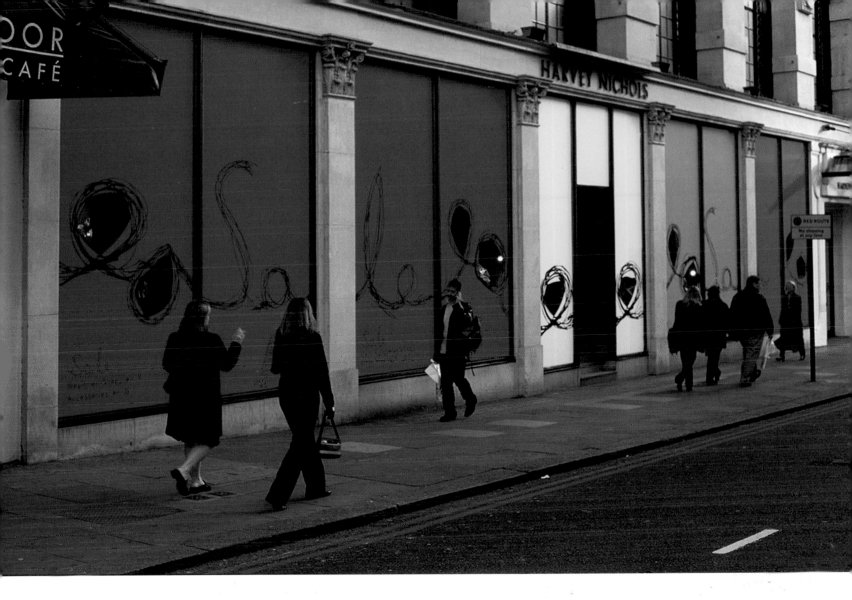

Hot Soups **Salads** **Snacks** **Smoothies** **Vegetable juices** **Wraps** **Fruit Juices**

Above: These logos for Jus Café use complementary colour schemes to create a fresh and vibrant look. Note the avoidance of additive primary colours: used plainly, these could be read as denoting a basic or child-oriented product.

Top: Harvey Nichols has won a number of recent awards for its window displays. In this case, designer Matt Wingfield filled panes with huge banners of flat colour, attracting the attention of passersby before offering a keyhole view of the goods inside. Who could resist a peek?

SIGNS OF THE TIMES Big buildings can be hard to navigate, even for those who work in them, but especially for anyone visiting for the first time. The solution is signage. Colour can help make sense of the building's internal layout by drawing the eye to on-site navigational aids and by coding wings or levels. On the outside, colour can advertise an institution's presence to the public.

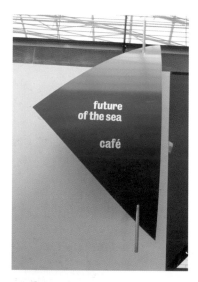

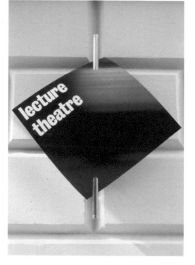

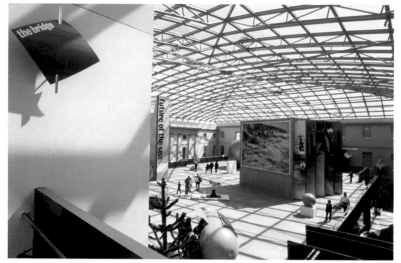

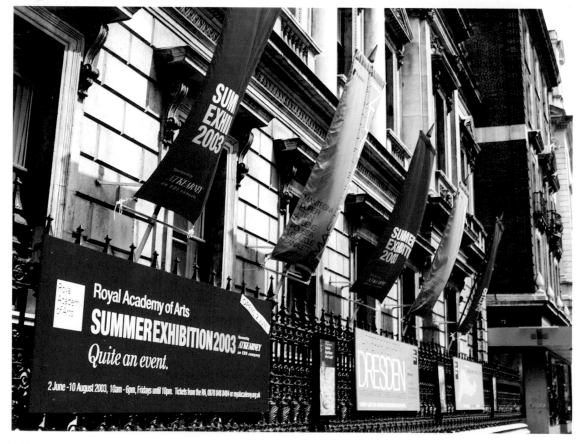

Above: **Established in 1934, the National Maritime Museum at Greenwich was extended in 1999 by architect Rick Mather, and a new signage system was commissioned from Pentagram partner David Hillman to guide visitors through the resulting complex. Aluminium panels, powder-coated in primary colours, are pierced by wall-mounted poles, giving a mast-and-sail effect. The colours denote north, south, east and west sections of the site.**

Left: **Every summer, the Royal Academy of Arts holds an open exhibition to which anyone can submit paintings. The event is traditionally popular with the public, and these brightly coloured banners were designed to maximize visitor numbers. Projecting several feet from the frontage, they could be seen from some distance down the street.**

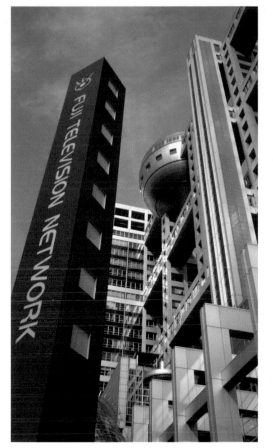

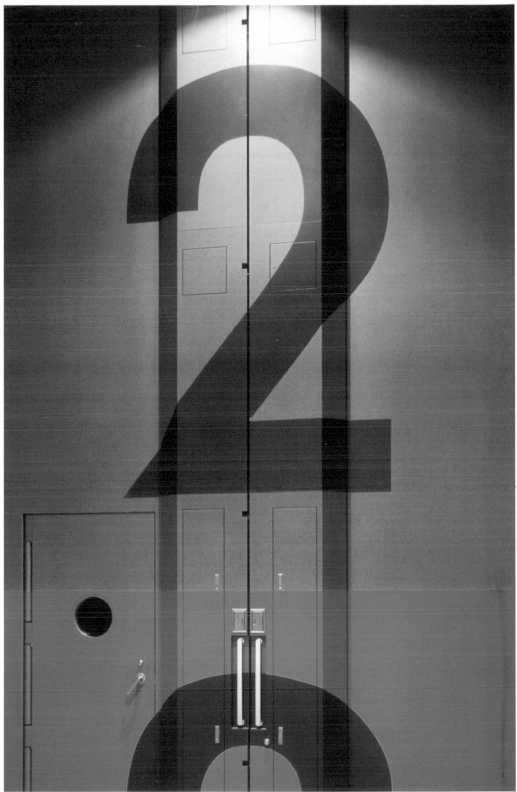

Above and right: **The architecture of Kenzo Tange (b. 1913) makes this broadcasting company headquarters an imposing, even daunting, building. A signage scheme by Pentagram uses oversized graphics in brilliant colours to make it visually accessible. The framing motif (seen above) derives from the architecture itself; the dark rectangle with a lighter frame can be read as a reference to a TV set.**

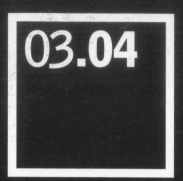

03.04

COLOUR IN BRANDING AND ADVERTISING

Nowhere is colour psychology of more direct practical significance than in the visual development of brands. The colour of a corporate logo can have a huge impact on public perception of a company, the success of its products, and even the workplace culture of its staff. Imagine the Virgin logo, for example, in an autumnal green rather than bright red. What we now think of as a brash, ground-breaking company undoubtedly would take on a completely different image.

With the increasing dominance of global brands, the use of colour becomes trickier and inevitably more conservative. Just as linguistic consultants are hired to ensure that a name that tests positively in Peoria does not mean something rude in Beijing, colour experts must assess the associations of corporate colours around the world. As an ever-smaller number of single colours meets the standards of universal acceptability, more and more logos incorporate a combination of several hues, an option made more practical by the rise of cheap and controllable full-colour reproduction.

Some established corporations have already shifted the connotations of colours by their own usage. Among the many other things red may mean to people, the addition of even a fragment of white script lettering screams 'Coke' – an association to which Virgin's logo is not entirely immune, though whether that is by accident or design it is impossible to say.

Advertising across all forms of media relies heavily on colour in order to get its message across, and since the message is now less often 'Buy this now!' than 'Covet the lifestyle this represents', the use of colour may be guided by psychological subtlety rather than the quest for maximum impact. Besides the choice of hues, the use of shading can indicate the attitude associated with a brand or product. Sophisticated, moody application of light and shadow can give a classic conservative feel, while flatter, more graphical compositions suggest modern, progressive values. Perceptions may be challenged by switching from one mode to the other.

Coca-Cola

Life tastes good

Unlike the shape of a bottle, a colour can't legally be 'owned' by a corporation. But the corporation can do everything possible to associate a colour scheme with its brand. Many other companies may use red and white, but on glimpsing a corner of a hoarding with curved white forms on a red background, most people will think first of Coke.

COLOUR MY WORLD Brand advertising – the kind that sells an attitude more than a product – works by evoking a carefully constructed world into which the audience is invited. After smells, colours are probably the sensory cue that can most immediately manipulate our feelings, before we even start to read what's said about the the brand – or decide whether we believe a word of it.

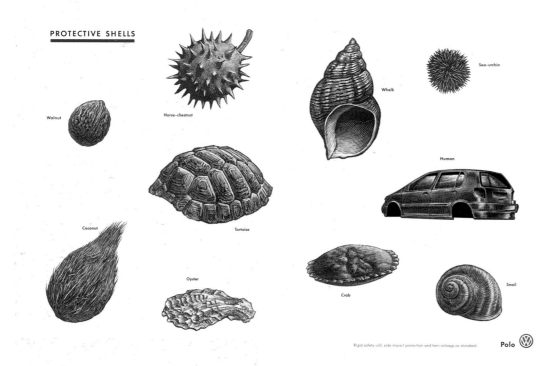

PROTECTIVE SHELLS

Walnut

Horse-chestnut

Whelk

Sea-urchin

Coconut

Tortoise

Human

Oyster

Crab

Snail

Rigid safety cell, side impact protection and twin airbags as standard.

Polo ⓋⓌ

Left: **This ad by agency BMP DDB for Volkswagen's Polo compact likens the car, which boasts numerous safety features, to natural forms of protection. The soft colours and yellowish background, along with illustrations in the style of engravings, tell us we're looking at a facsimile of a textbook, lending authority – and a touch of humour – to the comparison.**

Below: **NB:Studio's series of posters created an ultramodern image for long-established furniture maker Knoll. Clean line drawings in white on coloured backgrounds are reminiscent of blueprints, emphasizing the company's focus on design excellence. The bright colours lighten up the message.**

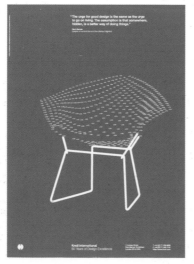

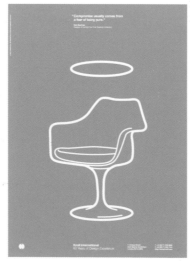

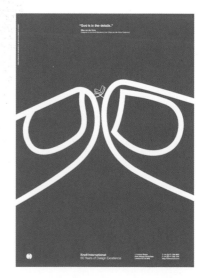

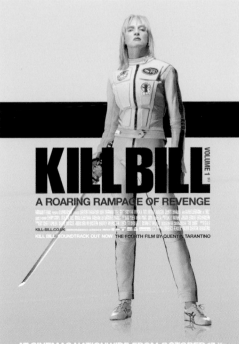

Left: Products don't come with more attitude than a Quentin Tarantino movie. The advertising campaign for *Kill Bill* (2003) used a black stripe on yellow – one of nature's most potent warning signs – to establish a motif so distinctive that it was recognizable without words or pictures.
Design: Empire Design
© 2003 Supercool Manchu, Inc. Reproduced with permission from Buena Vista International (UK) Ltd.

Below: These advertising spreads pair hard, monochromic images of the product with colour images suggesting the emotional state it might provoke in the wearer. Flowers, leaves and feathers in complementary colours give 'Strut' a cheerful look, but the exclusion of the rest of the spectrum creates a slightly threatening feeling of unreality. There's a different attitude in the angry red of 'Stomp'.
Design: Jonathan Raimes & Tim Peplow–Foundation

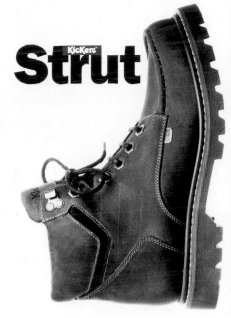

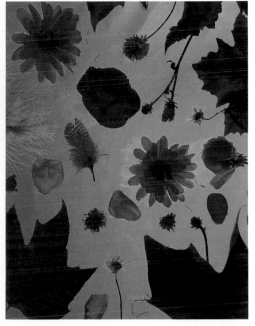

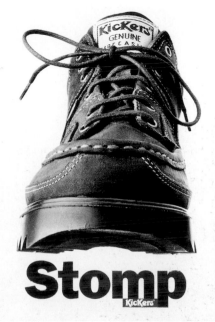

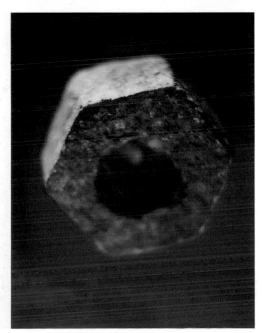

THE LANGUAGE OF COLOUR A colour scheme can stand for something specific – such as a brand – or invoke a more general mood. If they're used well, colours can convey an advertiser's message as clearly and unambiguously as words. And if you doubt the power of colour, compare the number of ads without words to the number without colours.

Left: **This campaign by agency AMV.BBDO for** *The Economist* **flatters its audience by expecting readers to figure out ironies and hidden meanings in the copy (bottom). So familiar has the white-on-red colour coding become that the name of the product can be omitted altogether, creating especially clever branding (top).**

"I never read The Economist."

Management trainee. Aged 42.

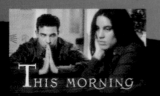

THIS MORNING

THEY WERE

AT EACH OTHER'S

THROATS.

FOR YOUR FREE BROCHURE
FREEPHONE 080 80 1000 000

WALES CYMRU
TWO HOURS AND A MILLION MILES AWAY

Above: What could a trip to Wales do for your state of mind? The cool, calm evening blues of this poster help the words explain.

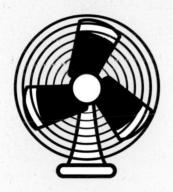

NEW **GUINNESS** EXTRA COLD

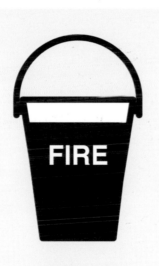

NEW **GUINNESS** EXTRA COLD

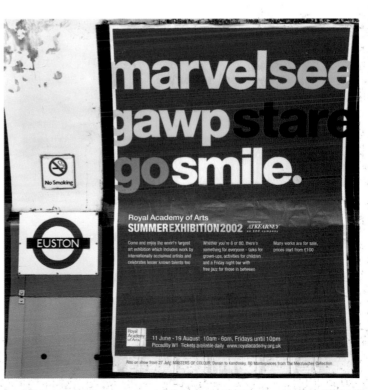

Above: The favourite Irish stout serves as its own corporate identity, the distinctive dark body and creamy head providing an instantly recognizable motif. The pictograms in this series of ads by AMV.BBDO symbolize the drink's thirst-quenching qualities.
Agency: AMV.BBDO
Art Director: Jeremy Carr
Illustrator: Jon Rogers

Right: This poster for a Royal Academy of Arts exhibition caught the eyes of London Underground commuters with multicoloured large type on a hot pink (magenta) background. The colours not only make the billboards impossible to ignore, but they suggest the show itself will be anything but dull.
Design by Heard

COLOUR MARKS There are many colours under the sun, but nowhere near as many as there are multinational corporations. With only a limited number of schemes to go round, each company's choice is made more by a process of elimination than by experimentation on a blank canvas. Yet the right combination of colour and form can be utterly distinctive.

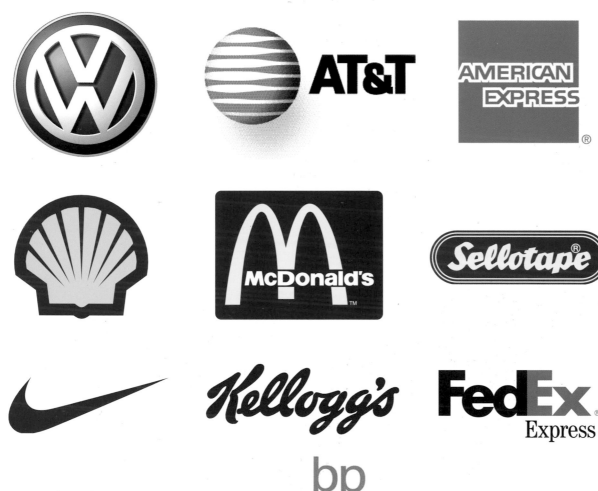

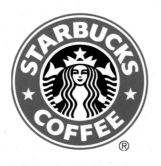

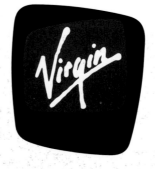

Left: **Red, yellow, green and blue account for the vast majority of logos. Red is strong and bold, signifying everything and nothing but always looking solid and inviting. Blue conveys authority and efficiency but needs its complement, yellow, to make it friendly. Red and blue together – fusing warm and cold, excitement and restraint – are patriotic in some countries and authoritative in all. Green indicates nature and wholesomeness, whether or not those are qualities logically associated with the products they represent.**

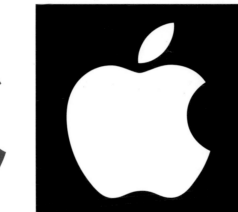

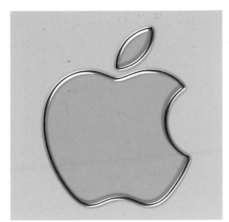

Above: **Apple Computer's original logo, by designer Rob Janoff, is one of the world's most affectionately regarded corporate symbols. Its rainbow pattern was in tune with the spirit of the 1970s but was quietly removed in the late 1990s, leaving behind a monochromic shape. Apple's latest operating system, Panther, features a shiny chrome version. "It's great to take an image and keep revising it and making it better. I'm totally into it," says Janoff, who is no longer involved with the company.**

Above: **BT changed its logo in 2003 to reflect its 'multifaceted nature' and 'being in tune with the multimedia age'. The new identity, known as 'connected world', uses six primary and secondary colours, compared to just red and blue in its previous logo. Tellingly, it was originally developed for a broadband Internet division, but it expressed values that were later felt to apply to the whole company.**

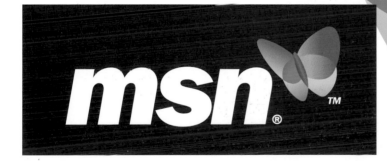

Left: **MSN, Microsoft's personalized online service, is another brand that has opted for a multicoloured logo. The company needed a mark that was instantly recognizable, even at small sizes, as it would be used to flag recommended Internet content. The butterfly is effectively an adaptation of the familiar Microsoft Windows logo, which is made up of four shapes in the same colours.**

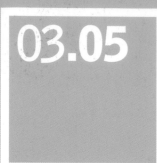

03.05

COLOUR ON THE WEB

Web designers have an amazing palette of colours at their disposal, although they must be careful not to exploit it too enthusiastically if they want their creations to be appreciated by the maximum number of viewers (*see chapter 04.04*). In theory, then, the Web should be filled with examples of exciting, innovative design. Given a brand-new medium in which companies are struggling to exert a presence, you would think that the finest graphic artists in the business would have made the territory their own as they forged new paradigms of visual experience.

Even a cursory bit of surfing quickly dashes such hopes. An initial proliferation of IT (information technology) specialists took their poor understanding of already-dated user-interface design techniques to the Internet, establishing some curious expectations in the minds of users. (Little 3-D–effect buttons were not part of the original conception of the Web.) Then a surge of professional print designers decided to switch to the screen with even less training in user interaction and little clue knowledge of what the Internet was all about. The result? An epidemic of unnavigable sites, bloated animations and the kind of pointless decoration and random use of colour that had blighted the beginnings of desktop publishing a decade earlier.

Fortunately, things have started to improve. More foolproof software is available to help design-oriented users create basic sites that work properly, while at the high end, major sites are produced by properly organized technical and creative teams. While many commercial sites do still rely on a simple-minded application of corporate colours to a grid-like template, others use colour more intelligently to create a mood and aid navigation.

Many of the best designers devote at least part of their efforts to purely experimental sites. These outer reaches of online design remain the best source of inspiration, even when working for the most conservative client. Ideas about how users interact with sites (as opposed to magazines, hoardings, and so on), how conventional rules of composition may need to be modified, and how the impact of colours on screen and in print differs are still at an immature stage. Anyone going in search of established paradigms will find that an open mind is the most valuable tool at this point.

Right: This website designed for furniture maker Knoll by NB:Studio uses a different color scheme for each section. The visually striking oversized type combined with the colours create a strong graphical feel even where no images are shown – and without requiring a huge data download.

Knoll

Products

Profile, History, Philos

Knoll

© Service

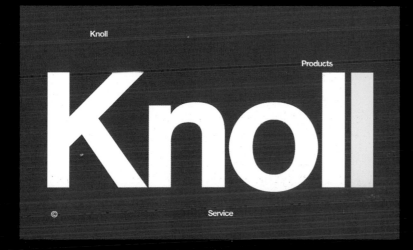

Knoll

Products

Knoll

© Service

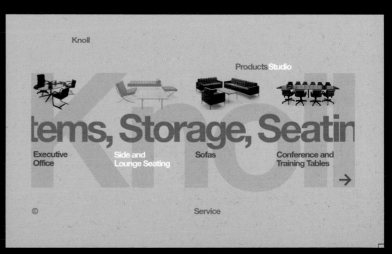

Knoll

Products Studio

tems, Storage, Seatin

Executive Office

Side and Lounge Seating

Sofas

Conference and Training Tables

→

© Service

ART FOR ART'S SAKE Not surprisingly, some of the best Web graphics are found on the sites of individuals and organizations who are in the art and design business. While others may dabble half-heartedly with colour, being unsure what to do with it, these innovators have already mastered it and can now explore its full potential in a new medium.

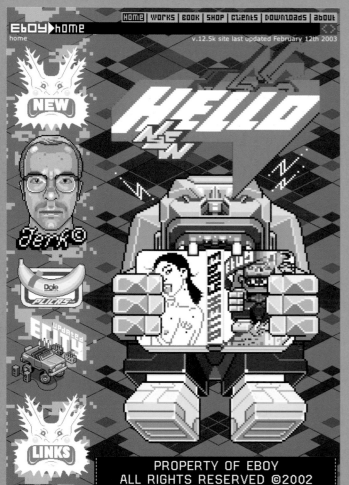

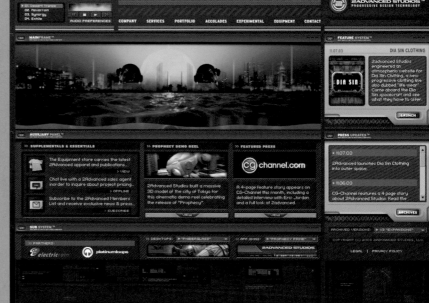

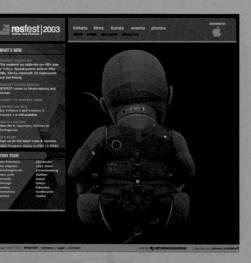

Above: US/European graphics collective eBoy offers challenging content in challenging colours. Inspired by the diversity – and perversity – of contemporary life, they list their influences as 'shopping, supermarkets, TV, toy commercials, Lego, computer games, the news, magazines...'

Right: The same principle has been applied to very different effect to publicize a more avant-garde cultural icon, the Resfest digital film festival. Designed by New York agency Infornographic using an identity by British filmmaker Johnny Hardstaff, the site re-creates the feeling of anticipation on entering a dark cinema. Splashes of orange and cyan are the only colours.

Above: Web-design agency 2advanced Studios operates a self-promotional site whose periodic redesigns are eagerly awaited by aficionados. The split complementary colour scheme of this latest incarnation is typical of the team's sophisticated approach. Every pixel seems to have been carefully constructed, and dozens of animated elements bring the page alive as the user moves the mouse around. This 'advanced user interface' comes at a price: download speeds on anything but the fastest connection are glacial.

part 03. designing with colour

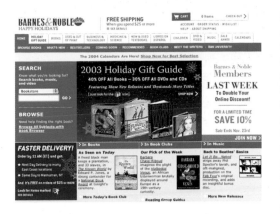

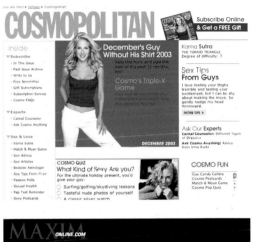

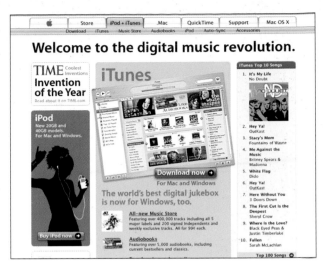

Commercial websites are based on many different business models – they may want visitors to buy goods, or subscribe to services, or just to add their clicks to the total reported to advertisers – but two universal aims are to hold visitors' attention and to project the brand. Colour is often essential to both.

Above left: Barnes & Noble covers most of its site window with tint blocks, leaving only a narrow band of white at the top. Blues and greens give the content a restful mood.

Left and below left: Men are from Mars, women are from Venus, and their preferred colour palettes are also separated by a few million miles if these magazine home pages have the right idea. Both employ the same part of the spectrum, but the women's title, *Cosmopolitan*, uses softer tints. Along with bold colour, the men's offering, *Maxim*, has sharper, higher-contrast photography, so the whole composition jumps out toward the viewer.

Below: The Collage Foundation doesn't want to sell you anything: it's a charitable organization dedicated to positive social and environmental change. It does, however, want to attract public attention and express its ethos. This website, by Web-design innovator Joshua Davis, has a unique look powered by vibrant colour.

Above: Apple's website, like its latest computers and accessories, is largely monochromic and dominated by white. As in print design, this gives a sophisticated feel. The page promoting its commercially successful iTunes music download service, however, makes strong use of colour to entice users to sign up.

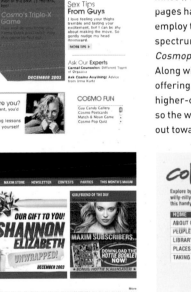

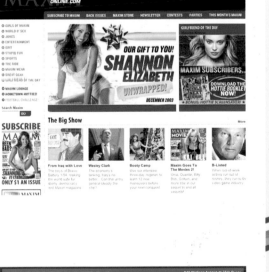

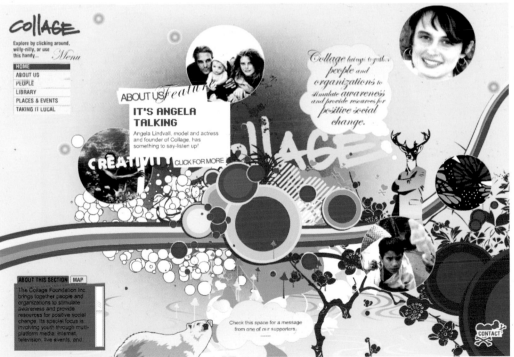

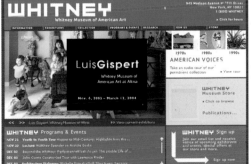

Left: The Whitney Museum of American Art uses white text and dark tints to give a distinctive and serious look to its site. Modern typefaces and varied images prevent things getting too heavy.

DIGITAL COLOUR

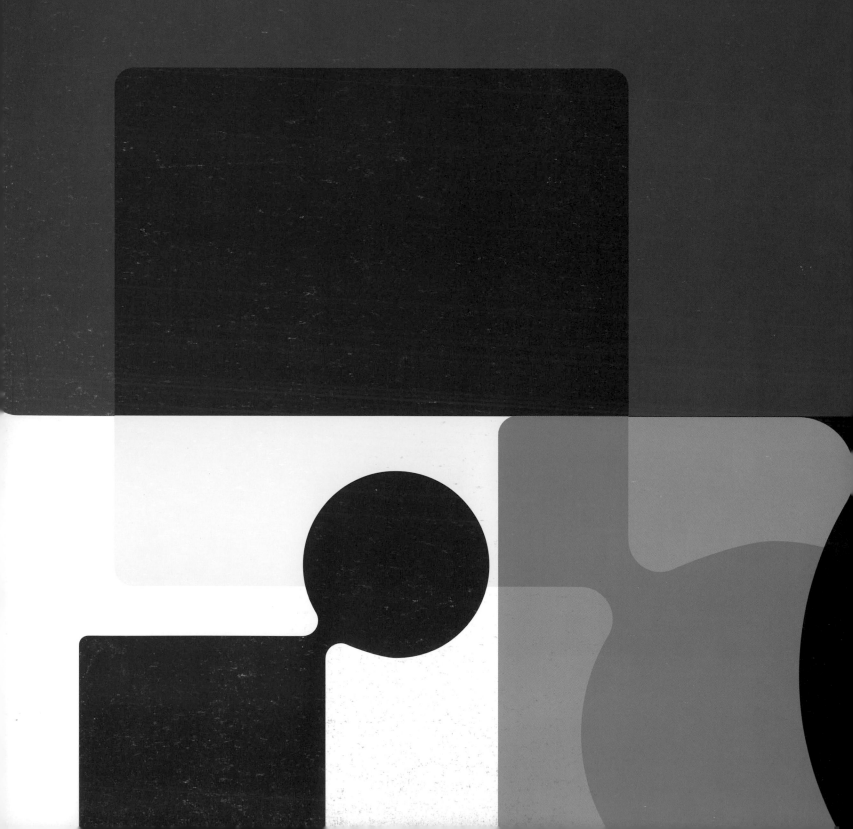

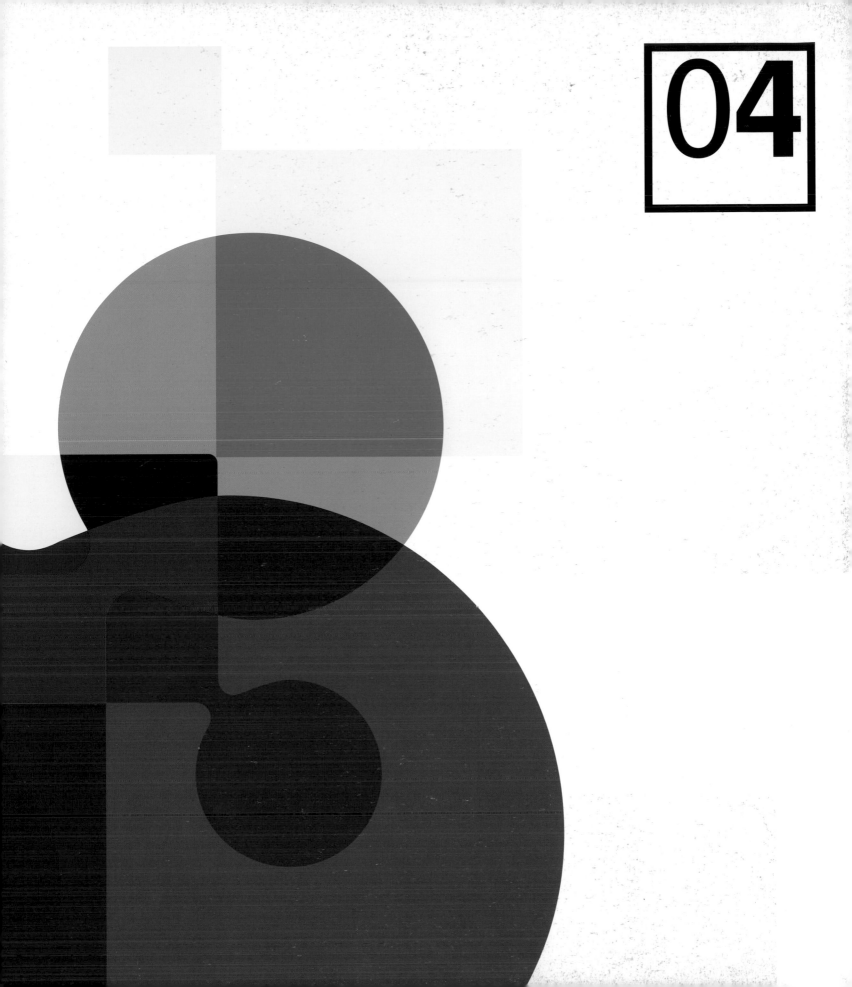

04

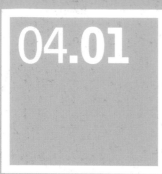

04.01

PART 04. DIGITAL COLOUR

CHAPTER ONE

DESIGNING FOR THE SCREEN

It is only thanks to a small number of independent thinkers, and some fortuitous coincidences, that colour and computers came together at all. In the early 1970s, Richard Shoup, an engineer at Xerox's PARC Computer Science Lab, constructed a system called Superpaint that could manipulate colour video frames. Along with an artist friend, Alvy Ray Smith, he developed Superpaint to the point where its fashionably psychedelic graphics caught the attention of the local media. His superiors reacted by withdrawing funding from the project, which they saw as a distraction from the development of business computers. The same attitude would pervade the industry for more than a decade.

Smith moved on to work for a movie-effects company founded by *Star Wars* director George Lucas. Meanwhile, the advent of affordable personal computers allowed others to experiment with digital graphics. The Apple Macintosh, launched in 1984, did not support colour: in fact, it could not even display shades of grey, only black and white. Nonetheless, it started the desktop publishing revolution, aided by the PostScript page-description technology developed by two other former PARC employees, Chuck Geschke (b. 1939) and John Warnock (b. 1940), who named their company Adobe. Users would typeset pages on the screen, output them with the newly invented laser printer and add colour images by traditional means.

In the late 1980s, Thomas Knoll began to program image-processing routines on the Mac, which would soon gain a colour display. Knoll's brother John recognized some of the image-processing principles being explored at his place of work: George Lucas's Industrial Light and Magic. Together, the brothers completed an image-editing program, eventually named Photoshop, which they sold to Adobe. It was released as a commercial product in 1990, and it remains the most popular professional colour-graphics software to this day.

Image processing is not the only approach to colour graphics. Adobe also developed a drawing program, Illustrator, based on PostScript, which manipulated geometrically defined elements. Illustrator could not work with photos, but instead gave artists and designers a blank canvas on which they could build up drawings from coloured shapes. Because each shape could be precisely edited and reproduced, the method was ideal for technical illustration. The distinction between image processing and drawing programs persists, and graphics programs are thus divisible into bitmap editing and vector drawing camps, although each now borrows from the other's armory.

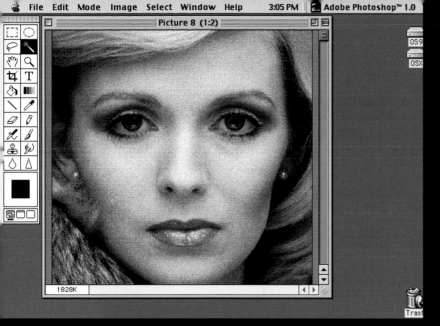

Colour was not a priority in the early development of personal computers, and colour-graphics pioneers were regarded as timewasters playing around with impractical technologies. Photoshop, the image-manipulation program that, perhaps more than any other digital product, has revolutionized the way colour is handled by designers, was originated not by a major corporation but by two brothers in a back room. Its evolution from a simple editing tool (left) to an immensely complex and powerful application (below) has followed the upwards trend of computer processing power.

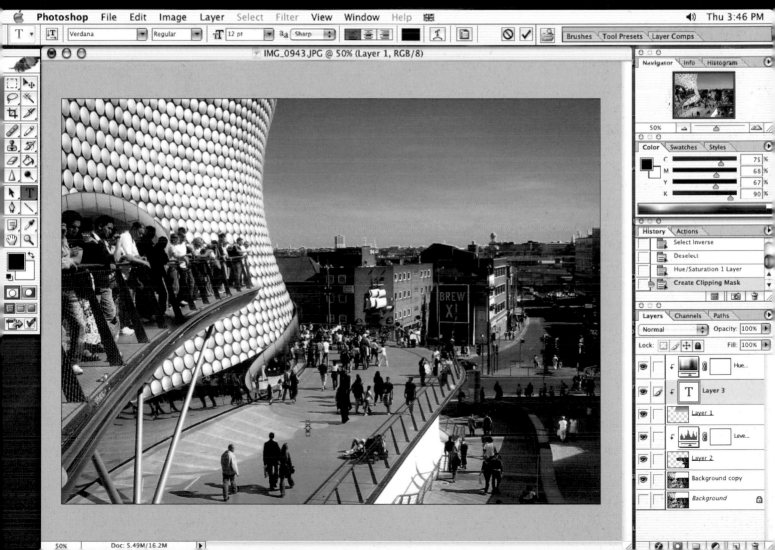

VECTOR VERSUS BITMAP Vector and bitmap pictures possess very different qualities. Any image captured from the real world – usually through a digital camera or a scanner – will be a bitmap, consisting of coloured squares, or pixels (from 'picture elements'), arranged in a grid. The more pixels are packed into each square inch of the image, the crisper and more detailed it appears. Thus, bitmaps are resolution-dependent. Once an image is created or stored with a given number of pixels, it can be reproduced at a larger size only by enlarging them. This will quickly start to reduce image clarity and give a mosaicked, or 'pixelated', appearance.

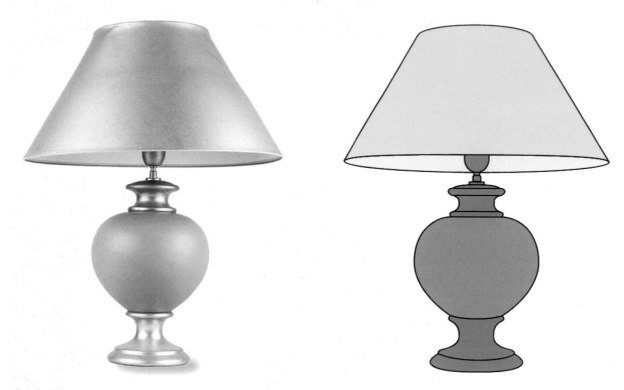

On the illuminated computer screen, pixelation is not noticeable even at low image resolution. When colour monitors first became commonplace, they displayed around 72 dots per inch (dpi): that is, 72 pixels across and down every inch. Today, this has crept up to around 96 dpi. So bitmap images for use in websites are created at this resolution. In print, however, pixels are more easily distinguished, and our expectation of clarity is higher. Colour images are therefore reproduced at around 300 dpi, although resolutions as low as half that may be used in lower-grade print such as colour newspapers.

Images occupy a large amount of computer memory, and the higher their resolution, the longer it takes to process them. So, just as resolution must be high enough to maintain output quality, it must also be low enough to be efficient. This balance is a constant preoccupation in image editing.

Vector-based artwork, on the other hand, is made up of objects that are mathematically scalable and therefore resolution-independent. Although vector images are ultimately bitmapped, or rasterized, when displayed or printed, the artist can resize the objects at will without any change in quality. Because the same number of coordinates describes any given shape no matter how large it appears, vector images usually take up much less memory than bitmaps and are much quicker to process.

This is not to imply that vectors are inherently more efficient, just that they are suited to a different kind of image. Although you can convert a photograph into vectors by an automated process known as tracing, the results are highly stylized. It is possible, however, to create photorealistic vector images from scratch, producing results that are reminiscent of airbrush art. The latest vector-drawing software resorts to

A photographic image (above left) is stored as a grid of pixels. Scaling it up too far will only increase the size of the pixels, resulting in a mosaic appearance. A vector image (above right) is created as a set of geometrically defined shapes and can be scaled to any size, but images cannot be captured from the real world in this format.
Image: Steve Caplin

combining bitmaps with vectors for more advanced effects, and in doing so, it relinquishes speed and size advantages.

Vector imaging lends itself well to animation, as flat artwork – of the kind traditionally seen in cartoons – can be stored efficiently, and changes between one frame and the next can be achieved by adjusting a few coordinates rather than thousands of pixels. Macromedia Flash is a vector-based technology that has become the standard tool for animated artwork on the Web; the free plug-in software required to view it is now included with Web browsers like Microsoft Internet Explorer and Apple Safari.

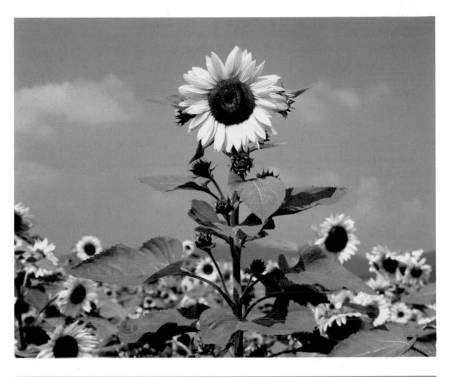

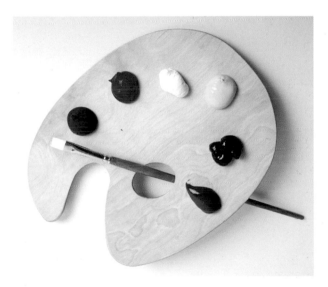

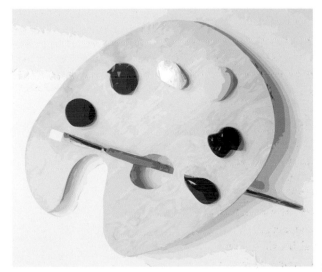

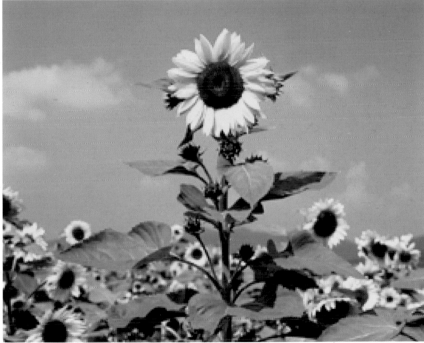

Left: **Bitmapped images can be automatically converted to vectors by autotracing routines in software. The results are inevitably imperfect, but with the right settings, an artistically stylized rendering can be produced.**

Above: **Although images displayed at around 70 to 100 dpi on the monitor may look sharp, this resolution is not sufficient for printing. Compare the same image printed at 300 dpi (top) and 72 dpi (bottom).**

HOW COMPUTERS REPRESENT COLOUR
The real world is characterized by infinite variety, but in the computer, variation must be precisely quantified by dividing an input signal into sections of a fixed size, then measuring and storing the value of each section. The fidelity of the result to the original depends on two factors: the number of sections, and the precision with which each section's value is measured. We have already seen that digital images are divided into sections called pixels, and that the number of pixels per inch determines image clarity. The second factor is the colour fidelity of each pixel, which depends on its bit depth.

Think of the computer's memory as an array of on/off switches. These can store binary (or base 2) numbers and perform mathematical operations on them. A pair of binary digits, or bits, can represent four binary numbers, which would be written down in figures as 00, 01, 10 and 11 – and in the case of image processing, 00 represents black and 11 represents white. Four bits (0000 as black and 1111 as white) can represent sixteen numbers (0 to 15), and eight bits can represent 256 (0 to 255), with 00000000 as black, 11111111 as white and 254 intermediate shades of grey. A group of eight bits is known by the now-familiar term 'byte'. At this complexity, the image has become what is known as a continuous tone. While practically no image is truly continuous – even traditional photographs are made up of tiny coloured dots – the term is used here to refer to images that appear to be so when viewed at normal size with the unassisted eye. But how does a continuous grey image become a coloured one?

Most digital images are stored in 24-bit RGB colour. This means that each pixel is described by 24 bits grouped into three bytes, each devoted to the red, green and blue components, or channels. (We saw in chapter 01.02 how red, green, and blue primaries can be combined to create any visible colour.) There are thus 256 possible values for each colour channel, and

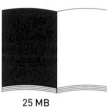

6 MB

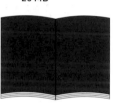

25 MB

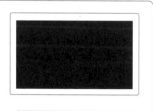

50 MB

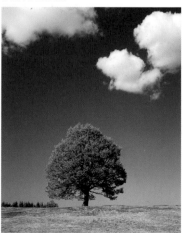

2 MB

multiplying these together (256 x 256 x 256) yields a total of 16.7 million possible colours – more than the human eye can distinguish.

Simple arithmetic will tell you how much computer memory is required to store a bitmapped image of a given resolution and bit depth. For example, a 15-by-10-cm photo captured at 300 dpi print resolution will take up 15-by-10 cms x 300 by 300 dots x 3 bytes = 6,480,000 bytes, or 6.18 megabytes. A kilobyte (KB) is 1,024 bytes, and a megabyte (MB) is 1,024 kilobytes.

It should now be clear that colour is one of the reasons why vector drawings occupy so much less space. An A4-size rectangle, for example, would be stored in vector format as an instruction to draw a rectangle, four sets of coordinates defining its corner points, and a single colour value – just a few bytes in total. In a bitmap editor like Photoshop, however, working at 300 dpi, the same rectangle would consist of 8,699,840 pixels, each with a colour value, totaling 25 MB of data.

1-BIT COLOUR

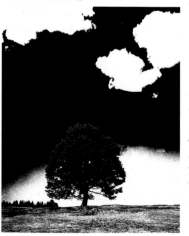

2-BIT COLOUR

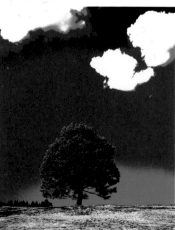

4-BIT COLOUR

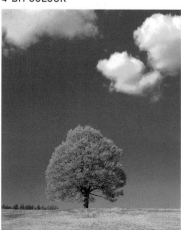

8-BIT COLOUR

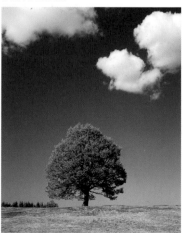

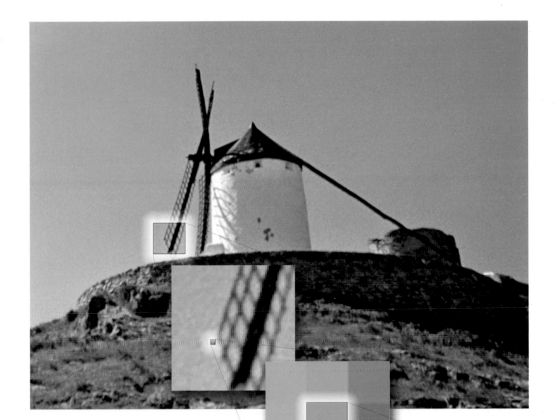

Below: HSV (also called HSL or HSB) is an alternative colour model to RGB. H (hue) describes the pixel's hue – its position in the spectrum. S (saturation) dictates how strong the colour is, with zero values creating greys. V (value) ranges from dark to light.

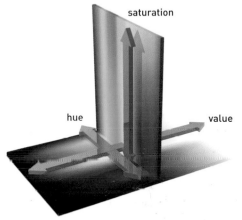

Above: Every pixel in a bitmapped image has a colour value. This is usually specified as proportions of red, green and blue, the primary colours of additive mixing. In 24-bit colour, the most commonly used format, each primary colour is represented by eight binary digits, giving a total of 256 possible values (from 0 to 255).

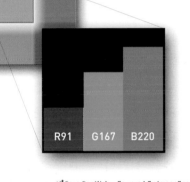

R91   G167   B220

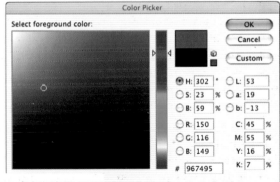

16-BIT COLOUR

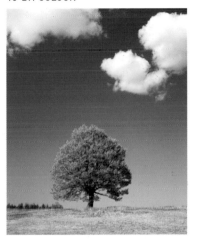

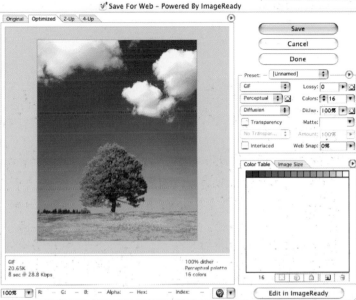

Above: In graphics software like Photoshop, you can specify colours by typing numeric values, or pick them from a visual colour mixer.

Left: Images with low colour depth are stored with a list of the colour values found in their pixels. An 8-bit image, for example, can have a maximum of 256 colours. The fewer colours allowed, the smaller the image file will be.

DIGITAL COLOUR SPACES Although the RGB model arises naturally from the way we perceive colour, it is not the only way colour can be represented digitally, nor is it as straightforward as it might appear. Let's take a step back. As we saw in chapter 01.03, to define colours meaningfully, we need to follow some kind of system that represents the visible spectrum.

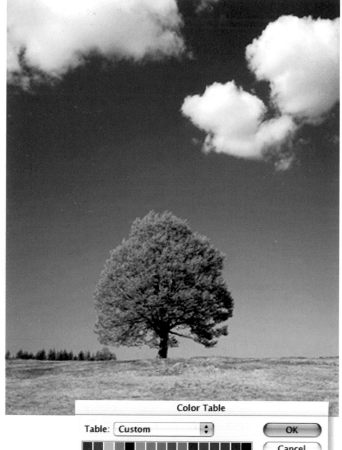

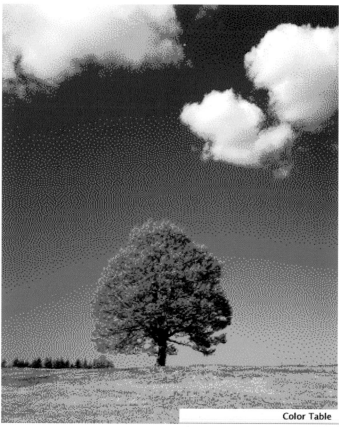

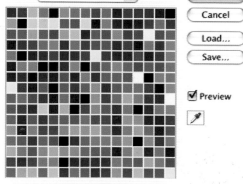

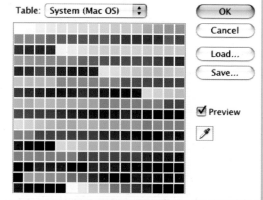

This page: An 8-bit file converted from a full-colour image using an adaptive palette, which includes as many as possible of its existing colours, may be almost indistinguishable from the original. If a predefined Color Table is used, such as the Web-safe palette or the system palette of a particular computer system, quality will be much reduced. This is rarely necessary nowadays.

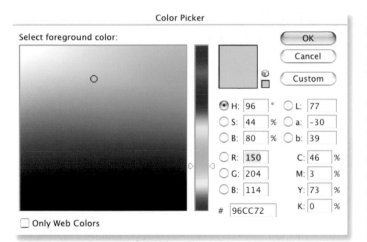

Left: Color Pickers in most graphics software allow you to use whichever colour model you prefer. Conversions between them are made automatically.

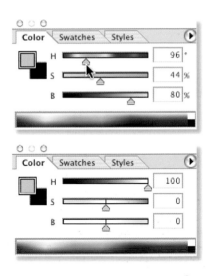

Right: The HSV system makes mixing more intuitive. Having selected a hue from the spectrum, its saturation and brightness can be adjusted independently. Lab colour, which relates to the opponent process in human vision (see page 25), is not so easy to understand, and is less often used for colour specification, although it can be useful for processing images in this mode (see page 198).

In the early days of colour computing, the engineers of each system would come up with their own 'good enough' systems. Things were simpler then because memory was scarce, and rather than define precise RGB recipes for each pixel, a limited number of colours would be used to define the pixels.

Typically, one byte was allocated to each pixel, giving a total of 256 possible values. These values did not represent an actual colour but a position in a list of predefined colours – known as a colour look-up table, or CLUT – already stored in memory. The standard colour table built into the computer was the system palette. Ideally, users would be able to substitute a different palette at will, so that they could apply the colours included to the image being displayed. (Users quickly discovered that they could also create groovy rippling effects by rapidly switching palettes.)

With 16.7 million colours to play with, the colour spaces we now use are complex mathematical models and a more sophisticated system is called for. The paragon of colour spaces is CIE-Lab, first proposed by the International Commission on Illumination (CIE) in 1960 and published in 1976. This is a transformation of the CIE-XYZ space (see page 47) in which, instead of a combination of three primaries, colours are defined by values called L, a and b. The L represents lightness or luminosity, while a and b can be described as red/greenness and yellow/blueness.

Lab colour is designed to be perceptually uniform, so that the mathematical relationships between colour values correspond to the visual relationships we see: 'half as dark', 'twice as red', and so on. The main drawback of Lab colour is that it is too mathematically intensive for efficient digital image processing. This is why we come back to RGB for

everyday storage and manipulation. An RGB colour space is defined as a triangle drawn with three points (primaries) within the CIE diagram of the visible spectrum. The actual colour space of your computer screen, for example, is referred to as Monitor RGB. But other RGB spaces can be defined using arbitrary primaries to cover a helpful gamut (range of colours). Examples include sRGB and Adobe RGB (1998).

Because most people do not instinctively think about colour in terms of RGB combinations, let alone the unnameable properties of Lab, other types of colour space have been devised to allow colours to be defined more intuitively. HSV, sometimes called HSB, expresses colour numerically in terms of hue (green, yellow, purple or whatever), saturation (how 'ungrey' it is) and value (brightness). These correspond to the physical properties of dominant wavelength, excitation purity and luminance (see chapter 01.02).

Below: An RGB colour space is described by a triangle within the CIE diagram of human colour perception. Although the gamuts of different RGB models vary, a large part of the visible spectrum is always excluded. Nonetheless, an RGB space is large enough to encompass almost all of the colours you can see on your monitor or printout.

COLOUR MANAGEMENT We have seen that images may be stored and manipulated in any number of arbitrarily defined colour spaces. It follows that a numeric colour value is not enough in itself to tell a digital device or software program what colour a pixel or vector shape should be. The device or program will also need to know what colour space this value refers to, and be equipped with a formula to convert from that space to the one it is using itself.

The minimum information required is an indication of the type of colour space being used: RGB, Lab, HSL and so on. Graphics file formats either include this information with each image or handle only one type, so as long as the relevant model is one that the hardware or software is capable of interpreting, it will make some kind of sense of the data. To reproduce colours exactly, however, requires precise information about the specific colour space in which the image was created.

Passing this information around and using it to convert accurately between colour spaces is the job of a colour management system (CMS). The industry standard for CMSs, established by the International Colour Consortium (ICC) in the mid-1990s, uses software files known as ICC profiles to define colour spaces. Profiles exist both for arbitrary spaces, such as Adobe RGB, and for the real colour spaces of products such as monitors, scanners and printers.

Below: In a colour-managed system, each digital device used has a colour profile. The system software uses this to convert image colours correctly between devices, whether their own colour space is additive (RGB) or subtractive (CMYK). All conversions are made via the CIE 'connection space', avoiding the need for conversion tables specific to each pair of devices.

What a profile actually defines is the relationship between a given colour model and the CIE-XYZ and CIE-Lab spaces, which are used as a reference model or profile conversion space (PCS). This means colour data can be translated between any two colour spaces as long as a profile has been installed for each of them.

ICC colour management systems are built into most computers. As a founding member of the ICC, Apple pioneered its own CMS, called ColorSync, which forms part of Mac OS. Microsoft has followed suit with ICC support in recent versions of Windows, although it prefers to promote its own form of colour management, which is simply to use

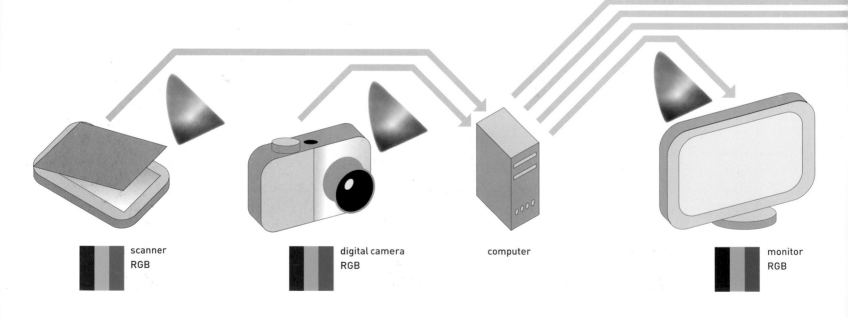

scanner
RGB

digital camera
RGB

computer

monitor
RGB

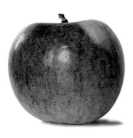

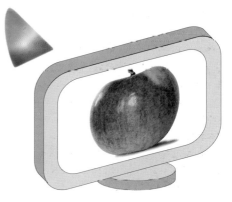

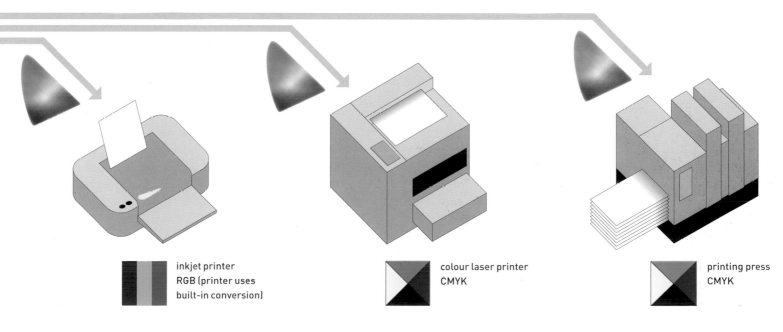

the sRGB colour space for everything. Unfortunately, sRGB has a rather poor gamut, making it inappropriate for serious use and particularly for the colour-conscious artist, photographer or designer. Because of this, professional imaging products are never likely to become standardized to sRGB. In any case, a single colour space cannot fulfil every need, and as soon as more than one is brought into play, a CMS is required to manage conversions.

Accordingly, although ICC colour management may seem tricky to grasp at first, applying it throughout your system is the only way to ensure that colours appear as you expect them to in your finished work.

Above. **If colour management is correctly implemented, the image captured by your camera should be faithfully transferred into software and accurately reproduced on the monitor. In practice, there will always be some degree of discrepancy; the goal is to reduce this as far as possible without spending impractical amounts of time or money.**

inkjet printer
RGB (printer uses
built-in conversion)

colour laser printer
CMYK

printing press
CMYK

CALIBRATION AND PROFILING The ICC profiles supplied with imaging hardware are predefined, or canned: they describe the colour behaviour specified in the design of that particular device. Whether the actual machine in your box matches up to that specification – and whether it will still match after six months of use – is impossible to know unless you test the device. The testing process, known as calibration, is always followed by the automated generation of a new ICC profile matching the device's performance as tested. In some cases, adjustments will also be made to the hardware itself to optimize its colour performance.

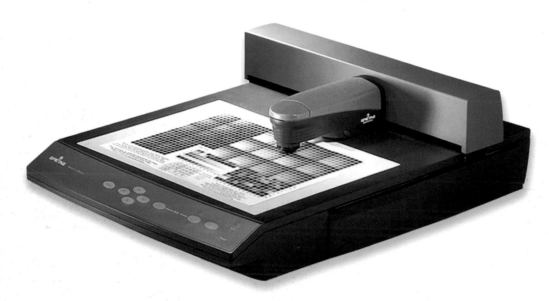

Calibration is optional, and the hardware and software you will need to perform it do not come standard: they will set you back several hundred to several thousand pounds. If you cannot justify that expense, you can colour-manage using only canned profiles, and you should still get considerably better results than without a CMS. But regular calibration and reprofiling will deliver the most reliably accurate colour reproduction.

Scanners are among the easiest devices to calibrate because the data they generate can be directly analysed by the computer. No extra hardware is required; the calibration kit will include software and a colour target, which consists of a piece of photographic paper (or a transparency, for checking transparency scanners) printed with hundreds of coloured patches. Most targets conform to a specification called IT8. To calibrate, you scan the target 'raw' – with colour management turned off – and import the scanned image into the calibration software, which compares the results to a predefined table of correct values. An ICC profile is then

Above: **A spectrophotometer with an automated scanning arm is used to read values from colour charts output by a printer. Software then compares these to a preset table of values to produce a profile for the printer. Even printing presses can be calibrated, greatly reducing the margin of error in colour reproduction.**

generated based on the discrepancies. There are many different mathematical approaches to this, and their relative complexity and efficacy accounts in part for the wide difference in price between entry-level and high-end calibration products.

Calibrating a printer is tougher because its end result is on paper rather than in the computer. Some products allow you to calibrate printer output with your scanner, but most scanners, even if previously calibrated, really are not accurate enough to do this well. Instead, it is preferable to invest in a spectrophotometer or colorimeter, devices dedicated to measuring colour. Colorimeters read values from a colour target, supplied as an image file, which you output on the printer to be calibrated.

One device that really must be calibrated is your monitor. Again, you can calibrate with a colorimeter; models from companies such as GretagMacbeth are available for less than the price of an image-editing program and work with most cathode ray tube (CRT) and liquid crystal display (LCD) screens. Alternatively, you can buy professional monitors that come with their own colorimeter and calibration software, such as the Sony Color Reference System. If neither of these options is within your budget, the next best thing is to calibrate your monitor subjectively, using either the Apple Display Calibrator (Mac OS only) or Adobe Gamma (supplied with Photoshop for both Mac and PC).

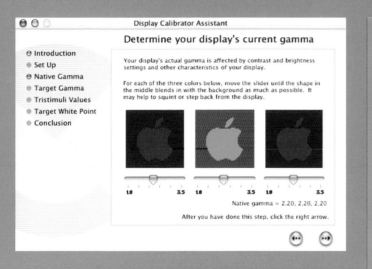

Above: **Monitors can be calibrated by eye to improve colour fidelity without incurring any extra expense.**

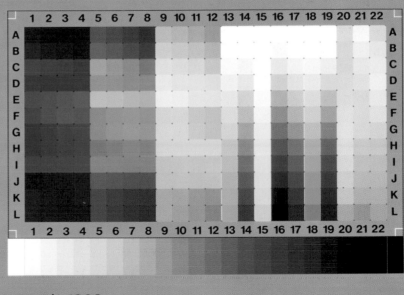

IT8.7/1-1993
2003:02

FUJICHROME PROVIA

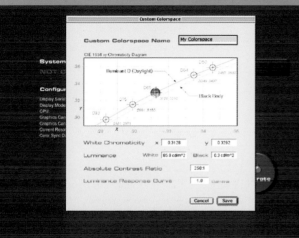

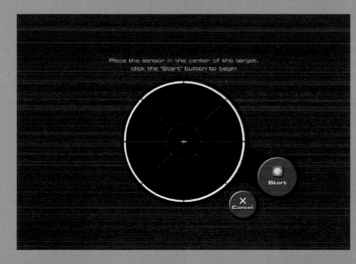

Left and below: **Professional monitors such as the Sony Color Reference System come with integral colour-management systems. A colorimeter is attached to the screen to enable automatic calibration, which should be updated every few weeks.**

Above: **IT8 colour targets are often used in calibration for colour management. The charts are supplied as photographic prints or transparencies for scanners and cameras, and as digital files for printers.**

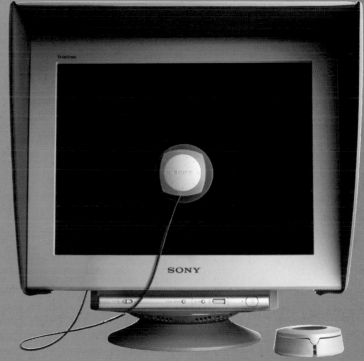

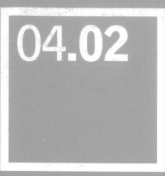

04.02

CAPTURING COLOUR

In October 1969, US physicists at Bell Labs in New Jersey sketched out a new semiconductor they called a charge-coupled device (CCD). A key element in digital imaging, the CCD is often likened to a set of buckets on a conveyor belt. When light, in the form of photons, falls on the CCD chip, free electrons are generated. These collect in millions of tiny packets of electrical charge – the buckets – which can then be moved along, a row at a time. At the end of the belt, the buckets are emptied into a separate memory. The number of electrons in each bucket corresponds to the brightness of the light that fell on that area of the chip, so the data from the whole array builds up a complete image.

CCD chips are divided into three main types: full-frame, interline and linear. Full-frame CCDs collect electrons for as long as light is allowed to fall on them and so, just like film, will only record an image successfully if their exposure is limited mechanically by a camera shutter. Once the shutter closes, all the data is shunted off at once, which takes a significant fraction of a second. Interline CCDs have additional components – extra buckets – into which data can be shifted at any time, thus registering the amount of light that has fallen on the chip so far and acting as a virtual shutter. This allows much faster updating but means that the sensor itself is squashed into less than half the space allocated to it in the array, limiting image quality. Linear chips are used in scanners, grabbing small amounts of data and moving on very quickly.

All CCDs are monochromic – they can detect only the amount of light striking them, not its colour – so colour images are captured via a colour filter array (CFA), which is placed over the CCD during the manufacturing process. This blocks out all but one primary colour from each cell in the array, so that some record only red, some only green and some only blue. The result is three colour channels, each with holes where the other-coloured pixels lie; the holes are then filled by interpolation to complete the image.

Although CCDs predominate, some digital cameras use image sensors based on complementary metal-oxide semiconductor (CMOS) technology -- similar to the transistors used inside computers – and some scanners have contact image sensor (CIS) components in place of CCDs. In both cases, the benefits are in cost and space savings, not in improved quality. On the other hand, many drum scanners used by reprographics houses are based on the older technology of the photomultiplier tube (PMT). PMTs are more accurate than CCDs, but the machinery surrounding them is complicated.

photosensitive cells in a charge-coupled device
(CCD). The chips are used in digital cameras and
scanners to convert light into digital signals,
bringing images of the real world into the computer.

USING A FLATBED SCANNER The flatbed scanner may not be featured in many lists of the twentieth century's greatest technological innovations, but its development has been remarkable. In the early 1990s, it was an expensive luxury for large creative agencies and publishing houses. Today, scanners have dropped in price to such an extent that the cheapest, starting at £50, are almost disposable – yet they offer resolutions of up to 1,200 dpi at fair speeds. Professional-quality models are now available for under £1,500.

Why such a broad price range? Resolution is a bit of a red herring here: you can buy a machine capable of 4,800 dpi for under £500, yet a specialist machine costing three times that much may offer less. Remember that image quality is determined not only by the number of pixels, but by how accurately the colour of each pixel is measured. Most scanners now devote extra memory to each pixel, using 36 or 48 bits instead of 24. This says nothing, however, about how well the hardware initially captures colour. One indication of fidelity is dynamic range. Optical density is measured on a scale of 0 (pure white) to 4 (pure black), and the dynamic range of a scanner is expressed by a figure representing the proportion of this range it can distinguish. A cheap scanner may be rated as low as 2.4, while a high-quality model might claim 3.8.

This is still by no means the whole story, and to understand the rest we need to look under the lid. The image to be digitized is placed face down on the glass bed. Below this, the image sensor (CCD or CIS) is mounted on a motorized arm, along with a lamp, in an assembly referred to as the scanning head. After you close the lid and initiate the scan, the lamp comes on and the image sensor begins to record a line of pixels across the width of the bed. Since a full-width sensor is expensive and unwieldy, a complicated array of lenses and mirrors is used to direct light from successive sections

Above: **Low-cost flatbed colour scanners can now be bought for well under £150 and produce reasonable results, though they won't satisfy serious users. Unlike cheap printers, they don't incur any running costs.**

Below: **Professional desktop scanners like the Creo Eversmart cost several thousand pounds, but they justify their price with significantly higher accuracy and colour fidelity.**

onto the sensor, which rolls the data into memory. Having completed the width, the scanning head moves a fraction of an inch down the length of the bed and the process begins again.

Given the high speed at which all this is done and the tiny size of the image sensor, the quality of the lenses and mirrors – the optics – can have as significant an effect on the final result as that of the electronics. In fact, these mechanical components are rather difficult to manufacture and assemble with absolute precision: hence the price premium for better-quality flatbeds.

The across-and-down method of scanning also gives rise to the dual-resolution figures quoted for flatbeds, such as 2,400 x 4,800 dpi. The smaller figure is a function of the image sensor, while the larger one refers to the smallest step in which the scanning head can move. Before the image is delivered to your computer, extra pixels are interpolated to bring the width into proportion with the height. Interpolation can also enlarge the whole image, but it gives no better results than scaling up in your image editor – and any manufacturers' claims for interpolated resolution should be ignored.

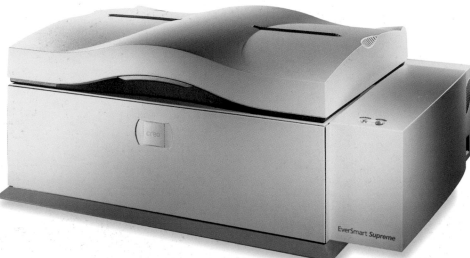

SilverFast v6.1.0r7

SilverFast Ai

General | **Frame** | Densitometer

Scan Type: 48->24 Bit ...
Filter: Auto Sharpen
Setting: Save
Image Type: Standard

Name
Paint_Wall

	Original	Scale %		Output	
↔	3.0	100.0		3.0	inch
↕	4.0	100.0		4.0	inch

Q-Factor | Screen | | Mbyte
1.5 | 100 | lpi | 0.77
| | | 150 | dpi

(Prescan) (Scan) (Quit)

SilverFast EPSON GT-9800

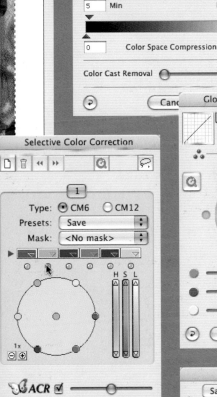

Histogram

25 Shadow | L | 0 | Highlight 232
5 Min | | Max 249
0 | Color Space Compression | 255
Color Cast Removal | --- %

(Cancel)

Global Color Correction

192	128	64
192	128	64
192	128	64

(Cancel) (OK)

Selective Color Correction

1

Type: ⦿ CM6 ◯ CM12
Presets: Save
Mask: <No mask>

H S L

1x

ACR ☑

(Cancel) (OK)

Gradation Curves

Save...

| 0 | 29 | 67 | 139 | 178 | 222 | 255 |

L | 0
| 2
△ | -6
▲ | 1
☼ | 0

(Cancel) (OK)

This page: **The image-capture software supplied with your scanner will display a preview image of whatever is on the scanning bed alongside various options to control how it will be digitized. Resolution and colour mode are the ones everyone needs to master. Tonal controls should generally be left on automatic, but some adjusting may be necessary either to correct individual images or to tailor the scanner's general performance to the designer's preference or the visual style of a particular job. Sharpening can be applied to** compensate for the slight softening inevitably incurred by digitization, and descreening can remove interference patterns from images scanned from halftoned originals (such as newspapers). The usual sequence of events is to generate a preview image first, which should only take a few seconds; drag the rectangle in the preview window to capture the area within it; adjust the settings if necessary, based on the appearance of the preview; and finally click Scan. Very high-resolution scans may take several minutes to complete.

USM & Descreening

not Descreened | Descreened and Sharpened

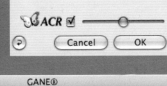

☑ preview Moiré | 1x | (Prescan) | ☐ Monochrome

Descreening Parameters
Screen: Magazine (... | 133 | lpi

☑ use Unsharp Masking
Unsharp Masking Parameters
Intensity: | 50 | %
Threshold: | 1.0 | % K
Matrix: 3 x 3 Pixel
Presets: <Save>

(Cancel) (OK)

GANE®

Grain & Noise visible | Grain & Noise eliminated

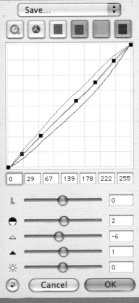

1x | (Prescan) | ☐ Monochrome

GANE® Parameters
Presets: Medium G...

(Cancel) (OK)

USING A DIGITAL CAMERA After many false starts that provoked photographers to write them off as expensive novelties, digital cameras are finally starting to compete seriously with film. By early 2003, good-quality compacts were available for well under £400, and for around £800, you could buy a single-lens reflex (SLR) model suitable for at least semiprofessional use. The Four Thirds format, established in late 2003, uses much larger CCDs for better image quality and sets standards for components and accessories designed specifically for digital cameras, rather than using those borrowed from film camera technology.

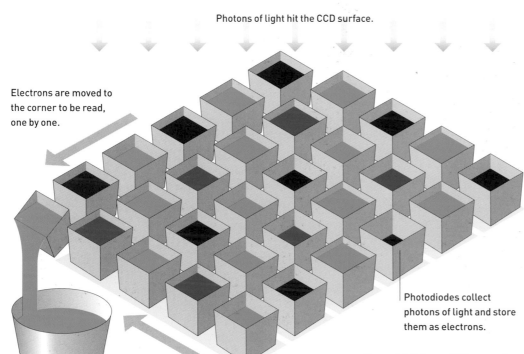

Photons of light hit the CCD surface.

Electrons are moved to the corner to be read, one by one.

Photodiodes collect photons of light and store them as electrons.

Above: A full-frame CCD, as used in professional digital cameras, continues to gather light as long as the shutter is open, much like film. The cells are then read one by one – hence the lag time digital cameras are prone to. Interline CCDs, typically used in cheaper cameras, are less effective but update continuously for live LCD previews.

counts, note that the total number of pixels in the image sensor is not the best indicator of image resolution. The legitimate reason for this is that some pixels at the edges are covered with a black dye, and the reading taken from this is used to calibrate the image. This may account for the number of pixels actually recorded being up to 10 per cent lower than the total. A less legitimate reason for larger discrepancies is that manufacturers may build an existing CCD into a less capable camera model, disabling the pixels that cannot be recorded because, for example, the lens is smaller. Always check the number of recorded pixels or effective pixels. As with scanners, also beware of quoted image-size options that refer to interpolated results.

The higher the resolution, of course, the more memory is required to store pictures. Most cameras accept cards in standard formats such as SmartMedia, CompactFlash and Memory Stick, which are now quite cheap to buy in sizes from 16 MB to 256 MB. You can carry around as many cards as you like and swap them in and out. For larger storage requirements, the better cameras support MicroDrive hard disks, tiny plug-in units with capacities of several gigabytes (thousands of megabytes). When you get back to the computer, you can transfer images from the camera either through a USB cable or by removing the memory card and inserting it into a card-reading device attached (again, usually through USB) to the computer.

Resolution remains the chief limitation of affordable units. Image size is quoted in megapixels, an invented unit that may mean either 1,048,576 pixels, as binary arithmetic would dictate, or 1 million pixels, as some manufacturers prefer to think. So a 15-by-10-cm photo at 300 dpi – 1,800 by 1,200 pixels – would require 2 megapixels. By late 2003, cameras costing under £1,000 were limited to a maximum of 5 to 6 megapixels – barely enough to fill an 20-by-25-cm page at print resolution, let alone catering to the need to blow up or crop pictures, which multiplies the number of pixels required. Specifications should continue to improve rapidly, however. For example, Foveon® has developed a sensor array in which three photo-sensors are embedded vertically in the silicon wafer at each pixel site. Although this doesn't directly affect the resolution, it will lead to greater colour accuracy, which in turn may help when interpolating images. When comparing pixel

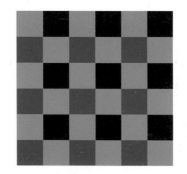

Left: The GRGB pattern is commonly used in CCD colour-filter arrays. To construct a complete image, the camera interpolates the missing pixels of each colour.

To minimize storage requirements, most consumer cameras use JPEG file compression (*see page 202*), which means that image quality has already been compromised before you get the picture into the computer. Better models offer the alternative of compressed TIFF format, which saves some space without affecting the pixels. But the best option of all is RAW, which preserves all of the data recorded and ensures that colour is correctly interpreted when the image is downloaded to the computer. This requires camera-specific software that is normally supplied with your camera as a standalone program, but it may also be available as a Photoshop plug-in.

Digital cameras are by far the hardest type of device to colour-calibrate, since the colour recorded on any given occasion will be strongly affected by the colour temperature of the light source. Unless you work as a studio photographer who needs to accurately match a known colour – as opposed to using a digital camera just to generate raw material that will be creatively reworked on the computer – the tools, skills and time required for meaningful calibration will probably not be worth the effort.

If you do want to calibrate your camera, products and advice are available from companies such as Integrated Color Corporation (www.integrated-colour.com).

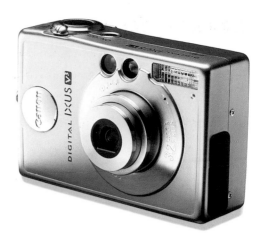

Right: **Compact digital cameras such as the Canon Ixus series pack a lot of technology into a tiny case, but then usually lack the manual controls that serious photographers look for.**
Below: **Professional digital cameras have generally been based on existing SLR film camera components, but there is now a trend towards formats that have been developed for digital from the ground up. Resolutions up to 13 megapixels are now available.**

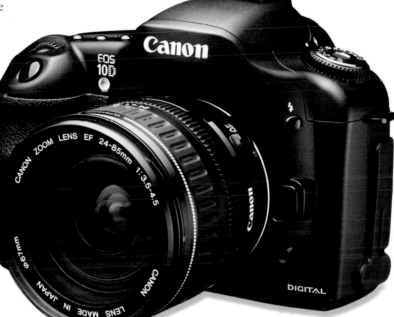

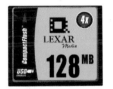

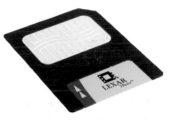

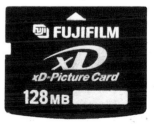

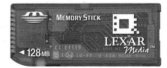

Right: **Various types of memory card are used to store images in the camera. If you're working at high resolutions, even a 128-MB card will quickly fill up. Some cameras allow a MicroDrive format hard disk to be attached so you can take gigabytes of pictures without returning to the computer.**

Left: **This chart compares the pixel dimensions and physical reproduction size of camera images from 0.3 to 4.3 megapixels.**

6

4

2

2400x1800
4.3m

2048x1536
3m

1600x1200
2m

1280x960
1.2m

640x480
0.3m

inches
at 300dpi

2   4   6   8

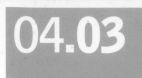

04.03

PART 04. DIGITAL COLOUR

CHAPTER THREE

PRINTING COLOUR

While a monitor emits light, enabling additive mixing of red, green and blue frequencies, printing out artwork takes us back into the realm of pigments and subtractive mixing of reflected light. The primary colours, therefore, are cyan, magenta and yellow. As we saw in chapter 01.04, these are mixed in the printing process not by combining pigments before applying them to the page, as in traditional painting techniques, but by dividing images into proportional numbers or sizes of dots of each ink.

Colour printing based on inks of these hues is referred to as 'process' or 'CMYK' (*see page 27*). The fourth ink is black, termed K to avoid confusion with blue (B), although the initial can also stand for 'key', since the black plate in a process colour job may be used as the reference to which the other three colours are aligned. The order of the letters refers to the order in which the plates are printed, which is significant because the inks used are translucent, and dots of each may overlap. Cyan, the strongest of the three primaries, goes first, since it will be least compromised by any overlying dots of subsequent inks. Black, on the other hand, goes last, mainly so that solid black text and line work can overprint, obliterating any inks underneath without having to erase corresponding areas of the relevant plates.

Progress in the manufacturing of pigments has resulted in inks that are optimized to give the best possible results. Nonetheless, three problems are inherent in subtractive mixing. The first is generating black: overlaying 100 per cent of all the primaries never gives an absolutely pure and solid black. The second is linearization: equal percentages of all three primaries may not give a neutral grey. Both of these are addressed by the use of black ink. The third problem is gamut: the total proportion of the visible spectrum covered by combinations of CMY inks is significantly smaller than that of most RGB spaces.

Here again, the answer is to add more inks. Spot colours can be used on their own for jobs requiring only black and one or two solid colours (as opposed to continuous-tone work like photos), or in conjunction with CMYK to reproduce a particular colour that cannot be achieved in process colour. These inks are specified as reference numbers within a recognized palette such as Pantone or Toyo. A magazine cover might use CMYK plus a fluorescent or metallic spot for the masthead. A more recent trend is to use spot colours as extra primaries in 'hi-fi colour' processes. Pantone's Hexachrome system, for example, uses vivid orange and green inks with slightly adjusted cyan, magenta and yellow to give a considerably extended gamut.

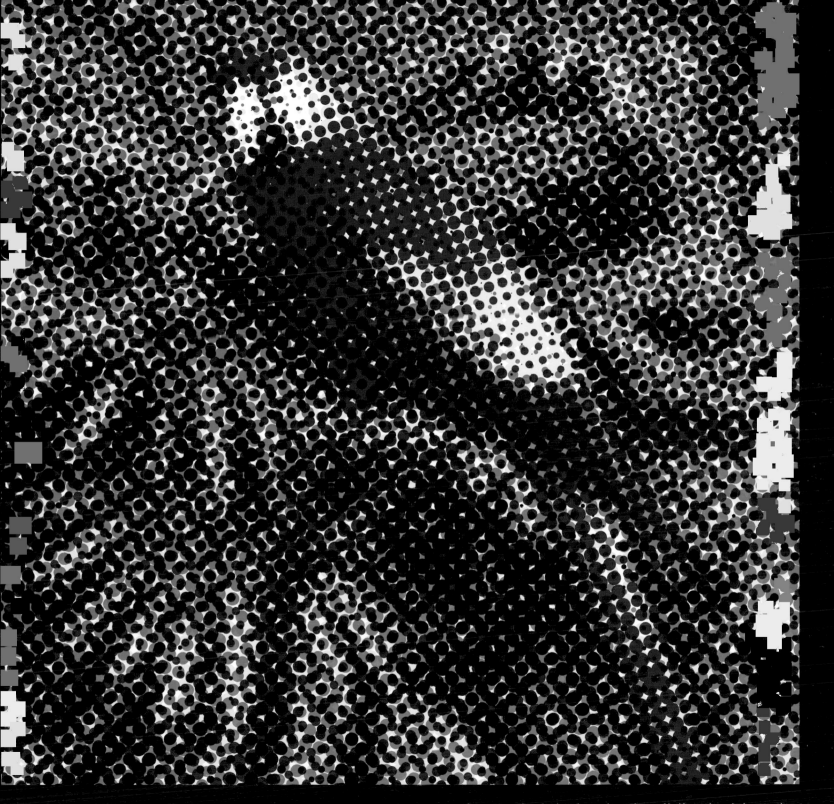

A process-printed colour image is made up of halftone dots. As long as the
line screen – the distance between dot centres – is small enough, we see
the picture, not the dots. In practice, halftone 'rosettes' are quite easily
visible in certain tints. Try looking closely at other pictures in this book.

COLOUR PRINTING PRINCIPLES Offset lithography is the method used to print most magazines and illustrated books. Although it seems complicated, in practice it can offer excellent quality at a reasonable price. The cost of setting up a job on a press, however, means that short runs work out to be very expensive. Digital presses are usually the best option in these cases.

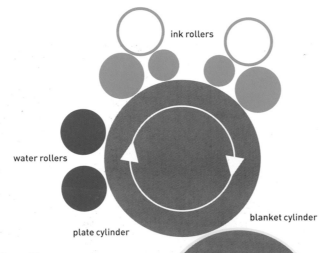

ink rollers

water rollers

plate cylinder

blanket cylinder

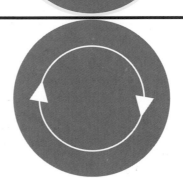

press sheet

impression cylinder

Plates are conventionally generated from film separations, acetate sheets printed with the cyan, magenta, yellow and black components of a page. The acetates are produced by a machine called an imagesetter. More recently, since the advent of computer-to-plate (CTP) technology, plates are increasingly being made by a platesetter, which use lasers in the creation of the plates. Either way, software called an RIP (raster image processor) generates the colour separations from the original digital artwork.

The time-honoured method of preparing images for reproduction is halftone screening (*see page 58*), and this is simulated by the RIP. Each plate is broken up into dots whose centres are fixed to a grid but whose size varies according to the amount of colour required. The size of the grid, or line screen ruling, is quoted in lines per inch (lpi). A typical value for a high-quality colour print, as used in magazine work, is 133 lpi.

A further step is necessary for digital output: the halftone dots themselves must be converted into a bitmap of fixed resolution. To provide sufficient resolution to render the halftone dots clearly, imagesetters work at around 2,400 dpi. Any solid colour fields, such as vector text and line work, need not be halftoned and are rasterized directly at this high resolution, producing crisp edges.

Where does the 300 dpi image resolution recommended for print output (*see page 158*) fit into all this? Since only 133 discrete coloured points per inch can be formed in a 133 lpi screen, an image resolution of 133 dpi would seem adequate. In practice, however, the pixels will not line up precisely with the screen. As a result, increasing the resolution does improve print quality, but only up to between two and two-and-a-half times the line screen: hence the 300 dpi norm for 133 lpi output.

The somewhat roundabout approach of halftoning the image, then bitmapping the halftone, was adopted by early prepress systems mostly because conventional printing techniques were based on halftoned plates. A more direct approach is to rasterize each plate

Left: The most common technology for commercial process colour printing is offset lithography. An aluminium or plastic plate is produced from the artwork, with non-image areas chemically treated to repel ink. The plate is then wrapped round a cylinder that rotates in contact with an ink roller and a rubber cylinder, or blanket. Ink coats the image areas and is transferred to the blanket, which in turn rolls it onto the paper. The process is repeated for each of the four (or more) colours, often in one pass, with paper passing between cylinders for each ink colour.

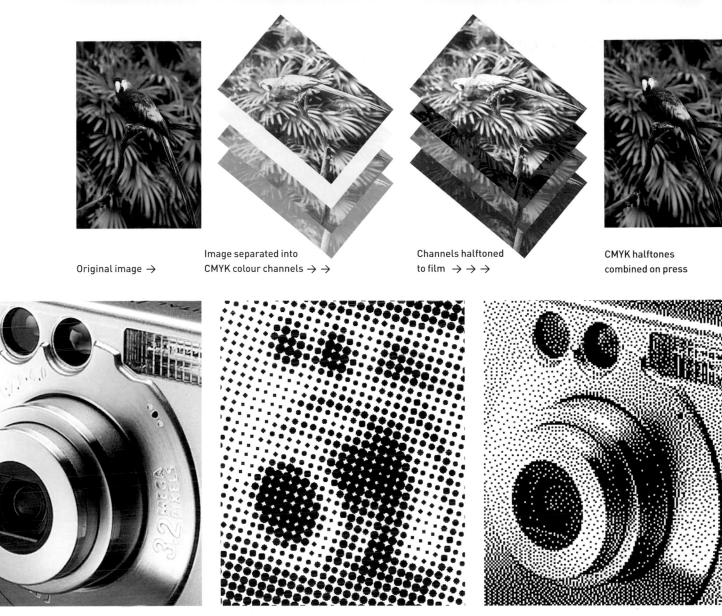

Original image →

Image separated into
CMYK colour channels → →

Channels halftoned
to film → → →

CMYK halftones
combined on press

using a form of dithering. This is described as frequency modulated (FM), or stochastic, screening, since it works by varying the number of dots, as opposed to amplitude modulated (AM), in which the size of the dots varies. FM screening has several advantages. The line screens of halftoned separations must be precisely angled in relation to each other to avoid moiré, an unwanted large-scale rippling effect formed by interference between regular patterns. This is unnecessary with FM screening, since the arrangement of the dots is random. Hi-fi colour processes such as Hexachrome rely on FM screening, because there are not enough non-conflicting angles to cover all the plates, and it is also the norm in desktop inkjet printers.

Because dots do not have to be shoehorned into a halftone pattern, FM screening can produce smoother-looking print. One catch, however, is that completely random placement risks clumping of dots, so pseudo-random programming methods or algorithms are used to optimize quality.

Above: **Halftone, or AM, screening** (centre) started life as an optical method of dividing images into printable dots. Now that computer technology allows us to break up images any way we want, FM, or stochastic, screening (right, shown in monochrome for clarity) is looking like a better way for most purposes.

Top: **Once the colour data in an image is converted from RGB to CMYK, each pixel has cyan, magenta, yellow and black values. Separating these results in four colour channels, greyscale images from which the printing plates are made, either directly from computer or by first printing onto acetate film. After the plates are used to print each separation in the appropriate ink, the image is reproduced.**

COLOUR PRINTING TECHNOLOGIES

Inkjet is the most versatile option for everyday digital colour output. Printers available for under £100 can produce pages rivalling any glossy magazine, as well as photos almost indistinguishable from an original print. Pricier models offer a number of extra advantages.

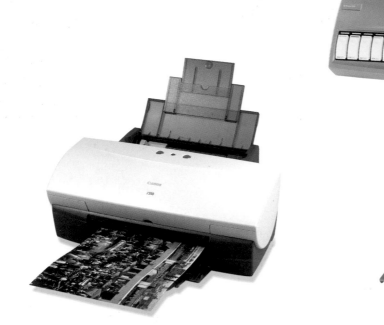

Size is one: while letter-size printers may suffice for business use, the graphic artist will often be working on a larger scale. Full-bleed A4 printers are available from around £300, while A3 devices start at a little more than twice this price.

Colour fidelity is another differentiating factor. Low-cost inkjets are designed to turn out crowd-pleasing results, often oversaturating colours and sacrificing accuracy as they do so. Machines designed for faithful reproduction of ICC-managed colour, however, start at around £700. These have revolutionized proofing, the task of producing printed output that simulates what will appear on press, without having to run the press to produce an expensive wet proof.

Until a few years ago, accurate colour proofs could only be generated using film-based chemical transfer systems with brand names such as Cromalin and Matchprint, owned by imagesetting companies rather than designers, at a total cost to the client of

Above left: Desktop inkjet printers can be purchased at very low prices, and even the cheapest should produce reasonable colour. The catch is, the cost of the inks can outstrip the hardware purchase price within a year.

Above right: Large-format inkjet printers are now common in print shops and design studios, and can work with a variety of printable media to produce striking display graphics.

around £50 per sheet. Inkjets can now deliver comparable results on your own desktop for a tenth of that price, partly thanks to six-ink processes whose gamut exceeds that of any CMYK press. A prerequisite for proof-quality output is a good RIP, either built into the printer or supplied as a software package for your computer. More basic inkjet devices do not have an RIP and cannot interpret PostScript, instead relying on your graphics software to rasterize pages.

Inkjet technology also powers a growing number of digital presses. Digital presses compete for short-run jobs, where the digital press's relatively high cost per page and low speed are outweighed by the platemaking and setup costs of litho. Rather than hire an imagesetting company to produce film separations, you can simply send a digital file to the printer, normally in PostScript or PDF format. This must be correctly created, however, with all the appropriate prepress settings – a tricky job for anyone not already well versed in reprographic lore. Your printer should be able to offer advice on the specifics.

Digital presses incorporate ICC colour management, as do RIPs, but what happens after plates go on a litho press is another matter. Traditionally, the press would be calibrated using its manufacturer's own system, and a skilled operator might check the first few pages of a job against a supplied

Right: Continuous-tone printing would allow the amount of ink applied to vary without screening, but few technologies allow this in practice.

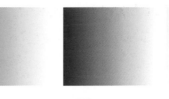

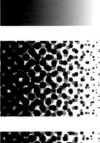

Right: CMYK printing halftones each colour channel using a different screen angle. Light tints tend to 'drop out' to white as very tiny dots disappear.

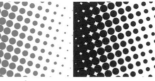

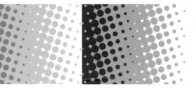

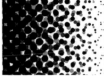

Right: Some inkjet printers add paler cyan and magenta inks to the usual four. This helps fill in the gaps, giving smoother tints and rescuing light areas.

Below: Digital presses have become commonplace over the last few years. The technologies used and the most economical run lengths vary among models, but all tend to be easier to operate and maintain than offset litho presses. As with litho, more than four inks can be used to extend the range of colours reproducible.

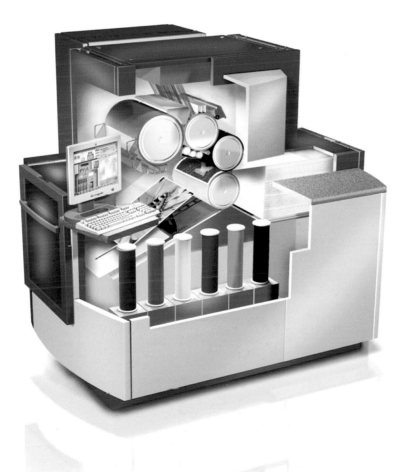

proof before making any necessary adjustments. Nonetheless, a degree of variation is to be expected. Some presses now use feedback from sensors to recalibrate output automatically during the course of a job, helping to keep colour more consistent. If precise colour matching is critical, discuss this with the printer.

Alternative colour-output technologies include laser printing, solid ink, dye sublimation and laser-exposed photographic printing. Desktop colour laser printers have fallen to reasonable prices, from under £700, but are still chosen for speed – typically in an office context – rather than image quality. Solid ink printers, available almost exclusively under the Tektronix brand from Xerox, squirt liquefied wax onto the paper to build up an image. Although affordable, they are not as attractive as inkjets to most users, although solid-ink printers can cope with a wider range of paper types.

Dye sublimation allows ink quantity to vary continually over the page, without the need for screening, but printing tends to be slow and materials expensive; dedicated photo printers, which plug directly into digital cameras, are their most common incarnation. Finally, the laser exposure method, mainly used in photo processing stores, constructs a digital image in place of a negative. It is then reproduced by conventional photographic processing, allowing traditional photo prints to be generated from digital camera shots or other image files.

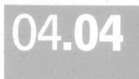

PART 04. DIGITAL COLOUR

CHAPTER FOUR

DISPLAYING COLOUR

Producing artwork to be published on screen – whether on a Web site or in a physical location such as an interactive kiosk – could not be more different from designing for print. Not only do you have your pick of all those millions of colours, but you can work directly on the final image. Rather than go through processes such as halftoning, which are beyond your direct control, your artwork remains exactly as you create it.

The issue of resolution has quite different implications in display work than in print production. When you view a bitmapped image that you are planning to print, there is no such thing as actual size. If your image is destined for the screen, however, you can work at the same resolution on the same pixels your audience will see. One benefit of this is that you can work in extremely fine detail. Very small lettering and very fine shading will not survive the printing process unscathed. On screen, you can draw a dotted line consisting of spaced single pixels in the knowledge that everything will remain intact.

Images for print need not be precisely sized, since it makes little difference whether the final output works out to 300 dpi or, say, 287 dpi. On screen, however, the number of pixels dictates physical size, so at some point you must resize your image to exactly the required dimensions. Because this involves resampling (*see page 158*), resizing can disrupt pixels in a way similar to printing, so it should be done before working on any fine detail. On the other hand, filters and effects are best applied before downsizing – with the image at twice the final resolution or greater – so that any pixel-level glitches will be smoothed out in resampling.

Vector graphics remain resolution-independent whether printed or displayed (*see page 158*), but the advantages of this are limited in on-screen work. Rather than exploiting the high resolution of the imagesetter, the quality of a vector graphic is limited by the dot pitch of the screen, and any slight inaccuracies in rasterizing will be more visible than in print. Due to their low resolution, bitmaps for display take up much less memory than those for print, so the efficiency benefit of vectors is reduced. And the viewer needs more complex software to interpret vector graphics. As a result, most still images for display are delivered as bitmaps; even artwork produced in vector-drawing packages is converted to a bitmap before being incorporated into a website or CD-ROM. Vector delivery is very popular for animation, however, with the Macromedia Flash format accounting for the majority of animated content on the Web.

Apple's Cinema Display epitomizes the quality and fidelity of today's LCD colour monitors. Unfortunately, most users have rather less impressive screens on their desks, and anyone designing for the Internet must consider how these are likely to display their work.

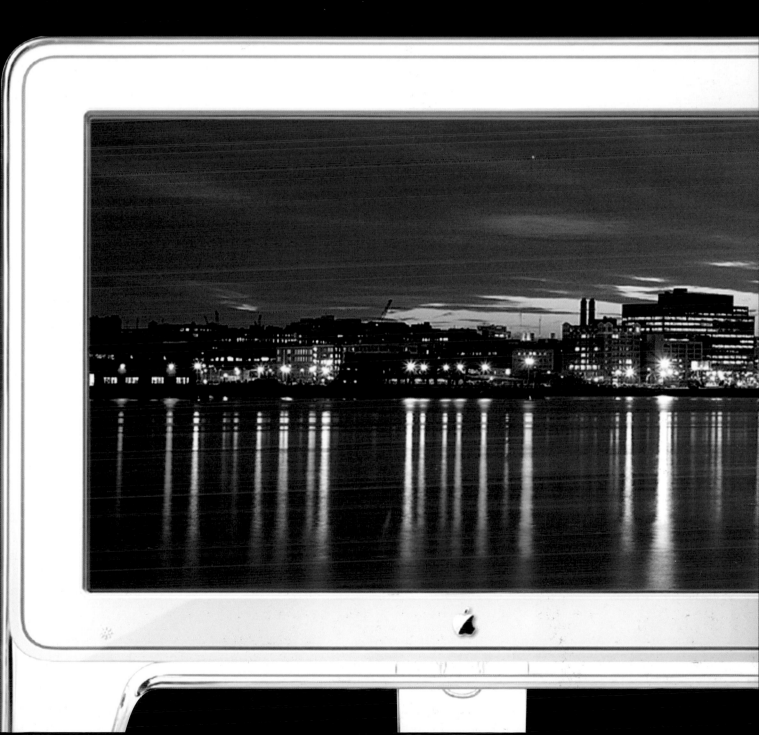

COLOUR DISPLAY TECHNOLOGIES

COLOUR DISPLAY TECHNOLOGIES Most computers are equipped with monitors based on a cathode ray tube (CRT), the same technology used in TV sets. Compared with the elegant solid-state electronics inside the computer, the CRT is an unwieldy contraption that resists all attempts at miniaturization. But it does deliver excellent picture quality, not least owing to its high brightness.

LCD monitor

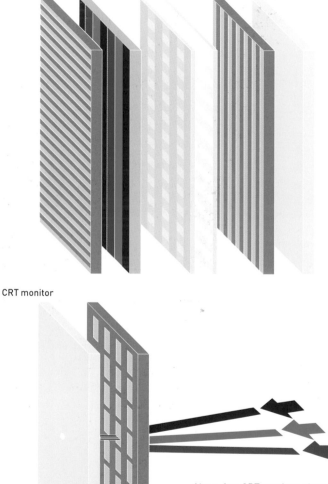

CRT monitor

This is a key factor in colour reproduction, because the difference between black (no illumination) and white (maximum illumination) dictates the overall tonal range of the display. Since the monitor cannot generate black any darker than the manufactured colour of the screen, it needs to make white as light as possible.

LCD (liquid crystal display), the most successful solid-state monitor technology, struggles to compete with the brightness of CRT. Illumination is provided by an array of lamps that 'backlight' the entire screen, and the luminance of each dot is determined by the variable opacity of a liquid crystal cell in front. Not only does this arrangement tend to limit brightness, but it means that perceived luminance varies depending on the angle of view. This effect may even be detectable within the area of the screen, so that colours at the edges look different from those in the middle. The best LCD monitors do now offer brightness and consistency comparable to CRTs and are increasingly being adopted by graphics professionals.

Monitors offer a number of user controls, the two most familiar being brightness and contrast. Confusingly, it is the contrast control that dictates the maximum luminance level, or what in plain English we might call brightness. It should now be obvious that reducing contrast limits the display's tonal range, and that the contrast setting should therefore normally be set to maximum. The brightness control governs the black point: the higher the setting, the more luminance is applied to nominally black areas. So if the setting is too high, blacks will be too light, effectively reducing tonal range; if it is too low, dark colours will be 'clipped' to maximum black. LCDs have no brightness control, as their black point is fixed.

Above: In a CRT monitor, phosphors lining the screen are struck by streams of electrons from three cathodes, which are checked by a 'shadow mask' or 'aperture grille'. The phosphors emit red, green or blue light. In an LCD monitor, voltage applied to liquid crystal cells determines whether or not light is allowed to pass through; a colour filter produces the RGB elements of each pixel.

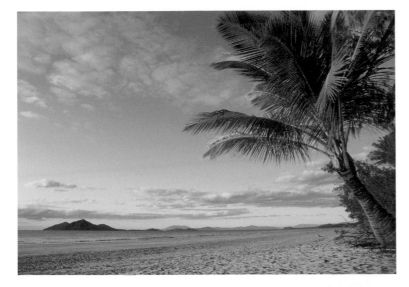
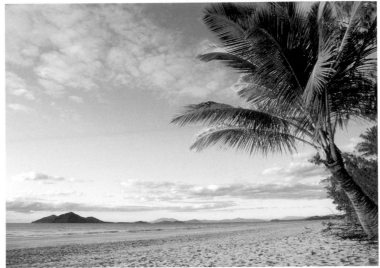
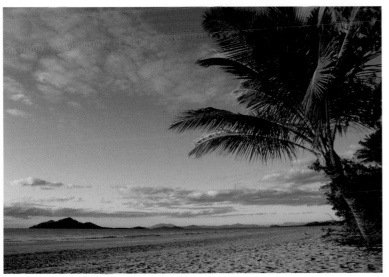
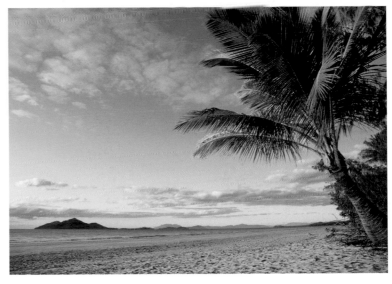

An important setting not usually provided on the monitor itself, but controllable by the computer driving the monitor, is gamma. Gamma describes the relationship between the colour value received by the monitor and the degree of illumination the monitor generates. A simple linear relationship would leave darker areas looking dim and muddy. Gamma correction makes brightness increase quickly as colour values rise from zero, then level off as they approach maximum. A higher value thus brings out detail in shadows and midtones without compromising highlights. Too high, however, and the whole image will look pale and washed-out.

Above, clockwise from top left: **An image will look best when its native colour space is translated into the widest tonal range with the least clipping. With the monitor's contrast setting reduced, a smaller tonal range is available, and the picture looks lifeless. Given maximum contrast, the brightness must also be set correctly. If it's too high, dark areas will be lightened, again reducing tonal range. Too low, and they will be clipped, losing detail from shadows. Because errors in both brightness and contrast settings can leave the picture lacking contrast, you may be unsure which to adjust, but the simple answer is always to turn contrast up fully and then alter brightness.**

Another key aspect of monitor colour reproduction is colour temperature. This governs the display's overall colour balance by defining the hue generated in white areas, where maximum illumination is applied. The scale refers to the colours generated by heating a black body, such as an electric stove element. So fairly hot is red, hotter still yellow and very hot is blue.

Since all of these controls are preset variously by manufacturers, and can then be adjusted at will by users, it is an unfortunate fact that every monitor displays colour differently. Colour management (*see page 164*) can greatly increase consistency, but few owners outside the graphics industry will practice it. This means that, no matter how effective your own colour management, you cannot rely on colours in your artwork to appear the same on the viewer's monitor as on yours.

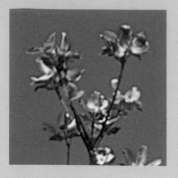

Original image at 300dpi. It is reduced to 64 x 64 pixels to the right, and a dotted border added to compare compression effects.

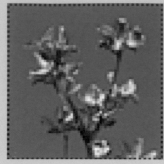

Compression: None (TIFF)
File size: 628 K
Download – 56 K modem: 90 secs

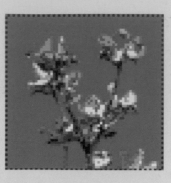

Compression: GIF 16 colours
File size: 1.129 K
Download – 56 K modem: 1 sec

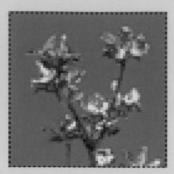

Compression: GIF 32 colours
File size: 1.772 K
Download – 56 K modem: 1 sec

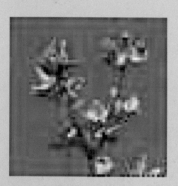

Compression: JPEG Low
File size: 0.91 K
Download – 56 K modem: 1 sec

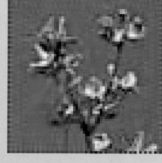

Compression: JPEG Medium
File size: 1.356 K
Download – 56 K modem: 1 sec

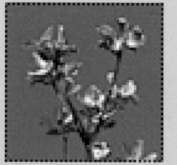

Compression: JPEG High
File size: 2.615 K
Download – 56 K modem: 1 sec

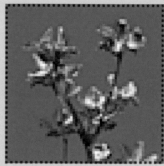

Compression: JPEG 100%
File size: 7.617 K
Download – 56 K modem: 2 secs

Above: A comparison of files sizes using various compression algorithms. All create significantly smaller files than the original, but the trade off can be seen in quality. In larger images, the effect on download times can be dramatic, so when saving for Web it's important to examine your options.

Below: In commercial websites, colour can be used to convey a mood (left) or provide navigational structure (right).

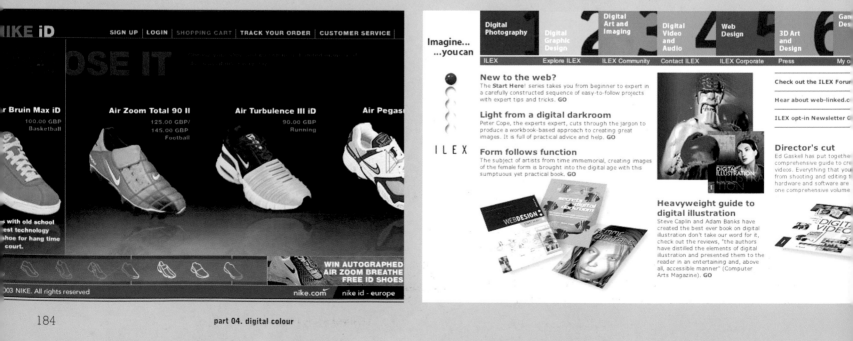

COLOUR ON THE WORLD WIDE WEB
The immediacy of designing for the screen is most keenly appreciated on the Web, where your artwork can be uploaded and accessible to millions of viewers within moments of being finished. Not that it necessarily has to be considered finished: unlike a file sent to the printer, a webpage can be altered at will, and you are rarely committed to the result for any great length of time. The Web does, however, impose its own restrictions.

While working in print, your concerns are all to do with reproduction; online, you also need to consider delivery. Imagine a parallel universe where print designers have to take into account the weight of ink: if they employ too many colours over too great an area, bookshops will find their shelves bending, distributors' vans will grind to a halt and readers will abandon books because it takes too much effort to turn the pages.

This illustrates the effects of limited Internet bandwidth. As we have seen (*see page 158*), every bitmapped image consists of a fixed number of pixels, each using a fixed amount of data to represent its colour. All of this data has to be conveyed from the server – the computer on which a website is stored – to the user trying to view it. The connection between the server and the Internet can handle only so much data; its owner, the Internet service provider (ISP), will operate a scale of charges to limit the amount its clients transfer. So the 'heavier' your website, the more it will cost to run.

The user's connection will be even more tightly limited. With a dial-up connection via modem, speed is limited to about 5 K (5 kilobytes) per second. A broadband connection, through a cable TV point or DSL (digital subscriber line) telephone line, typically offers about ten times this speed. Either way, the more data included in a webpage, the longer the user must wait for it to appear. Because an image filling the smallest typical Web browser window, 544 by 376 pixels, takes up 600 K, image size is a significant issue for users.

There are many ways to reduce the quantity of image data. One is to avoid using images, but in today's online environment, this is usually unacceptable. Another is to limit images to fairly small sizes, and a glance around the Web shows that this is the general practice. Fortunately, there are also technical solutions. The simplest is to reduce the number of bits per pixel. The GIF file format, which uses 8-bit colour rather than 24-bit, is widely utilized for this purpose. A colour look-up table (*see page 163*) is stored along with each image and is usually optimized to represent it as accurately as possible. A standard CLUT called the Web-safe colour palette was briefly popular, but it is now rarely used except in sites specifically designed to work on devices that do not support full 24-bit display.

A more versatile approach is data compression. In 'lossless' compression methods such as LZW (used in the TIFF file format), software analyses the image data and encodes it more efficiently – replacing 20 pixels of the same colour with an instruction giving the colour and the number of repeats, for example. Files are often reduced by 30 to 50 per cent. 'Lossy' methods, such as JPEG, do not preserve individual pixel values but break up the image into fields that are represented accurately enough to fool the eye and brain. Files can be reduced by almost any factor, at the expense of quality. JPEG is now very widely used on the Web for photographic images, while GIF is still the better option for graphics where every pixel counts, such as dividing lines and decorative details.

Below: **Aggressive data compression can squeeze almost anything into a website without demanding huge bandwidth, as long as you are preprared to sacrifice image quality. The home page of TV channel Five uses moving video as a background, with overlaid graphics in analogous colours.**

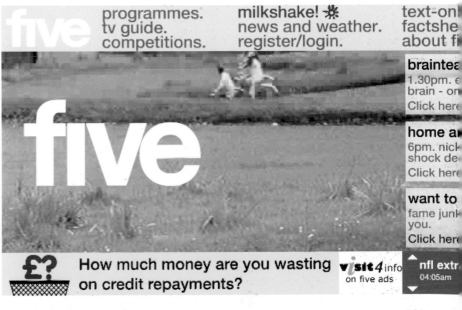

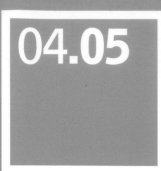

04.05

IMAGE MANIPULATION

Bitmap editing programs such as Photoshop provide many different ways to manipulate digitized photographs. All of these work by altering the colour values of pixels.

While you work, you should get into the habit of consulting Photoshop's Info palette. This shows the colour value wherever you hold the cursor over your image. When you bring up a dialog box to apply an adjustment, the Info palette shows what the current unadjusted colour value will be after the adjustment has been made. This allows you to check the effect of an adjustment before committing to it.

Not only does the Info palette show colour specifications in the mode you are working in – normally RGB – but it can also show what values will be produced when the image is converted to a different colour space, such as CMYK, using your current colour management settings (*see page 206*). If the value has to be adjusted to bring it within that colour space, an exclamation mark is shown next to it. For example, if you increase the saturation of an image, it may appear more vibrant in RGB, but it may not be possible to reproduce the effect in print. By watching the Info palette, you can avoid this problem.

Photoshop can work optionally with 16-colour bits per channel instead of the usual 8 bits (*see page 160*). The former is vastly more accurate and less prone to data loss during adjustments. It is debatable whether this feature will really benefit most users, however, and it can slow things down. The greatest benefits will be seen with images originally opened in 48-bit, whether from a scanner, a digital camera or a file supplied by another user. Check under Mode on the Image menu to see whether the image has 8 bits per channel or 16.

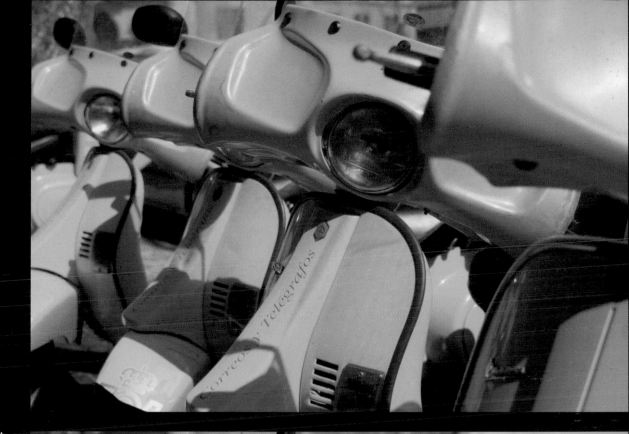

Right: The camera may not lie, but once you get the photo into the computer, you can make it say anything you want. Here a simple hue shift has been applied in Photoshop to give these scooters an instant paint job.

Below: The Info palette provides a constant colour reference, showing the specifications of the pixel under your cursor.

R :	35	C :	83%
G :	152	M :	6%
B :	142	Y :	43%
		K :	0%
X :	121.5	W :	
Y :	109.1	H :	

BASICS OF TONAL ADJUSTMENT

Anyone who has ever fiddled with the brightness, contrast and colour settings on their TV set has some experience manipulating the tone of a picture. To work successfully with photographic images, however, and produce results of professional quality, you need to familiarize yourself with smarter tools than these.

As we have seen, a digital image consists of a grid of pixels, each with a colour value. Most software tools for manipulating images work by applying a mathematical formula to all the colour values in an image. The simplest operations are linear, affecting all values equally. This is the case with the Brightness and Contrast controls provided in software. Their effects do not correspond directly to those of the knobs on the TV or monitor (*see page 182*) but they may still seem comfortably familiar. Unfortunately, they will rarely improve an image and are very likely to destroy colour information by compressing values into a narrower range or 'clipping' values near the ends of the scale, so that pixels that were previously different from each other, generating detail in the image, end up with the same value.

Nonlinear tonal adjustments may be harder to grasp at first but are much more successful. You can get a clearer idea of their effects by looking at a bar graph, or histogram, of an image's tonal range. Most image-editing programs can generate histograms, and the latest version of Photoshop can display it continually so that you can see the effect of any changes. The histogram plots value (dark to light) from left to right against pixel count (few to many) from bottom to top.

Below: The histogram seen here (displayed in Photoshop's Histogram palette) is typical of an image with good tonal range and balance. There is a fairly even distribution of values across the range from dark to light (left to right). About half the area is filled by the black bars, indicating that the graph has not been distorted by large numbers of pixels clustered around the same value. The 'humpbacked' shape of the graph shows pixel counts dropping off relatively smoothly towards each end of the scale, indicating that highlights and shadows have not been clipped.

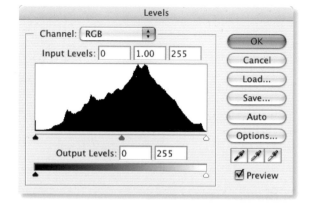

Above: The Levels dialog box provides the most versatile tonal controls. Like the other main correction tools, it is found under Adjustments on the Image menu in Photoshop. A histogram is displayed with the black (shadow), white (highlight) and midpoints marked by sliders. Dragging the black slider to the right pushes shadows towards the dark end of the scale; values to the left of this point will be clipped to black. The highlight slider works similarly. Moving the midpoint slider adjusts gamma (*see page 183*), making the image darker or lighter overall without affecting shadows or highlights. You can recall the last settings you applied by holding the Alt key (labelled Option on some Macintosh keyboards) while selecting the command from the menu or using its key shortcut (Command-L on the Mac, Ctrl-L on the PC). The same trick works with other adjustments.

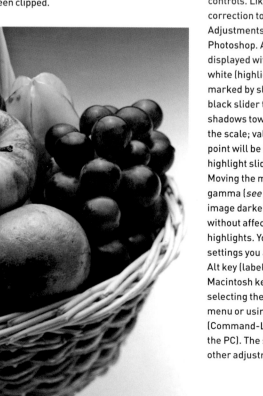

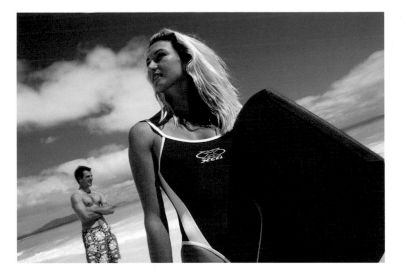

Above: This picture looks pretty good, and its histogram confirms the impression. Slightly excessive shadow is revealed by the peaks at the dark (left) end of the scale, indicating large numbers of pixels at these values.

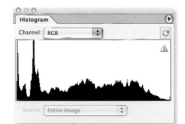

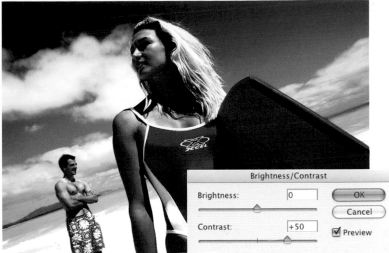

Above: Increasing the contrast makes the picture bolder, but at the expense of realism. Notice the 'spikes' off the very top of the scale at each end, showing that large numbers of pixels have been clipped to the same values. This leaves fewer pixels in between to give tonal variation.

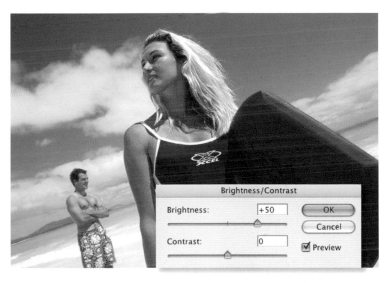

Above: Increasing the brightness of the image may seem the obvious way to bring out detail obscured by shadow. In fact, it squashes all the pixel values up towards the light end of the histogram, decreasing the overall tonal range and making the picture look washed out.

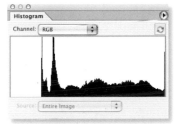

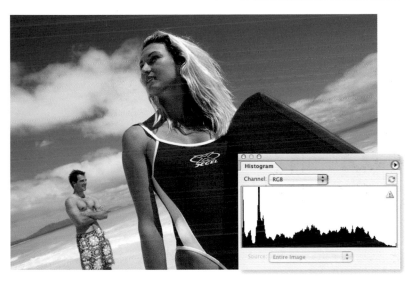

Above: Adjusting levels is a better method. The white slider is dragged to the last occupied value on the right. The grey (gamma) slider is then dragged slightly to the left to lighten midtones. There is no clipping, and the histogram is left looking healthy.

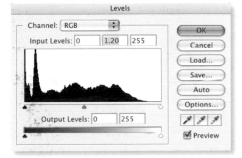

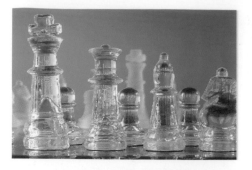

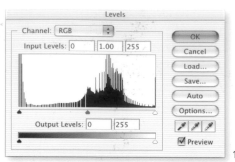

1

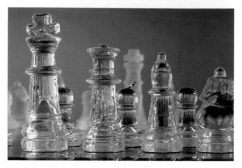

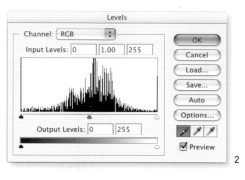

2

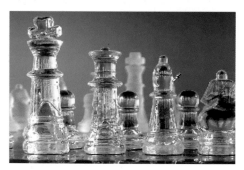

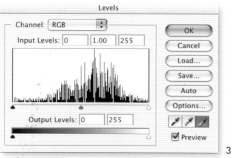

3

CURVES

The Curves dialog box (below) provides a different form of control over tonal range. Here, input is plotted on the horizontal axis and output on the vertical, with the relationship between the two represented by a curve. Initially this is a diagonal line, indicating a direct correspondence between input and output – no change to the image. By changing the shape of the line, you can vary the output. Click on the line to add a point, then drag it, and the line curves follow.

Dragging a point upwards generates a higher output for a given input, lightening midtones around that point. This can reveal detail in a picture that has been shot in moody lighting but is not simply too dark. Here, some areas are already bright, but we need to bring out others.

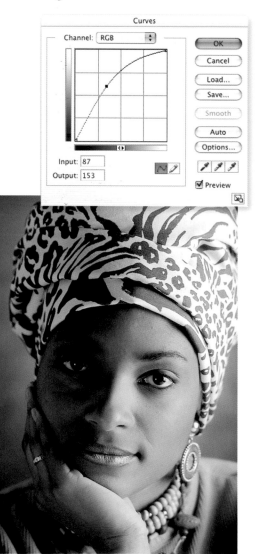

SETTING BLACK, WHITE AND MIDPOINTS

The Levels dialog box (above) also has three eyedropper tools that can pick values from within an image to use as the black, grey and white points. This can be very effective when it is not obvious where to move the sliders to improve a picture (1). Click the black eyedropper, then click on the darkest shadow in the image (2). Then click the white eyedropper and click on the brightest highlight (3). The midpoint is trickier to select, not least because it must be a neutral grey to give the correct colour balance; you may find it easier to adjust gamma using the grey slider. Try choosing different points to enhance contrast or correct colour. Photographers can include a test card showing pure black, grey and white swatches in a shot, then eyedropper these to correct the image automatically.

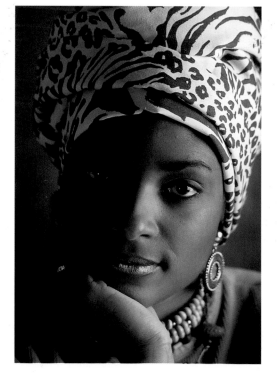

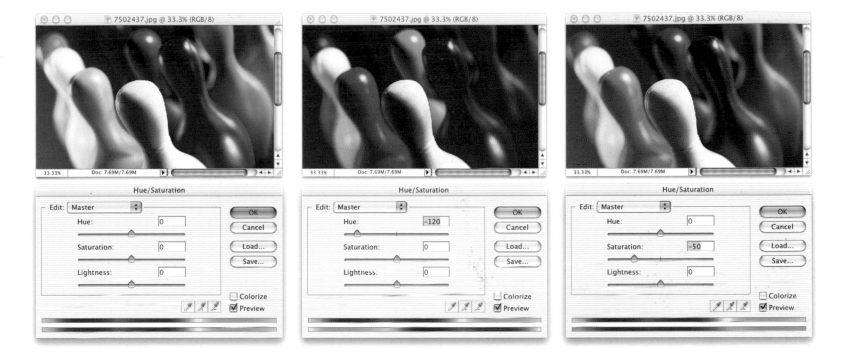

HUE/SATURATION

You can adjust the three fundamental properties of colour using the Hue/Saturation dialog box (above). Hue is shown on a linear scale that represents the circumference of a colour wheel, so the lowest setting gives the same result as the highest. Drag the slider either way to shift the hues within the image, changing, say, red objects to green. You can increase or decrease saturation to make colours more or less vibrant than in the original image. Lightness, like Brightness, is usually best left alone because it reduces the dynamic range of the image.

If you select Colorize, the image is converted to greyscale, and the selected hue, saturation and lightness are then applied, giving the effect of a colour tint. The result is not as sophisticated as a duotone (*see page 199*) but can be a useful effect, and the image will optimize very efficiently.

HIGHLIGHTS/SHADOWS

Photoshop CS has a new Shadow/Highlight function (*shown at right*) that very effectively assists corrections involving the outer ends of the tonal scale. The default settings often give useful results right away, but by clicking Show More Options, you can display an array of sliders for precise control. Using these sliders, you can often make significant improvements to images with tonal problems that do not respond well to Levels or Curves adjustments.

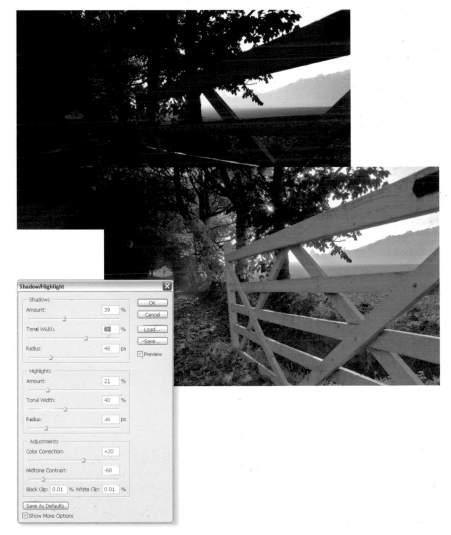

GLOBAL COLOUR CORRECTIONS

Some photos have a colour cast: a general bias towards one part of the spectrum. A colour cast is typically caused by unusual lighting – tungsten or fluorescent light indoors, or sunlight going through colour changes near dawn or dusk – but it can also be introduced by film stock or poor calibration of a digital camera, or deliberately by lens filters.

You can try to counteract a colour cast by shifting the Hue (*see page 191*), but the effect is usually too complex to be tackled this way. Shadows, midtones and highlights may need different amounts of correction, which Photoshop's Color Balance dialog box addresses.

Often, some objects within a picture will be flattered by a scene's lighting, while others appear dull and lifeless. Or correcting a colour cast may improve certain areas but make others worse. It would be useful to be able to adjust certain areas while leaving others alone. Photoshop provides a

Below: **Colour casts affect the psychological impact of a picture. These two shots share almost identical composition, yet the food on the right looks far more appetizing. The blue-green lighting of the other scene might suit other subjects just fine, but it is a gastronomic turnoff.**

Right: **When you are adjusting colour balance for subjective effect rather than 'correctness', Photoshop's Variations can help. Found at the foot of the Image/Adjustments menu, Variations shows the effect of several possible Color Balance settings at the same time, so you can compare the effects.**

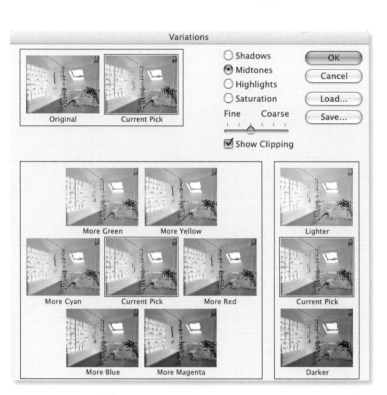

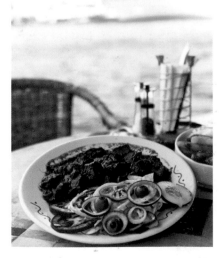

number of ways to do this, which we explore later. They must be used with care, however, to avoid creating unnatural effects and making images look obviously manipulated – even if it's hard to put your finger on why.

When making global adjustments, you may need to prioritize certain elements and aspects of your image at the expense of others. A face in the foreground will often be more important than an object in the background. There may be a particular object that needs to be bright and clear, or to match a predefined colour specification. In the latter case, use the Info palette to monitor values as you adjust, rolling the cursor over midtone areas of the object rather than shadows or highlights.

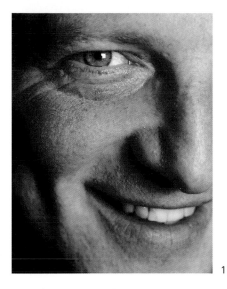

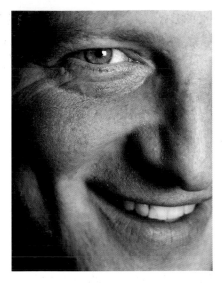

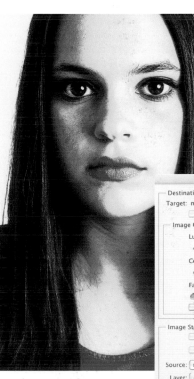

1

2

3

COLOR BALANCE

Photoshop's Color Balance dialog box (above right) divides the image's tonal range into shadows, midtones and highlights and allows you to adjust the colour of each by moving sliders between opposing (complementary) primary colours: cyan/red, magenta/green and yellow/blue. Clicking on the Preserve Luminosity option ensures that the image gets no lighter or darker overall.

1. The photographer has complemented this subject's avuncular expression with a very warm light. This is acceptable in itself, but alongside other images the red cast could look wrong.

2. The Color Balance sliders affect whichever tone region is selected at the bottom of the dialog box; you can adjust each in turn before clicking OK to apply all the corrections at once. The first step is usually to adjust the midtones. In this case, the excess red is removed by shifting the first slider towards cyan. The third slider is then moved towards yellow so that the tone does not become too cold.

3. In the highlights, red is not so dominant, and a smaller adjustment is made towards cyan. There is already too much yellow, however, so the third slider is moved towards blue. Making contrary adjustments to different tone regions can often help preserve or enhance depth and realism.

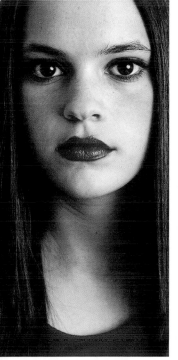

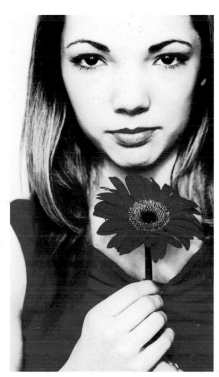

Left: Match Color, a feature recently introduced in Photoshop, analyses the colour palette of one image and applies it to another. This can help establish consistency to a series of photos. It can even (although less reliably) reproduce a special colour effect from an existing photo, giving pictures a similar appearance.

SELECTIVE COLOUR CORRECTIONS
Image-editing programs offer various tools for selecting parts of a picture, including the Marquee, Lasso and Magic Wand. The selection is shown outlined by flashing dots known as dancing ants. Any adjustments you then apply will take effect only within the selection. A selection is stored as an alpha channel, a greyscale image in which black represents selected areas, white represents unselected areas (or vice versa) and shades of grey indicate partial selection, so that those areas will be affected only to a certain degree.

It is quite difficult and time-consuming to make accurate selections that will give seamless results. If your aim is to adjust everything that falls within a certain colour range, rather than a discrete object, Photoshop provides a number of ways to select only the required part of the spectrum.

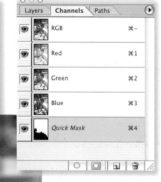

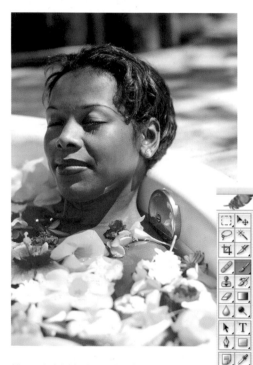

Above: Quick Mask is a simple way to make a selection in Photoshop. Press Q or click the button at the bottom right of the Tools palette. Then use the Paintbrush tool to paint over the area you want to mask. For large areas, you can just paint around the edge, then use the Paint Bucket tool to fill the area. The mask is displayed as a red tint superimposed on the picture.

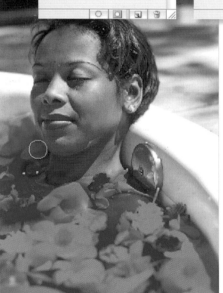

1. After global adjustments to colour-balance the subject's face, the flowers looked dull and had a slight green cast. To help correct this, a Quick Mask has been painted on. Since it is easier in this case to paint over the flowers than the remainder of the image, the Quick Mask mode was first switched (using Quick Mask Options in the Channels palette's options menu) so that painted areas are selected rather than masked.

2. When the mask is finished, click on the RGB channel to edit the image. The Quick Mask remains in place, and when a Hue/Saturation adjustment is now applied, it affects only the tinted area. Note that the Quick Mask is shown in italics in the Channels palette: this indicates that it is temporary and will disappear when you click Q to exit Quick Mask mode. To save the mask as an alpha channel, drag its name onto the New Channel icon (it resembles a turned page) at the bottom right of the palette.

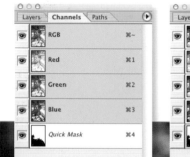

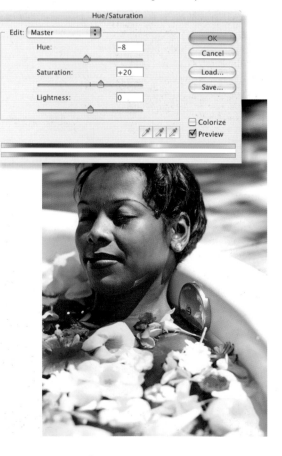

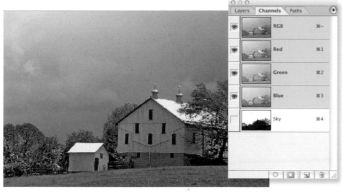

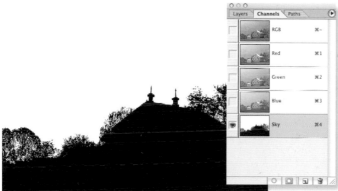

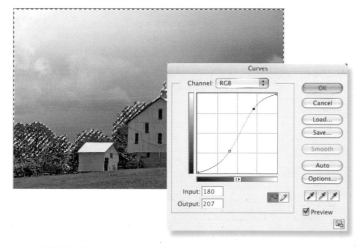

Right: We have already seen (*see page 191*) how Hue/Saturation can globally alter the colour of an image. The pop-up menu at the top of this dialog box also allows adjustments to be made to a specified colour range. Here, by switching from Master to Blues, you have adjusted the hue of blue tones without affecting the rest of the image. If necessary, you can move the sliders on the colour spectrum at the bottom to expand or contract the range of colours selected.

Left: Creating an alpha channel enables you to make subtle changes to selected areas only.

1. The Magic Wand and Lasso tools were used to create a selection of the sky in this picture. This has been saved as an alpha channel with the name Sky using the Select/Save Selection command.

2. Click on the alpha channel in the Channels palette to display its content. You can edit this greyscale image using most of Photoshop's usual tools. For example, if you noticed a stray black (unselected) patch in the sky, you could paint it out with the Eraser.

3. To load the alpha channel as a selection, click the dotted circle icon at the bottom left of the Channels palette. You can now apply a Curves adjustment to boost the sky's colour without affecting the landscape.

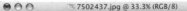

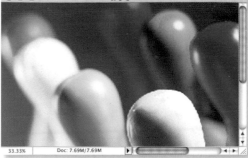

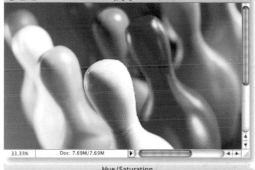

Below left: Photoshop's Replace Color feature integrates selection and correction. Here, the model's bright blue jeans distract from the room's interior. With the Replace Color dialog box open (from Image/ Adjustments), an eyedropper appears when the cursor is placed over either the selection preview or the image itself. Click with this to choose the colour that will be replaced and increase the Fuzziness setting to include a greater area of similar colour. You can also use the + and − eyedroppers to add or subtract extra colours – for example, picking up both the shadows and the highlights in the jeans. The Hue, Saturation and Lightness settings under Replacement dictate the colour to which the selection will be shifted, shown in the Result swatch. Click this swatch to bring up a colour picker with its own eyedropper, which you can then use to select an existing colour from the image. Here, a sample has been taken from the sofa cushion, shifting the jeans to a similar neutral shade.

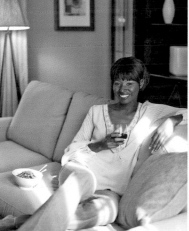

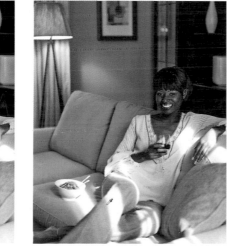

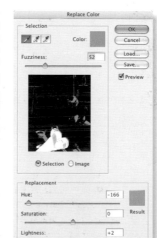

COMBINING IMAGES A powerful feature of today's image-editing software is its ability to superimpose images in many different ways. Superimpose images for montage – where elements of several pictures are cut out and put together to make a new composition – and for manipulating individual pictures.

LAYERS AND BLEND MODES

Any document in Photoshop (and other advanced image editors) can contain multiple layers, each a full-colour image in its own right. Looking at a layered image is something like stacking several photographic slides (transparencies) and holding them all up to the light at once: each image is partially visible, filtered by those in front. But you can adjust the opacity of each layer and change the way each layer filters the next by applying different blend modes. You can also use blend modes in a number of adjustment operations.

Unlike single flat images, layers also have a property of transparency. Besides its colour, each pixel has a transparency value that determines how much it affects the colour of the layer beneath. In fully transparent areas the underlying layer shows through unaffected. Each layer can also have a layer mask – a type of alpha channel that dictates which parts are visible. This allows you to cut away parts of a picture within a montage while leaving the picture itself intact, so changes can be made later.

Adjustment layers are special layers that contain no image data. Instead, they represent an adjustment operation such as Levels or Color Balance. Rather than applying such adjustments directly to an image, you add it as an adjustment layer so that you can tweak or remove it later, leaving the original image intact.

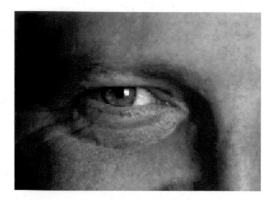

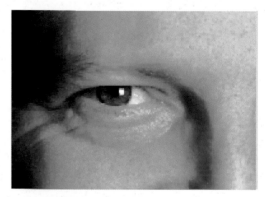

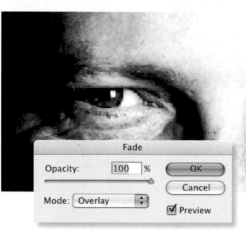

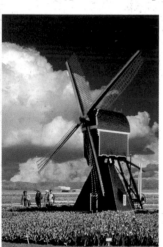
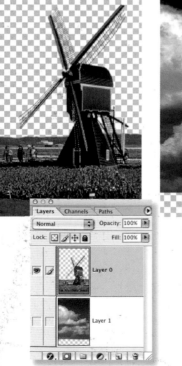
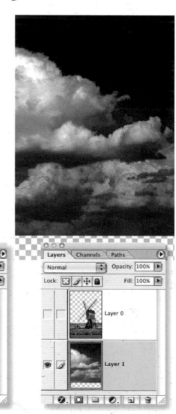

Above and right: **This montage is composited from two layers, one containing the windmill image and another the sky. The original sky in the windmill photo was selected, then erased to transparency by pressing the Backspace key. The eye icon to the left of each layer in the Layers palette makes it visible or invisible. Notice how, when you view a single channel, transparent areas are shown as a checkerboard pattern.**

Above: **The Fade dialog box allows you to modify the adjustment you have just applied. In effect, the adjustment result is combined with the original image. In this example, Hue/Saturation was used to shift the colour of the image to its complement. By following this operation with Fade using Overlay mode, you can combine the two colour schemes, and arrive at a more neutral image.**

BLEND MODES

Photoshop offers a large choice of blending modes. Technical descriptions of each are provided in the software manual, but experimentation and experience are likely to be just as useful in deciding which will serve your particular purposes, whether corrective or creative.

The following samples show the results of applying different blend modes to the upper layer in a document.

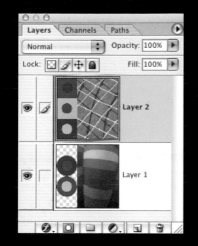

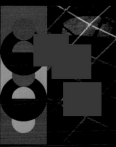

Darken

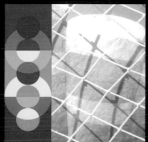

Lighten

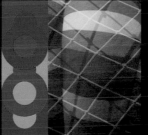

Overlay

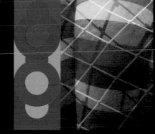

Linear light

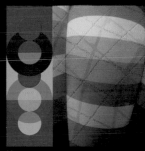

Hue

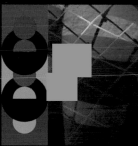

Multiply

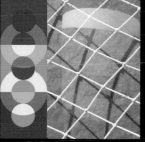

Screen

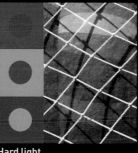

Soft light

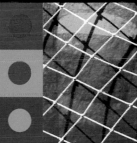

Pin light

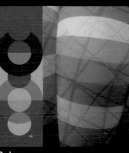

Saturation

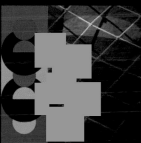

Color burn

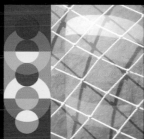

Color dodge

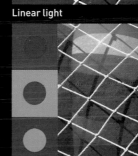

Hard light

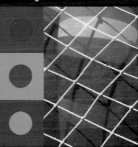

Hard mix

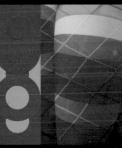

Color

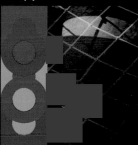

Linear burn

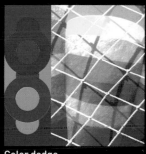

Linear dodge

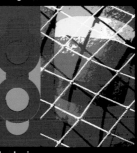

Vivid light

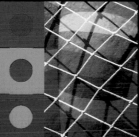

Difference

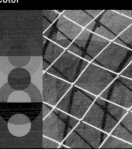

Luminosity

WORKING WITH COLOUR CHANNELS

All of our examples so far have shown images stored in the RGB colour space. As explained on page 163, this is the default mode for image manipulation, but other colour spaces are also commonly used, particularly CMYK and Lab. Editing the individual colour channels in any mode is another way to manipulate colour.

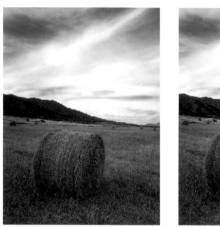
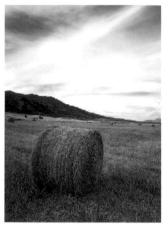
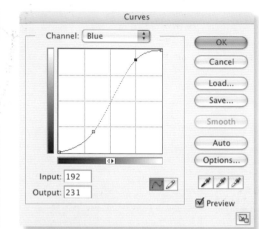

Left: Many tonal adjustments can be applied to a single channel rather than the composite image. This can be a very controllable way to correct colour casts. Here, a picture with what should be a classic colour scheme – warm earth colours in the foreground at the bottom, cool blue in the background at the top – has taken on a violet tinge. Applying an S-shaped curve to the blue channel reduces the amount of blue in near-shadow while slightly increasing it in lighter areas, leaving the hay yellow and the sky blue.

Although the red, green and blue components are all essential to the overall appearance of the full-colour, or composite, image, they have their own characteristics. Red generally contains the greatest tonal range and is important for shadows and highlights, but it often provides little detail in the midtones. Green, on the other hand, contains the most high-frequency detail, in which neighbouring areas differ significantly in value. The blue channel usually contains the most noise (random specks caused by film grain or digitization errors).

Applying monochrome adjustments to each channel accordingly can produce significant enhancements: for example, blurring the blue channel reduces noise without significantly damaging detail. It will sometimes be helpful to convert the image into Lab mode, where the three channels serve different functions. The L (luminosity) channel carries most of the visible detail in the image, while the a and b channels contain colour information. Adjusting the L channel can therefore improve tonal characteristics without affecting colour, while blurring colour channels can remove noise without damaging detail.

Images destined for commercial printing are normally converted to CMYK mode as a final step in the editing process. The only reason to convert earlier is if colours within the image must be precisely matched to a predefined specification or to others within a publication. Here, it is preferable to work directly on the CMYK ink values to avoid any colour shifts in conversion. By checking the Info palette during adjustment, you can ensure an exact match.

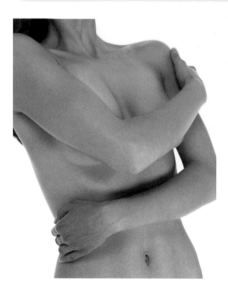
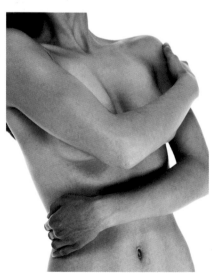

Above and right: The Apply Image operation combines one image with another using blend modes (see page 197). Apply Image can often be useful to recombine one channel of an image with the composite. The picture above has a soft feel, largely because the red channel contains mainly high values, with detail blown out. By adding a copy of the green channel – which contains the most detail – to the composite image, you can enhance detail and create a more realistic picture. Hard Light mode was used in this case.

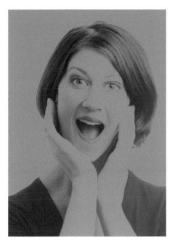

Left: A duotone is a monochromic image printed in two ink colours rather than only black. The main purpose of duotone as a photographic technique is to increase the available tonal range, but it can also be used purely creatively. You can print a duotone created on screen in Photoshop in CMYK – you do not have to use spot inks of the duotone colours. You must always convert the image to greyscale first, then to duotone (both options are on the Mode menu). Tritones and quadtones are also supported.

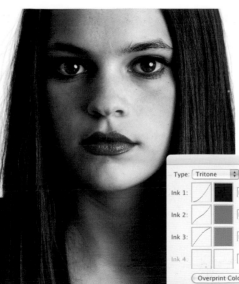

Left and below: Each of the plates in a duotone, tritone or quadtone has a colour specification and a curve. Adjusting the curves governs exactly how the image data are distributed between the plates. The first plate (shadows) should usually be black; if you use a different colour, contrast will be limited.

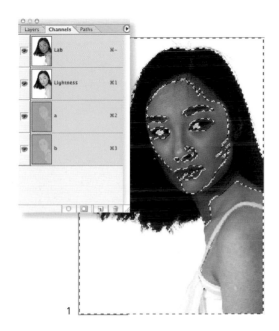

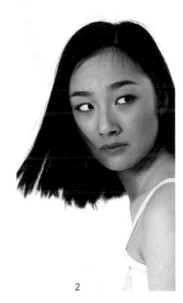

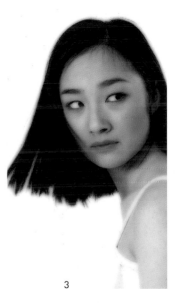

Left and right. We have already seen how an alpha channel resembles a colour channel. Conversely, you can load any colour channel as a mask by holding down Alt-Command on a Mac or Ctrl-Alt on a PC while typing the channel number.

1. The picture has been converted to Lab mode and the L channel loaded as a selection (Lightness).

2. This masks off shadows, leaving light areas most affected by any adjustment.

3. A Gaussian Blur has been applied, giving an effect reminiscent of a hand-tinted photo.

1   2   3

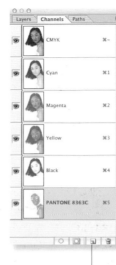

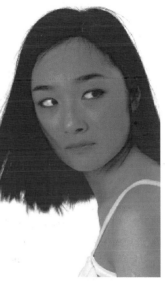

Right: If you are using spot inks in the printing process, you can add any number of colour channels to accommodate them, selecting the New Spot Channel command on the Channels palette options menu. Choose the ink colour for each channel from a standard system such as PANTONE, and Photoshop will display the composite colour image as it should appear when printed. Generating appropriate image data for each plate, however, is up to you. Use the Calculations command (from the Image menu) to combine tonal information from existing channels. Here, to enhance an image with metallic gold, the yellow channel was combined with the black using the Difference blending mode. The resulting channel (an alpha channel by default) was inverted, then converted to a spot ink channel by double-clicking it in the Channels palette and picking an ink reference from the PANTONE Metallic range. The result is a gold sheen highlighting flesh tones.

COLOUR EFFECTS In addition to tone and colour adjustment controls, image editors such as Photoshop provide dozens more filters and effects that can radically alter the colour make-up of a picture. These may be supplemented by plug-ins sold separately.

BASIC COLOUR EFFECTS

A number of simple colour effects are common to nearly all image editors and can be used creatively or for technical purposes to facilitate other adjustments. In Photoshop, you will find most of these on the Image/Adjustments menu. They work in all colour modes.

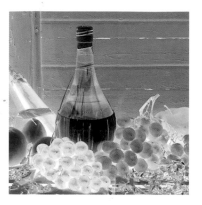

INVERT turns the image into a negative. The result depends on the colour mode; an RGB negative looks different from a CMYK version.

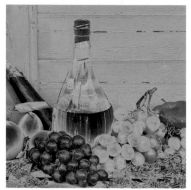

SOLARIZE combines a negative with a positive. The effect is similar to that of briefly exposing a photo during developing. (This is found under Filter/Stylize and does not work in Lab mode.)

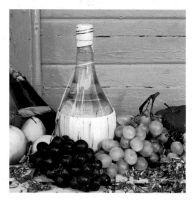

EQUALIZE distributes pixel values evenly from dark to light. Often useful to apply to a layer or channel that will be used to modify another.

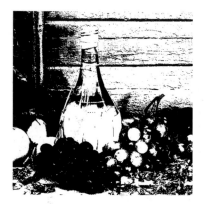

THRESHOLD All pixels darker than a specified value become black, and all lighter pixels, white. Can help produce a simplified mask from a channel, often followed by a blur.

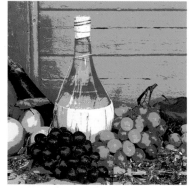

POSTERIZE has the effect of reducing the shades of colour in an image. Good for pop-art effects and turning photos into flat graphical compositions. For more sophistication, try Filters/Artistic/Cutout.

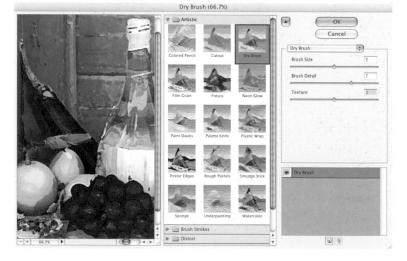

FILTER GALLERY previews the results of Photoshop's many creative filters, which manipulate colour in different ways to suggest anything from film grain to neon. Although the various simulations of traditional art media are not very sophisticated, they can be surprisingly convincing. Using the button at the bottom right of the dialog box, you can add multiple effects, which are all applied to the image at once. These filters work only in RGB with 8 bits per channel (24-bit colour).

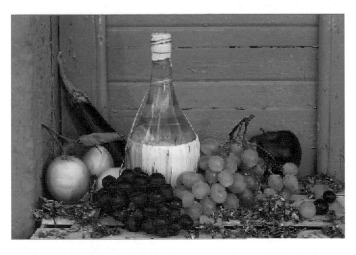

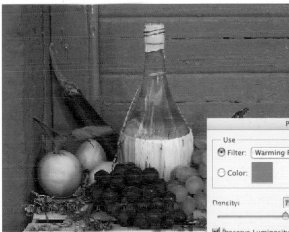

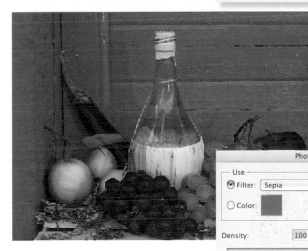

PHOTO FILTERS

Photoshop's recently introduced Photo Filters mimic traditional photographic techniques and effects. For example, colour casts can be applied in a way similar to fitting colour filters over the camera lens (centre), and a Sepia option recalls early film stock (bottom). Again, these can be used in any colour mode.

DIVISIONISM

Photoshop provides a number of filters that break up colour into discrete fields. The simplest way to do this with any digital image, of course, is to decrease its resolution, making the pixels visible. While you don't need a filter to do that, you can find most of these operations on the Filter menu under the heading Pixelate.

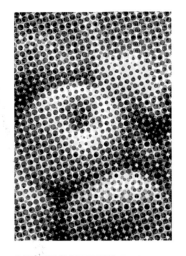

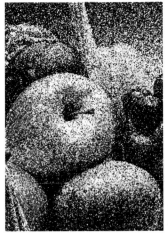

COLOUR HALFTONE simulates the halftoning process that occurs when you print an image, but with the dots much larger. Pop artists such as Roy Lichtenstein (*see page 110*) had to paint their versions of this trick by hand.

MEZZOTINT re-creates the random dot screening that resulted from early mechanical reprographic techniques, in which printing plates were finely stippled to break up colour.

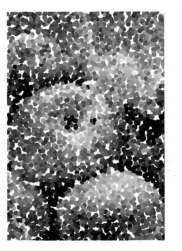

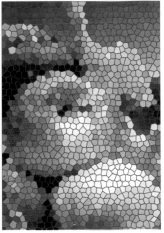

POINTILLIZE mimics the divisionist painting methods of the impressionists (*see page 102*). Although the results are interesting, they will leave you in no doubt that Georges Seurat's technique was more than mechanical.

STAINED GLASS (found under Texture) divides the image into irregularly shaped pieces reminiscent of traditional leaded glass. Like many other 'special-effects' filters, Stained Glass is clever but perhaps unlikely to prove very useful.

FILE FORMATS AND COMPRESSION The 'native' file format in which Photoshop stores your work (PSD) is fine for your own use, but few other programs can read it, and it includes a lot of information that is unnecessary for printing or online display. Image files are commonly exchanged in a number of industry standard formats.

GIF

Graphics Interchange Format was popularized by the online service Compuserve and is widely used on the Web for icons, graphics and blocks of preset text. It uses lossless compression but devotes only one byte (8 bits) of data to each pixel, giving 256 colours rather than millions. Certain pixels can be transparent, so a webpage's background will show up behind an irregularly shaped picture. With suitable software, you can also store several images within a file, and a Web browser will display them in turn, creating a simple animation. Animated GIFs are often found on online advertising banners. The name is supposed to be pronounced 'jif', but most people say it with a hard *g*.

JPEG

The lossy compression method devised by the Joint Photographic Experts Group cleverly removes the colour information you notice least. The more compression you apply, the smaller the file – down to around 1 per cent – and the more visible the degradation. JPEG is great for Web graphics and for sending full-page, full-colour images to press without uploading dozens of megabytes. But you should never use JPEG to store images you will be manipulating further, as compression artefacts - blocks and streaks – will become more and more obvious. The acronym is pronounced 'jay-peg'.

PNG

Portable Networks Graphic arose as an alternative to GIF after the patent holder of GIF's compression method demanded royalties. The patent expired in 2003, and PNG seems likely to wane. The acronym is pronounced 'ping'.

RAW

Camera Raw format delivers the data generated by the light-sensitive chip in a digital camera straight into software. This means you can control exactly how colour and tone are handled, rather than start from an image that has already been processed into a format such as JPEG or TIFF. Photoshop CS can read most popular Camera Raw files, earlier versions of Photoshop, however, need either a software plug-in or software supplied with your camera. Camera Raw is the best import format if your camera supports it.

TIFF (OR TIF)

Graphics professionals often use Tagged Image File Format (TIFF). TIFFs work with all serious graphics programs on all operating systems. Alpha channels can be stored, and programs can include information that is ignored by others that do not understand it. So, for example, Photoshop can store and read layered image as a TIFF, while other programs just see a flat image. Lossless compression can be applied, although not all programs can handle this, and compressed files are still quite large.

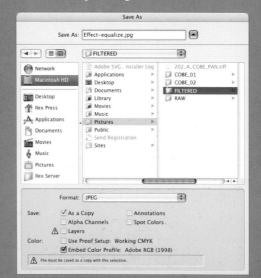

Left: **Not all file formats can incorporate all the kinds of information that may exist in a Photoshop image. Layers and extra channels are supported only in a few formats. When you try to save a complex document in a format such as JPEG, the Save As dialog box warns you about elements that cannot be included and forces you to save the document as a copy, leaving the complete document intact on screen so that you can save it in PSD format for later editing.**

Right: ImageReady, the Web graphics program supplied as part of Photoshop, provides this '4-up' view to compare the effects of compression settings. Here, three different JPEG levels are applied to the image seen at the top left. With a high-quality setting (top right), the image is almost indistinguishable from the original but occupies only 32 K, reduced from 501 K. A lower setting (bottom left) halves this size to 16 K, but quality is visibly suffering. At the lowest setting (bottom right), a small extra saving in size is probably not worth by the conspicuous deterioration. Note how comparative download times are also reduced (from 13 seconds to 5 seconds).

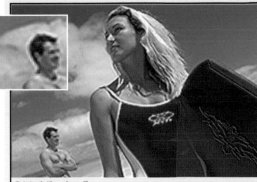
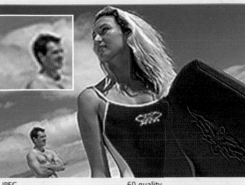

Original: "beach.psd"
501K

JPEG
33.75K
13 sec @ 28.8 Kbps

60 quality

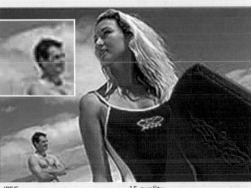

JPEG
16.41K
7 sec @ 28.8 Kbps

30 quality

JPEG
11.25K
5 sec @ 28.8 Kbps

15 quality

beach.psd @ 100% (4–Up)

Original Optimized 2–Up 4–Up

100% ▼ 11.25K / 5 sec @ 28.8 K... ▼ 501K / 11.25K JPEG ▼

Indexed Color

Palette: Local (Selective)
Colors: 256
Forced: Black and White
☐ Transparency

OK
Cancel
☑ Preview

Options
Matte: None
Dither: Diffusion
Amount: 75 %
☑ Preserve Exact Colors

Left and below: When you save a Photoshop image as a GIF, the settings in the Indexed Color dialog box govern the conversion to a palette of no more than 256 colours. A 'local' palette, created to suit the tones within the image, should normally be used for best visual quality. In ImageReady, you can build a 'master' palette from a set of images, ensuring that they will all display similarly. The Dither setting governs how the conversion copes with the shortage of available shades. With no dither, areas graduating between colours or from light to dark tend to resolve into bands (below centre). A diffusion dither randomly intersperses pixel values, making the image grainier, but sometimes more acceptable to the eye (below right).

original image

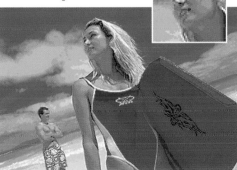

undithered image

dithered image

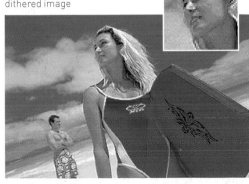

IMPLEMENTING COLOUR MANAGEMENT As we saw in chapter 04.01, calibration and colour management are important for anyone dealing seriously with colour on the computer. The first step is to calibrate your monitor, using software tools if you do not have calibration hardware.

CALIBRATING YOUR MONITOR

Macintosh computers come with the Display Calibrator Assistant. Go into Display in System Preferences and click Calibrate in the Color tab. PC users need to run Adobe Gamma – a similar utility supplied with Photoshop – and choose the Wizard method. These programs are suitable for both CRT and LCD screens; some of the steps do not apply to LCDs. Switch on your monitor and leave it running for at least half an hour before calibrating, to stabilize its performance. This form of calibration does not affect the monitor itself (except for your brightness and contrast adjustments) but changes the information that the computer sends to it. This is governed by an ICC profile generated at the end of the calibration process, which is applied in your operating system's colour management settings.

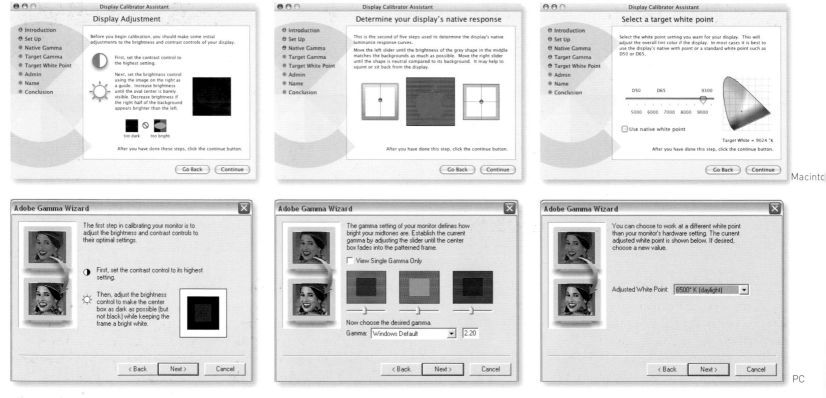

Macinto

PC

1. You start by turning the monitor contrast up to maximum, giving the broadest possible tonal range. You are then asked to adjust the brightness control with reference to a graphic displayed on screen. This creates the best hardware setup within which to calibrate as accurate a picture as possible.

2. To achieve the desired gamma setting (*see page 183*), the software first needs to know the screen's own 'native' gamma. It will ask you to adjust sliders until blocks of each primary colour match black-striped backgrounds. You can then choose the gamma setting you prefer. Print graphics professionals using PCs may prefer to switch from the Windows default of 2.2 to the lighter 1.8 setting normal on Macs. Mac Web designers, on the other hand, may switch to 2.2 to get a better idea of what images will look like in PC Web browsers.

3. You can also choose the colour temperature or white point. Most monitors default to a very high (blue) value, but a lower (yellower) value better represents colours as they appear on printed pages. Again, Mac and PC norms differ, but print designers should choose 6,500 K (also known as D65), while Web designers may go as high as 9,300 K to mimic the average Web-user's settings, although this makes images look bluer than they should.

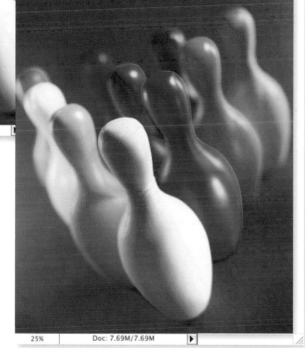

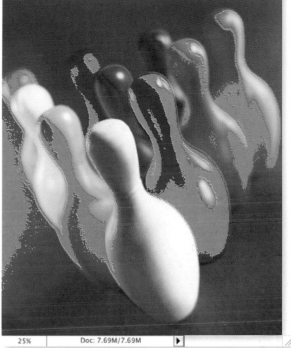

Below: With a CMYK press profile selected and Proof Colors turned on, you can see that the colours will not be as bright when printed.

Above: This picture contains highly saturated colours that look extremely vibrant on screen.

Above: Turn on Gamut Warning to highlight colours that are outside the range of the selected device.

HARDWARE CALIBRATION

If you invest in a calibration device with software that integrates with your colour-management system (CMS), the calibration process will be much less subjective. Instead of you having to select the gamma and white point you prefer, settings are made according to the requirements of the CMS, so that images will objectively match those colour specifications when displayed. If calibration is integrated with the monitor, brightness and contrast are set automatically and should not be changed by the user.

SOFT PROOFING

When you display an image in Photoshop – or other ICC-compatible graphics programs – on your calibrated monitor, its appearance will be as faithful as possible to the colour data in the file. Sometimes, however, you may want to see how the image will appear when output less faithfully. If you are designing for print, you will want to know how your work will look when it comes off a CMYK press; Web designers will want to check how graphics look on an average, uncalibrated monitor. This is known as soft proofing. In Photoshop, you use the Proof Setup command at the top of the View menu to choose what device profile to mimic. Choose Custom if you need to use a profile that is not listed, or to tweak the settings. You can then turn soft proofing on and off, using the Proof Colors command immediately below.

PHOTOSHOP COLOUR SETTINGS You will find Color Settings in the Edit menu if you are running Photoshop on a PC, or on the Photoshop menu on a Mac. This dialog box underpins all your work in Photoshop, so do not skip it because it looks complicated! Pass your cursor over each option to show a helpful description at the bottom of the box.

Color Settings

Settings: Custom

☑ Advanced Mode

Working Spaces
RGB: Adobe RGB (1998)
CMYK: U.S. Web Coated (SWOP) v2
Gray: Dot Gain 20%
Spot: Dot Gain 20%

OK
Cancel
Load...
Save...
☑ Preview

Color Management Policies
RGB: Convert to Working RGB
CMYK: Preserve Embedded Profiles
Gray: Preserve Embedded Profiles
Profile Mismatches: ☑ Ask When Opening ☑ Ask When Pasting
Missing Profiles: ☑ Ask When Opening

Conversion Options
Engine: Adobe (ACE)
Intent: Relative Colorimetric
☑ Use Black Point Compensation ☑ Use Dither (8–bit/channel images)

Advanced Controls
☐ Desaturate Monitor Colors By: 20 %
☐ Blend RGB Colors Using Gamma: 1.00

Description
Color Management Policies: Policies specify how you want colors in a particular color model managed. Policies handle the reading and embedding of color profiles, mismatches between embedded color profiles and the working space, and the moving of colors from one document to another.

Above: **Click the arrow to choose from the standard colour setups that come with Photoshop. US or Europe Prepress Defaults is a good start; Mac users may prefer ColorSync Workflow to help keep the whole system working consistently. When you alter settings, the name will change to Custom. Tick Advanced Mode.**

WORKING SPACES

Here you choose the colour spaces (*see chapter 04.01*) that will be used to handle RGB, CMYK and greyscale images. Since most of your editing will be in RGB, your RGB colour space should be device-independent – devised to represent colour in the abstract, rather than the characteristics of any particular hardware. Adobe RGB (1998) is a good choice. Some Web designers choose sRGB, the default colour space used by PCs, as it represents what most users will see, but this can compromise image quality.

Do not choose your monitor profile here. As long as you have applied the monitor profile in your operating system, the display will look correct. Your monitor's own colour space is not a good neutral working space.

Because you normally convert to CMYK in preparation for commercial printing, the CMYK working space should match the printing press. Choose a standard profile - Euroscale Coated v2 or US Web Coated (SWOP) v2 – unless you have a specific one. (Web here refers to web offset printing, not the World Wide Web.) Note that if you use a desktop inkjet or colour laser printer, data is normally sent to such devices in RGB, not CMYK.

The Gray setting affects only monochromic images. If these are for press, set a dot gain factor to compensate for ink spread, normally 20 per cent; for desktop printers, pick a standard gamma setting. If you use spot colours in offset printing, the usual dot gain is also 20 per cent, but check with your printer.

COLOUR MANAGEMENT POLICIES

This very important section governs what happens when you open an image that has been saved without a colour profile, or with a profile different from your working space. Most people should choose Convert to Working RGB, to keep all their work in the same colour space. If you typically receive images in CMYK because they have already been prepared correctly for press, choose Preserve Embedded Profiles for CMYK; otherwise, choose Convert to Working CMYK. Apply the same principle to the Gray setting. Tick all three Ask… options so that you are always told what is happening with conversions.

CONVERSION OPTIONS

It is not always possible to convert precisely between colour spaces (such as RGB to CMYK), but you can use various methods to compensate. The engine is the software that does the conversion; the conversion settings can be left as Adobe (ACE), but Mac users may prefer Apple ColorSync to match conversions in other software. You will generally get the most satisfactory colour if you choose Relative Colorimetric for the Intent and tick both the options here.

ADVANCED CONTROLS

Unless you know better, leave these turned off. They are specific controls that alter the colours in an image, and which you would only use if you wanted to override the management policies. Ultimately, adjusting the Advanced Controls means that the monitor display cannot be relied upon.

Below: If you capture the screen display (using the Prt Scrn key on a PC or the Grab utility on a Mac) then paste it into Photoshop, it may not look correct. Here, the window on the right contains a screen grab of the window on the left. To correct the colour, assign the monitor profile to the grabbed image. Then convert to your usual working space.

WORKING WITH COLOUR MANAGEMENT

Whenever you save an image, Photoshop gives you the option to embed the current working space profile. This ensures that when the file is opened in Photoshop or in any other ICC-aware program, the colour data is correctly interpreted. Always tick the box – unless you have a reason not to. If you are saving a JPEG for Web use, embedding a profile will enlarge the file, to little benefit, since most browsers will ignore it and most users' monitors are uncalibrated.

Under Mode on the Image menu are two special options: Assign Profile and Convert to Profile. Assign Profile tells Photoshop that the current image should be interpreted as if it had a certain profile embedded. This option will change the image's colour appearance, you hope, back to what was intended.

Convert to Profile switches the working space in which the image is held and should not change its appearance (unless, for example, you convert from an RGB to a CMYK profile). This is useful when you are delivering an image to a non-ICC user, but you know what profile might represent their system. When saving an image for the Web, for example, you could convert it to sRGB, then save it without a profile, since most PCs use sRGB by default.

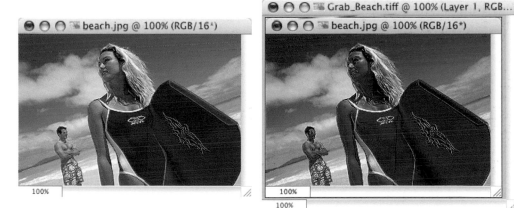

DIGITAL PAINTING Manipulating coloured pixels on the computer is not just about editing existing images such as photos. You can also create artwork from a blank canvas, using the digital equivalents of brushes, pens and pencils.

The basic principle behind Photoshop's Brush tool is that a small image is repeated along the line you draw. Aspects such as the shape of the brush's 'tip', its size, the amount and direction in which it is squashed, the repeat distance, how much the repeated shapes diverge from the path, variation in colour, opacity and so on can all be made to vary within defined parameters. If you have a graphics tablet, you can set the tilt of the stylus and the pressure you apply to its tip to control the degree of variation, allowing expressive 'painting'.

Although the 'natural media' are a worthwhile feature within Photoshop, programs dedicated to them offer much more sophisticated features. Corel Painter is the leading example. Like Photoshop, Corel Painter is fundamentally a bitmap editor, but its tools – including wet and dry brushes, chalks and crayons, inks and washes – are

Below left: A graphics tablet is a good aid to on-screen drawing and painting. The computer mouse is unwieldy and uses a relative positioning system, so while the cursor gives an indication of your current position, 'muscle memory' cannot be relied on to take your hand to a given position on the virtual canvas. The graphics tablet's stylus is more like a pen or brush and records its absolute position within the tablet area. You can even trace artwork on a piece of paper placed over the tablet.

Below right: This image uses colour techniques to convey an atmosphere. The artist has worked as a matte painter and lighting designer for companies including Disney and Industrial Light and Magic.
Courtesy Erik Tiemens,
Watersketch.com

aimed at the artist rather than the retoucher and have enticed many traditional painters into the digital realm.

Currently, the main limitation of Painter is that it imposes extremely heavy data-processing tasks on the computer. This means that the speed of operation may slow to a crawl when producing complex artwork, frustrating the artist or illustrator's expressive flow. Fortunately, successive generations of computer processors are gradually outstripping the demands of the software.

Creative House Expression, a program developed by a team of computer scientists and artists, takes a new approach. Paths are stored as vectors, using proprietary 'skeletal strokes' technology, so that you can rework individual brushstrokes within your artwork at any time. Expression capitalizes even further on perhaps the chief advantage of painting on the computer. You can edit and erase what you have painted in a way that is impossible with, say, real watercolours.

You can find out more about these products and download demonstration versions at www.corel.com/painter and www.creaturehouse.com, respectively.

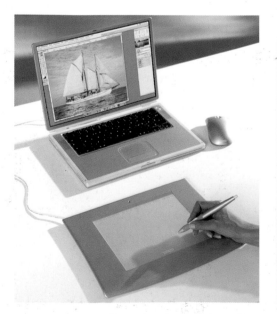

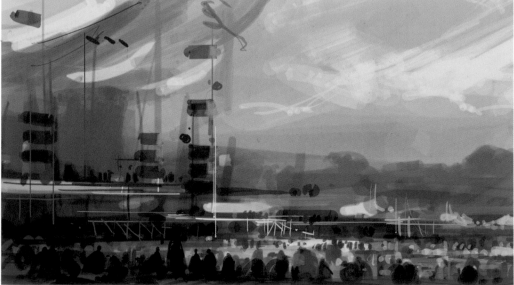

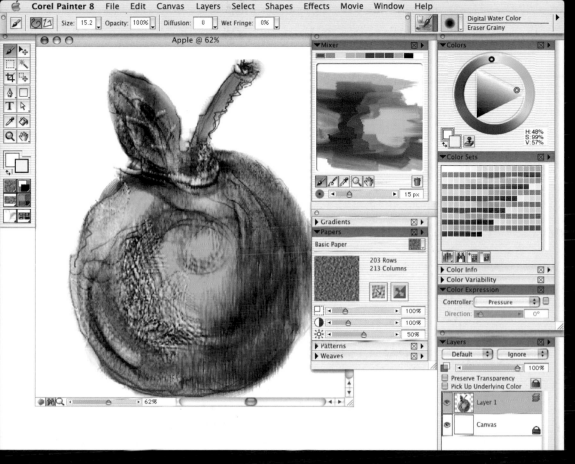

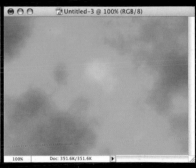

Left: **Corel Painter is a program** specifically designed to simulate working with real paints and surfaces. You can mix colours on a palette (top right) and then apply them to the canvas (left), using a huge variety of brush types. You can select the texture of the canvas (below Mixer) and add Water Colour layers to apply 'wet' effects, such as brushstrokes running into each other and washes diffusing strokes previously laid down. Graphics tablet attributes such as tilt and pressure allow you to vary your brushstrokes.

Below: **You don't have to imitate** traditional tools to 'paint' on the computer. Various image-editing filters can produce instant textures and washes over any area you define with a selection. Here, for example, Photoshop's Fibers (left) and Clouds (right), both found under Render on the Filter menu, have been used to generate patterns coloured according to the current Foreground and Background swatches.

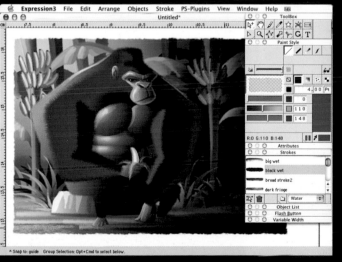

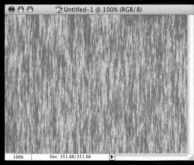

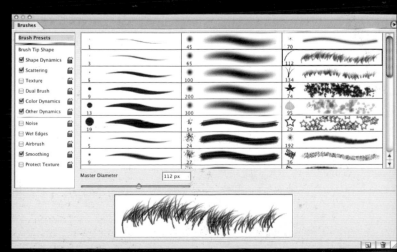

Above: **Creature House Expression** represents strokes as vector paths. Although the brushwork is still built up from bitmaps, Expression gives artwork a degree of editability and resolution-independence lacking in programs such as Painter.

Right: **Photoshop's Brush tool has a** large number of settings that you can customize to produce different effects. The brush sets included with the program range from simple calligraphic strokes to complex semirandom arrangements of preset graphics along the path you draw.

PART 04. DIGITAL COLOUR

CHAPTER SIX

COLOUR LINEWORK

While photo-editing and painting programs work with bitmaps, vectors are the basis for drawing and page-layout software, such as Adobe Illustrator and QuarkXPress respectively. A vector-based graphics program can be thought of as the digital equivalent of the felt shapes you may have played with as a child. You can cut each shape to any pattern you like and arrange any number of them on a background, overlapping where necessary, to build up a picture.

A vector shape, or object, is defined by a path: a straight or curved line formed between a number of points. You can give it a stroke, a line of specified colour and width, and/or a fill, a colour or effect that fills the area it encloses. To be filled, a path must be closed, finishing exactly where it started. Shapes with holes in their bounding (outer) line or edge are formed by compound paths: for example, a letter o consists of two ellipses, one for the outside and one for the inside.

Like pixels, then, paths are made visible by their colour values. Unlike a pixel, however, a stroke or fill can be removed, or set to None, so that it is not white, black or anything in between, but simply absent. Similarly, although vector-based software presents you with a rectangular area on which to compose your work, the result need not be rectangular. Any areas of the background not covered by objects are empty, not white; if your artwork is placed (within software) over the top of other material, any underlying graphics will be visible in these empty areas.

Digital typesetting is a special use of vectors. Font files are always stored on your hard disk as PostScript vector data (or, most often in Windows-based PCs, in the similar TrueType format). As you type text in a particular font at a given size, the computer's operating system rasterizes the letter shapes to the monitor. What is stored in the document you are editing, however, is not the rasterized dots but the words of the text and details of the font, size and other typographical settings. When you zoom in on your work, the text is rasterized from scratch at the new size, so it comes out looking just as smooth. When you come to print the document, it is rasterized again by the printer's RIP (or by your software on behalf of a less-capable printer) at its higher resolution.

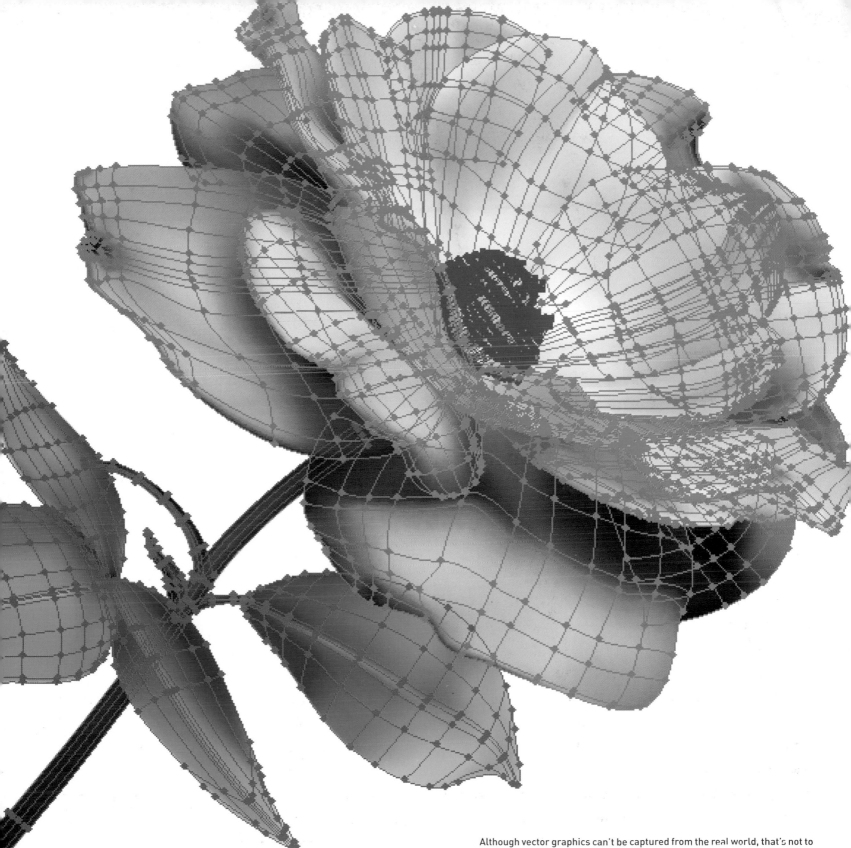

Although vector graphics can't be captured from the real world, that's not to say they can't be photorealistic. This subtly shaded flower was drawn using Adobe Illustrator's Gradient Mesh function. Object blends can be formed in any vector drawing package to create complex shading.

VECTOR-DRAWING PROGRAMS Vector drawing can seem at first like a black art. You construct shapes with Bézier curves, geometrical forms consisting of nodes and handles. It takes some time to master Bézier curves, but if you use them logically and methodically, your artwork will tend naturally towards elegance and uniformity. And having once created a shape, you can repeat it, scale it up or down or even generate concentric duplicates (offset paths), with a few clicks.

Above: **A hand is drawn, and appears as the first object in the stacking order. We have given it a name, Hand, to make it easier to keep track of later.**

Above: **Three stars are drawn and named. Since they'll want to remain together, we have grouped them, and this is shown in the list.**

Above: **A banknote shape is drawn and named. Being the most recent object, it appears on top, covering the other elements.**

Above: **The banknote is sent to the back. This places it lowest in the stacking order, behind the other objects and at the bottom of the list.**

Above: **A shape is drawn on a new layer. Although it is at the top within this layer, it underlies the other elements, as its layer is lower than theirs.**

There are many options for colouring your objects. Besides solid colours, you can apply gradient fills, which graduate smoothly from one colour to another. You can add multiple colours, creating effects ranging from psychedelic rainbows to metallic shimmers. Where these do not provide the exact shading effect you want, you can 'blend' between objects to create transitions between colour fields of any shape. Some drawing programs now also support transparency: each coloured object can have an opacity setting and even a blend mode (*see page 197*).

    Since vector objects are discrete, they can each have their own colour mode. This means you must take care, when designing for print, to ensure each colour you apply is defined as a process or spot colour as appropriate. Confusingly, you can use whatever colour model you prefer – RGB, CMYK, HSV and so on - to

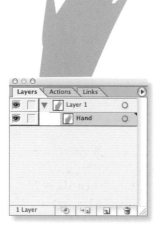

Above: **Drawings are built up from multiple objects with different fills. With all objects selected, you can see how they fit together to construct the artwork. Objects adding detail to larger shapes can be placed on top of them in the stacking order, so there's no need for one to be cut out around the other.**

specify a colour, regardless of whether it is tagged as a process or spot ink. Process colours will all be converted to CMYK on output, while spot colours will simply be allocated to the relevant plate. The ink used to print spot colours depends on what you ask the printer for. If you print the file to a desktop inkjet printer, all colour values will be translated into its inks to match their displayed appearance as closely as possible.

Rather than just applying a colour spec to a given object, you can make it a swatch, which is stored within the document and can easily be applied to other objects. You can later change all instances of a particular colour in a document by editing the swatch. Effects other than solid colours, including gradient fills and fancy strokes, can be stored as styles, which work similarly.

Some effects, like soft shadows and glows, are very hard to construct in vectors. The latest drawing programs support such effects by representing them as bitmaps. In theory, the user need not be aware of this, since the bitmap elements, or raster effects, are generated automatically and seamlessly integrated into the artwork. In practice, however, there are a few technical hitches. First, the designer has to decide on the resolution of the bitmaps. This is normally set for a whole document, according to whether the work is destined for display or print. Second, a lot of processing power is needed to generate the bitmaps, which can slow down the drawing program to the point of provoking frustration. Reducing the document-raster resolution can help – it can always be increased again just before output - but the designer must then take the visual quality of the effects for granted while working.

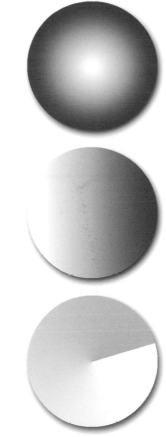

Above: **Standard gradient fills include radial (top) and linear (centre). Some programs offer extra types such as cone fills (bottom).**

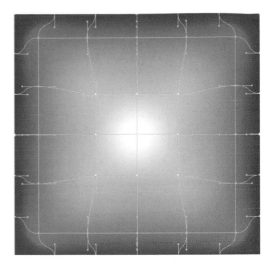

Above: **In Adobe Illustrator a gradient mesh is formed from Bézier curves, and its points and handles can be moved like any other Bézier curve. Here, the points nearest the edges have been selected together and scaled by 120%.**

Resolution is an even trickier issue with blends. The smoothness of the tonal graduation is a function of the number of objects, the distance over which they are distributed and the degree of variation between the colours in the blend. But the number of steps is left to the user's educated guesswork, and there is no automatic facility to redo blends when artwork is scaled up. Therefore, print designers should be especially aware that vector artwork is not as resolution-independent as its fundamental principles would suggest.

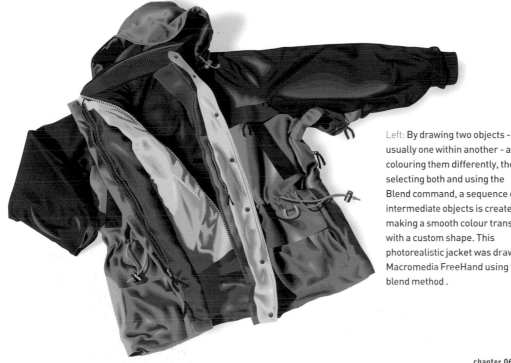

Left: **By drawing two objects - usually one within another - and colouring them differently, then selecting both and using the Blend command, a sequence of intermediate objects is created, making a smooth colour transition with a custom shape. This photorealistic jacket was drawn in Macromedia FreeHand using this blend method .**

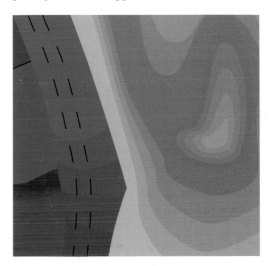

PAGE-LAYOUT APPLICATIONS Page-layout packages are a special class of vector-graphics program devoted to the production of documents combining simple vector shapes, imported bitmapped images and significant quantities of text. Their core features are typographic: type can be set with fine control over spacing and justification, and text can run over multiple columns and pages. Because the resulting file is usually a publication that will be sent for commercial printing, prepress features are also more advanced and comprehensive in page-layout programs than in drawing programs.

The first product in this field, Aldus PageMaker, was quickly challenged by QuarkXPress, which by the late 1990s dominated the publishing industry. Adobe, which acquired PageMaker in 1994, eventually relegated it to a less significant role, launching an innovative replacement, InDesign, to rival Quark. InDesign is based on a new document description technology called PDF (portable document format), developed by Adobe to advance the capabilities of PostScript.

Since PDF supports advanced colour features such as transparency, InDesign is able to integrate text, vector graphics and images much more comprehensively than earlier products. For example, you can run text with a soft shadow effect over a background image, something impossible in QuarkXPress, at least without the help of clumsy plug-ins.

Below: **Adobe InDesign, the newest of the leading page-layout programs, allows text and graphics to be made transparent and overlaid. In QuarkXPress, you can only achieve the same effect by re-creating all the relevant objects in a graphics program, such as Adobe Photoshop or Illustrator, setting up the required effect, then exporting the composition as an image and placing it in the Quark document. InDesign layouts using these features may suffer occasional glitches on output, however.**

QuarkXPress files are usually sent for output in the program's own file format, since its market dominance is such that every image-setting company and printer is set up to work with it. Over the past few years, however, PDF has become accepted as a universal format – independent of applications and operating systems – for viewing, checking, proofing and final output. Its flexibility is both a help and a hindrance in this regard. You can quickly convert documents created in your page-layout program into PDF files of exactly the right specification for the press, incorporating ICC colour management - but only if you make the correct settings in the software used to create the PDF, which may be within the page-layout program itself or in an external PDF-creation tool such as Adobe's Acrobat Distiller.

Page-layout packages lack serious image-editing or drawing tools, so pictures are usually imported from files created using other programs. An image 'placed' on the page can be 'embedded' within the page-layout file, so that a copy of it is stored; but the more usual option is to 'link' it, so that the original image file remains the sole copy, and

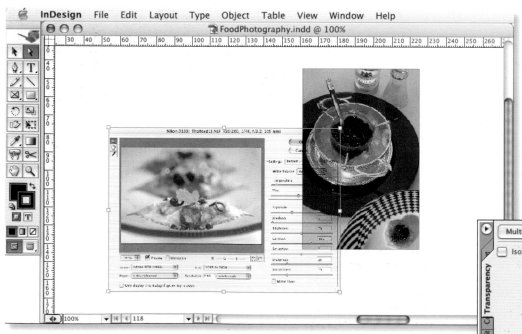

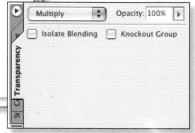

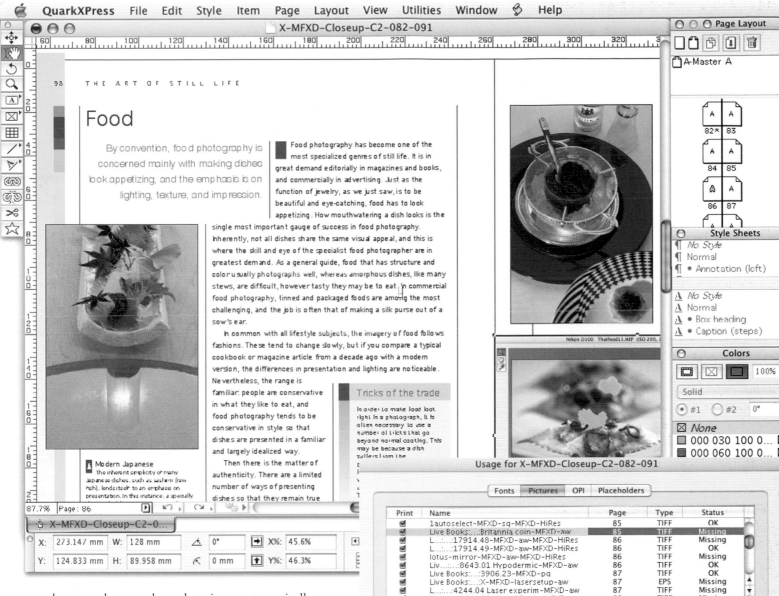

any changes subsequently made to it are automatically reproduced on the page when it is next loaded, updated or output. Documents containing linked images can be successfully printed only if the image files are present, so before sending a document for commercial printing, gather all the images together along with the page-layout file itself, a process known as collecting for output.

Because text similarly requires the specified font file to be present, fonts are also normally collected for output, even though sending them to a third party technically infringes the copyright of the font's manufacturer. (To avoid this, fonts can be embedded in PDFs.) 'Preflight' software – available in the form of standalone programs, utilities built into tools like Distiller, and Internet-based services – automates collecting for output, warns you if any required files are missing, and can check that all colour specs are ready for print.

Above: **Because page-layout programs are all about bringing elements together on the page, you will need to make sure all the elements are present when you send off a document to your printer. In this dialog box, Quark lists the pictures and fonts used, and warns you if their files are absent.**

When you are specifying the colours of vector fills and strokes from scratch, rather than modify existing colours in a bitmap image, guide your choices within a project with a colour palette.

Most computer operating systems and graphics programs use some kind of RGB colour wheel as their main 'colour picker'. Applications from Adobe, including Photoshop and Illustrator, are an exception, presenting hues in a vertical line and saturation/brightness variations in a chart progressing from dark to light on the vertical axis and from grey to saturated on the horizontal.

In Illustrator and FreeHand, along with other vector-drawing packages, a pop-out menu on the Swatches palette provides access to industry-standard colour systems such as Focoltone, Pantone, Toyo and Trumatch. These may look rather disorganized, partly because the swatches are arranged within an arbitrarily proportioned window: try resizing it until some sort of pattern emerges.

Each program also comes with a few colour sets of its own, which may be useful. If you prefer to start from scratch, the RGB colour picker does give you some idea of the relationship between hues. But there is no provision for alternative colour wheels, such as those explored on page 163, nor any way to find colour combinations except by eye. A number of software utilities have been developed to address these shortcomings.

Two leading examples are Color Consultant Pro on the Mac and Color Wheel Pro on the PC. Both offer a choice between the RGB wheel and an artist's wheel with yellow as an extra primary. Whichever you choose, the software can then show the various colour harmony schemes - analogous, complementary, monochromatic, and so on (*see page 42*) – based on a starting colour of your choice. The palette defined by your chosen scheme can then be saved for use in other programs.

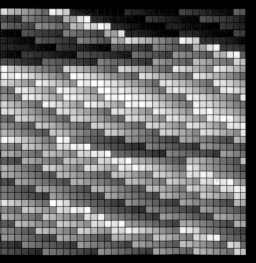

Below: **The Trumatch system is based on standard CMYK printing and organizes fifty hue families into forty perfectly proportioned tints of each.**

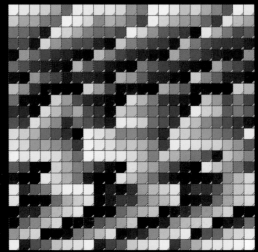

Below: **Pantone is the best-known colour specification system in the United Kingdom, Europe and the United States, while Toyo serves a similar purpose in the Far East. Each colour is defined by a formula that tells your printer how to mix ten primary colours to create the exact shade. Official CMYK conversion values are also available, but only about half will result in a perfect match to the spot colour.**

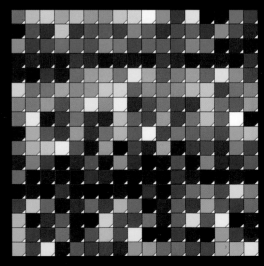

Below: **Focoltone (from four-colour tone) is also CMYK based. The 763 colours can be either process printed or premixed by your printer as solid spot colours.**

Right: Colour Consultant Pro, from Code Line Communications, derives palettes from three versions of the colour wheel. As well as RGB and Artistic (with yellow as a primary), there is an Artistic Full Spectrum option that sneaks cyan and magenta into the RGB wheel without affecting the relative positions of the primaries. This makes for some interesting palettes. Analogous, complementary, split complementary, monochromatic, triadic and tetradic schemes are supported, resulting in palettes of two to five colours with globally adjustable saturation and value (lightness). You can download a trial version of the program, which works a limited number of times, from www.code-line.com.

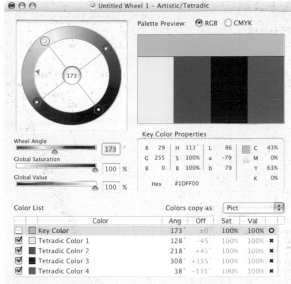

Left: With Adobe Illustrator, you can create your own colour palettes using the Blend command in most vector-graphics programs. For each row of swatches, draw only the first and last squares, and fill them with colours at the ends of your desired spectrum. Then go to Blend Options, under Blend on the Object menu, and set the number of steps. Select both squares and use Make Blend (Alt-Command-B on a Mac, Ctrl-Alt-B on a PC) to generate this number of intermediate swatches, which will have colour values precisely spaced between your original two fills. The above examples use pairs of hues differently spaced around the colour wheel to produce palettes of varying breadth. The same method can be used to mix any two colours. Note that complementary pairs – blue and yellow, for example – will result in grey intermediates: this demonstrates the painter's principle that a colour can be neutralized by mixing in a little of its complement.

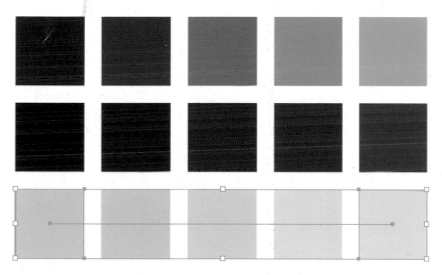

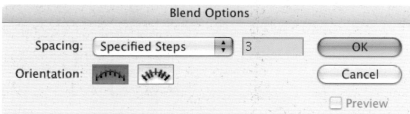

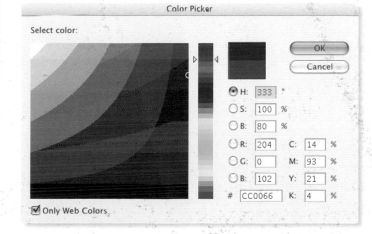

Right: Although it is rare (and usually pointless) to restrict photographic or continuous-tone images to the Web-safe palette, doing so can ensure an on-screen match between colours generated in different programs. The restricted nature of the palette (seen here in the Adobe Color Picker) also makes it useful as a design aid, since it narrows your choices to a limited but logically spread range of colours. Bear in mind, though, that there is no special guarantee that a Web-safe colour can be reproduced perfectly in CMYK, PANTONE or any other colour print system.

ANIMATING WITH VECTORS Most of the animated content on websites is delivered in Macromedia Flash format. A Flash 'movie' effectively comprises a series of vector drawings that are played back as frames at a preset rate. Thanks to the efficiency of vectors, high-quality animations can be delivered using a fraction of the number of kilobytes required for a video clip of the same length.

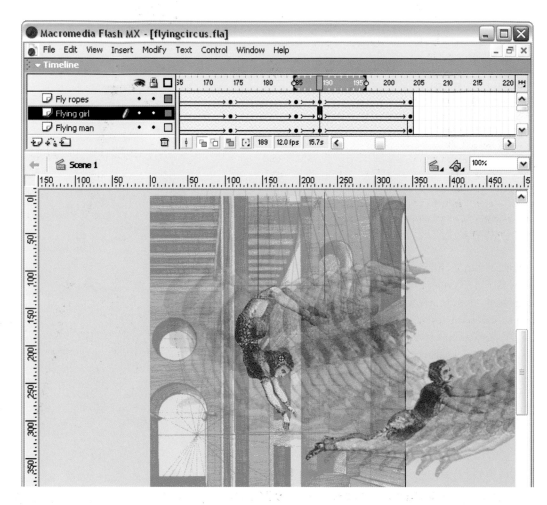

Flash animations can serve as welcome messages ('intros') and presentations, or an entire site can be constructed in Flash, giving the designer complete control over its appearance and behaviour.

In Flash, a time line is divided into scenes that in turn are split into frames. Graphical objects are then placed in selected frames called keyframes. An object may be edited to change subtly or dramatically from one keyframe to the next, and the software automatically generates the frames in between, creating smooth movement.

You can even create Flash movies in a vector-drawing program such as Macromedia FreeHand. A simple way to produce instant animations is to create a series of objects either by blending or using one of the various repeating options, which can generate multiple copies of an object that are progressively distorted or scaled. The Release to Layers command is then used to break up the series into a sequence of frames that can be exported as a Flash file.

To complete the multimedia experience, audio clips can be incorporated into movies and synchronized with frames. Bitmapped images and video clips can also be embedded if necessary. Alternatively, tools such as Wildform Flix (www.wildform.com) can 'vectorize' video clips – using a process similar to the autotracing of bitmapped images – to produce a stylized version of the original in vector form. Although not widely used, this technique can produce interesting and unusual results.

Viewers also need Macromedia software to interpret and play back the movie data. This software is not embedded in standard Web browsers but is offered as a free add-on or plug-in by Macromedia, which is now supplied with the leading browsers. Millions of people already have the plug-in, but as a considerable number still do not, it is good practice to provide an alternative, 'plain' version of any Flash content, containing only ordinary text and pictures viewable in all browsers.

Additionally, some users are unable to enjoy Flash movies because they have a disability, such as sight and/or hearing impairment, that prevents them from experiencing some aspect of the content, while other users may find themselves having to use a modified browser that has not been upgraded to support Flash. Flash and other browser

Above: The heart of Flash's animation toolset is the 'Timeline', shown at the top of the screen. This allows you to control exactly how long the animations (indicated by the arrows on each layer) last, and to keep them in sync with animations on other layers. In this example, it's a simple task to ensure that the girl on the trapeze catches the flying acrobat perfectly every time.

Right: Animated content can entertain users (left) or contribute to the information content of a site (right).

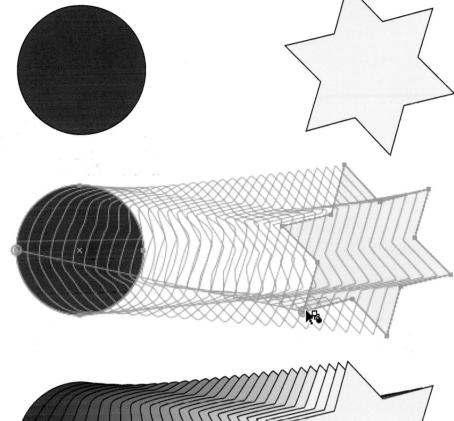

Above and right: **An easy way to create animations is to blend between two shapes in a vector drawing program, then convert the blend into a sequence of movie frames. In Macromedia FreeHand and Adobe Illustrator, the Release to Layers command places objects within the blend on separate layers. The document can then be saved as a Flash movie, with layers becoming frames.**

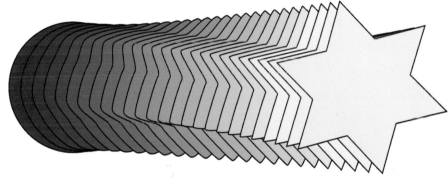

enhancement technologies are regarded as barriers to accessibility – a major concern for Web designers now that the United States, the United Kingdom, Australia and other countries have passed legislation obliging businesses to cater to the disabled.

In fact, however, multimedia content can improve accessibility if it is used thoughtfully. For example, a Flash presentation may be better able than plain text to convey information to users with reading difficulties, or who speak a different language.

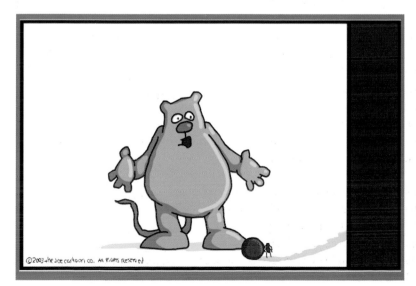

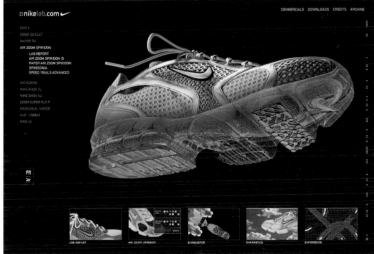

GLOSSARY

additive colour mixing The mixing of red, green and blue light to create white light (with all at equal strength), or one of the millions of other colours when mixed selectively. The basis of all screen display and digital image capture systems.

analogous scheme A colour scheme using two or more colours that would sit adjacent to each other on a colour wheel.

bit A contraction of 'binary digit', the smallest unit of information that a computer can use. A bit may have one of two potential values: on or off, positive or negative, 1 or 0. Eight bits form a byte, the unit that is required to store an alphabet character.

chroma The intensity or purity of a colour, and so its degree of saturation. Technically it refers to the mixture of wavelengths in a light source, where a single wavelength is the maximum chroma and an even mixture of all wavelengths is the minimum.

CMYK The four printing-process colours based on the subtractive colour model (black is represented by the letter K, which stands for key plate). In subtractive colour reproduction the colours are created by mixing cyan, magenta and yellow, the theory being that – when all three combine – they produce black. However, this is rarely achievable in real world printing, and if it were the print would use too much ink and take too long to dry. For this reason, black ink is used to add density to darker areas, replacing a percentage of the other inks.

clipping The loss or removal of colour image data outside certain tonal limits. Converting an image from RGB to CMYK for print typically involves clipping of the most saturated greens and blues as these colours cannot be reproduced in print.

colorimetry The technical term for the scientific measurement of colour.

ColorSync Apple Computer's system-level implementation of ICC-based colour management.

colour cast A bias in a colour image, which can either be intentional or undesirable. If the former, it is usually made at the image editing stage to enhance the mood or feel of an image. If the latter, the cast is due to faults or limitations in the capture or reproduction process, such as the lighting used in the original photograph or a printing error.

colour constancy the ability of the human eye and brain to perceive colours accurately under a variety of lighting conditions, compensating automatically for the difference in colour temperature. This phenomenon is also known as chromatic adaptation.

CMM (Color Matching Module) The 'engine' of a colour management system, the CMM uses device and working space profiles to transfer colour data between different platforms, software applications and devices.

colour space A description of the full range of colours achievable by any single device in the reproduction chain, along with any tonal and colour deviations. While the visible spectrum contains millions of colours, many of them are unachievable in digital imaging, and even when the colour gamuts of different devices overlap, they are unlikely to match exactly. For example, the colours that can be displayed on a monitor cannot all be printed on a commercial four-colour press and vice-versa – the press can print some colours that the monitor cannot display.

colour temperature A measure of the wavelength composition of white light. This is defined as the temperature (measured in degrees Kelvin) to which a theoretical 'black body radiator', reflecting no light at all but emitting it when heated, would need to be heated to produce a particular colour of light. A typical tungsten lamp, for example, measures 3200 K, whereas the temperature of sunlight is 5000 K.

colour wheel A circular diagram representing the complete spectrum of visible colours.

complementary colour The two colours that sit opposite each other on a colour wheel. Complementary colours intensify each other when used together, and create a neutral colour when mixed.

complementary scheme A colour scheme using two complementary colours.

cross-rendering To render colours from one colour space in another, usually in order to simulate the output of one device on another (e.g. simulating a press using an inkjet printer.)

curves A tool for precise control of tonal relationships in image-editing applications, such as Photoshop.

dithering A technique of simulating many colours from a few by arranging the available colours in patterns of dots or pixels. When viewed at an appropriate size or from an appropriate distance, the dithered image will resemble a continuous tone print.

gamut The full range of colours available within a particular colour space. For example, the range that can be captured by an input device, reproduced by an output device or described in a working colour space (which may be larger than that of any real-world device).

GIF (Graphics Interchange Format) A bitmap file format that uses up to 256 indexed colours to minimize file size and simulate a wider range of colours. Not a good choice for realistic colour reproduction but a favorite in Web design as it supports transparency and animation.

grey-balanced A property of an RGB colour space where equal levels of red, green and blue will always create a neutral gray. Working spaces are always gray-balanced.

halftone dot The basic element of a printed image, where a continuous tone original is reproduced ('screened') by breaking it up into patterns of equally spaced dots of varying sizes to simulate the tonal values. Colour images are reproduced by overprinting halftone patterns in each of the primary colours.

hue The attribute of a colour defined by its dominant wavelength and therefore position in the visible spectrum. Hue is what we normally mean when we ask, 'what colour is it?'

ICC (International Color Consortium) The organization responsible for defining cross-application colour standards for digital imaging and reproduction.

LAB The perceptually based colour model created by the Commission Internationale de l'Eclairage (CIE), an international scientific organization. The LAB model was created through a series of experiments, which involved subjects varying the strengths of red, green and blue lamps to match a set of sample colours. L is luminance (or brightness) and A and B are colour axes ranging from red to green and blue to yellow respectively.

levels An image-editing tool that maps tones in an image, from the darkest shadows to the brightest highlights, as a histogram. By adjusting sliders on the histogram, you can remap tones across the image to improve the use of available tonal range.

luminance The brightness of a colour, from solid black to the brightest possible value. *See also* hue; saturation

metamerism An undesirable property of printed material where the gray balance appears to change in response to the lighting conditions depending on the spectral content of the lighting. This is the effect responsible for items whose colours match under one lighting type (fluorescent, for example) no longer matching under another (daylight or incandescent).

partitive mixing A method of adding colour to an image. Fine dots or stripes of carefully chosen colours create the impression of a new colour with, in effect, the eye and brain mixing them. An old technique in traditional art, it forms the basis of dithering in printed media.

pixel Contraction of 'picture element'. The smallest component of a digital image.

PPI (pixels per inch) The measure of resolution for a digital image or screen display, in terms of how many pixels fit into a single inch of screen or image space.

primary colours Pure colours from which theoretically all other colours can be mixed and which themselves cannot be created by a mixture of other colours. In printing, the primaries are the 'subtractive' pigments (cyan, magenta and yellow). The 'additive' primaries are red, green and blue.

process colours The colours of the inks used in a particular printing process, usually assumed to be cyan, magenta, yellow and black unless otherwise specified. The process colours might be supplemented by spot colours that fall outside the gamut achievable using the primaries, such as very intense saturated colours and fluorescent or metallic colours.

profile The colorimetric description of the behavior of an input or output device, which can be used by an application to ensure accurate transfer of colour data. A profile describing the colour space used during image creation or editing should ideally be embedded in the image, so that it can later be used as a reference by other users, software applications or display and output devices.

resolution The degree of clarity and definition with which an image can be reproduced or displayed. Resolution is measured in terms of dots or pixels per inch or centimeter.

RGB (Red, Green, Blue) The primary colours of the additive colour model, and the colour system often (and preferably) used for digital images until the print output stage.

saturation The variation in 'purity' of colour of the same tonal brightness from none (gray), through pastel shades (low saturation), to pure colour with no gray (high or full saturation). *See also* Chroma.

separations The 'split' versions of a page or image that has been prepared for process printing. Each separation is used to print a single process colour or spot colour.

simultaneous contrast A human perceptual anomaly whereby colours or shapes are affected by surrounding colours or shapes. For example, a red square surrounded by a thick black border will seem brighter than the same red square surrounded by a white border.

soft proof A feature in professional publishing and graphics applications where the effects of a CMYK or RGB conversion or printing process are simulated onscreen as accurately as possible within the gamut limitations of the screen used.

subtractive colour mixing The colour model describing the primary colours of reflected light: cyan, magenta and yellow (CMY). Subtractive colour mixing is the basis of printed colour.

TIFF (Tagged Image File Format) A popular graphics file format which can be used for any bitmapped images and for colour separations. TIFF can be used for black-and-white, grayscale and colour images. It can contain embedded colour profiles and offers a lossless compression option.

triadic scheme A colour scheme that uses three colours spaced evenly around the colour wheel.

white point The colour of 'pure' white in an image. In an RGB image it corresponds to R, G and B values all at maximum, the brightest white that a monitor can show or scanner can read; in print or other CMYK hardcopy output it usually means the paper or other substrate colour.

working space A device-independent space that can be used as a predictable and controllable working environment for image editing.

INDEX

PICTURE ACKNOWLEDGEMENTS

AKG PHOTOS: pps.53T © DACS, London 2004, 103b Rudolph Staechelin family Foundation, 105b © DACS,London 2004, 108 Staatsgalerie Stuttgart, © ARS,NY and DACS,London 2004

AMV/BBDO: pps.146, Art Director J.Carr/Illustrator Jon Rogers: 147

ARCAID: p80b

BFI, LONDON: pps. 94 Courtesy of Pioneer Pictures, 96t Courtesy of Artificial Eye, 96b Courtesy of Paramount Pictures, 97tl Courtesy of de Laurentis, 97bl Courtesy of Touchstone, 99b Courtesy of Aardman,

BRIDGEMAN ART LIBRARY, LONDON: p53b © DACS,London 2004, 104 Stadische Galerie im Lenbachhaus © DACS,London 2004, 105tl Musée d'Arte Moderne de la Ville, © Succession Picasso, DACS, London 2004,105tr Christies © DACS, London 2004, 106 James Goodman Gallery, 107Ttr David Findlay Fine Art.NYC © Andrew Wyeth, 107b Christies,© DACS, London 2004, 109 National Gallery of Victoria, Melbourne © DACS, London 2004, 102 Galerie Nationale d'Arte Moderne,Rome © DACS, London 2004, 113t © Bridget Riley, 113b Saatchi Collection © ARS, NY and DACS,London 2004,

COURTESY OF BRITISH BAKERIES: p.136r&b

COURTESY OF CASEY PRODUCTIONS/ELDORADO FILMS: p95b

CORBIS: pps.13t Carl and Ann Purcell, 14 David Turnely, 15br,17tl Gavriel Jecan, 17tr Tom Brakefield, 17br Geoff Moon/Frank Lane Picture Agency, 23 Clyaton J.Price, 48b John van Hasselt/Sygma, 52bl Musée de Stadt Vienna/ Edimedia 52br Francis Meyer, 54 By Kind Permission of the Trustees of the National Gallery, London, 64l Massimo Listri, 79 Stockmarket, 97br Courtesy of Universal Pictures, 101 Pierre Vauther, 103t Archivo Icographico/Musée d'Orangerie, Paris © ADAGP, Paris and DACS,London 2004, 110 Burstein Collection © The Andy Warhol Foundation for the Visual Arts/ARS,NY and DACS, London 2004

COURTESY OF MUNSELL COLOR: pps.39, 46,47

© DISNEY ENTERPRISES, INC:p99t

FIREBRAND: p.134

HEARD DESIGN: pps.130, 135all, 140b, 147br

KOBAL COLLECTION: pps.95t Courtesy of Newline/Ralph Nelson Jnr,

COURTESY OF MGM: p.93

JOHN OUTRAM ASSOCIATES: p.81b

PENTAGRAM: pps.123, 129 all, 133, 126, 136t, 137, 138, 140t, 141

PHOTOS.COM: pps.11, 12t, 18 all, 19, 20, 33, 72bl, 73, 85, 118 both, 119 both

RAIMES, PEPLOW @ FOUNDATION: pps.65br, 137tr, 139b, 145r

COURTESY OF REM KOOLHAS: p.77

SAGMEISTER INC (NY): p.126t

© NIGEL SANDOR/DIGITAL VISION: p.120

THE TATE,LONDON: pps.102, 110/111 © DACS,London 2004

VINTAGE MAGAZINE PICTURE LIBRARY: p64r, 65t, 117, 124 tl, 124tr, 124l, 124r, 125tl, 125bl, 125bm, 125br, 128, 128tr, 128br

MATT WINGFIELD STUDIO for HARVEY NICHOLLS: p.139 (nominated for Silver in the design category of the 2002 D&AD awards)

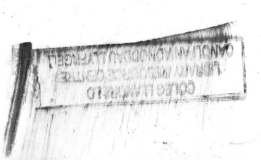